Falling in Love with America *Again*

Falling in Love with America *Again*

JIM DeMINT

and

THE HERITAGE FOUNDATION

CENTER
STREET

NEW YORK   BOSTON   NASHVILLE

Center Street
Hachette Book Group
237 Park Avenue
New York, NY 10017

www.CenterStreet.com

Printed in the United States of America

RRD-C

First edition: March 2014
10   9   8   7   6   5   4   3

Center Street is a division of Hachette Book Group, Inc.
The Center Street name and logo are trademarks of Hachette Book Group, Inc.

The Hachette Speakers Bureau provides a wide range of authors for speaking events. To
find out more, go to www.HachetteSpeakersBureau.com or call (866) 376-6591.

The publisher is not responsible for websites (or their content) that are not owned by the
publisher.

Library of Congress Cataloging-in-Publication Data has been applied for.

To my fellow freedom lovers at The Heritage Foundation, and the little platoons everywhere that make this country great

Table of Contents

Foreword

by

Dr. Ben Carson

When I was growing up in inner-city Detroit, and later in Boston, the civil rights movement was just getting started, and young African Americans like myself were confronted with vicious racism at virtually every turn. Sometimes I came across it in the park, when a group of older white boys tried to drown me in a lake. Sometimes I faced it in school, when one of my teachers was so upset by my high grades that she took all the white students to task for allowing a "mere black" to outperform them academically. I was shocked by episodes of blatant racism I witnessed within my own family as my two older cousins were the victims of brutal, racially motivated beatings by the police.

One of the worst effects of growing up in a racist society is that if everyone tells you that you're worthless and good for nothing, chances are high that you'll end up believing them. Fortunately, like many young blacks, I was a beneficiary of an extensive network of "little platoons" that African Americans had established over the years—supportive families (in my case, a remarkable single mom), dedicated ministers, and some truly caring neighbors. They shielded us from the most corrosive effects of racism. Our bodies may have been battered by white bigots, but our souls were unscathed.

Jim DeMint's important new book, *Falling in Love with*

America Again, is a love song to America's little platoons. At a time when so many in the media are bent on singing the praises of the high and mighty, Jim reminds us that America's real heroes are not to be found strolling through the corridors of power or ensconced in the mansions of the rich and famous. Rather, they're the modest man or woman who lives next door—who may not have attended an Ivy League university, or even graduated from high school, but who takes our Judeo-Christian heritage seriously and strives, day in and day out, to "do justice, love mercy, and walk humbly with God" (Micah 6:8).

These are the men and women whom we should honor and strive to emulate, but whom we usually overlook. Instead, too many of us pin our hopes and prayers on big government, believing it holds the solutions to our nation's most urgent problems. Jim regards this worship of the state as a modern-day form of idolatry, which he calls statism. In this book, he shows how damaging it is to our way of life, but it can be countered.

There are three things that I took away from Jim's compelling analysis. First, far from solving our problems, statism exacerbates them. Whether the goal is ending poverty, reforming education, protecting the environment, or improving health care (something I know a little about), big government's involvement takes a serious problem and makes it worse. That's because the incentives that motivate big government (as well as the other "Bigs" Jim describes) are geared toward enhancing its own power over the helpless masses who can't possibly manage their own lives, at least in the opinion of government bureaucrats. By contrast, the reason the little platoons are so effective is because they run on the most potent fuel of all—the power of love.

A second consequence of statism that Jim describes is the

harm it inflicts on our souls. Just as racism sought to make African Americans feel inferior, so statism tries to make all Americans feel that we're just not up to the many "complicated" (a favorite statist word) challenges facing us today. Instead of empowering Americans to take charge of our lives, statism diminishes us. It claims that we're not smart enough or educated enough or experienced enough to take responsibility for our own destinies. Far better, it urges us, to place our future in Big Brother's ready hands.

Jim fiercely opposes this approach, and the many stories he recounts all point to the same moral: Ordinary Americans are chock-full of talent, courage, and resourcefulness, and can manage quite well without Big Brother's interference.

But it's Jim's third point that I find most thought-provoking. Up until now, nearly all conservatives have pretty much made the same case against big government: It's too costly, too inefficient, and too overbearing. But Jim strikes an entirely new note. The main reason big government is so harmful, he maintains, is because it threatens to *destroy the love that we Americans should feel for our country.* This love is nurtured and sustained by the little platoons of everyday life, but as these little platoons are overshadowed and sidelined by the state, the wellsprings of our love for America are also drying up. In falling in love with big government, we risk falling out of love with America. Jim is determined to prevent that from happening.

In 1944, a Swedish social scientist named Gunnar Myrdal wrote a book called *An American Dilemma: The Negro Problem and Modern Democracy.* Myrdal correctly argued that racial segregation was seriously at odds with the American creed of liberty and equality. Although the book was in some ways seriously flawed (Myrdal was a socialist), it was hugely influential, and was cited by the U.S. Supreme Court in its 1954 landmark decision, *Brown v. Board of Education*, that outlawed segregation in our public schools.

I believe that Jim DeMint's *Falling in Love with America Again* compares very favorably with Myrdal's *An American Dilemma*. Although Jim is not a social scientist himself (and most definitely not a socialist!), it draws heavily on the insights of the brilliant thinkers and researchers who are Jim's colleagues at America's leading conservative think tank, The Heritage Foundation. Like Myrdal's earlier work, it too focuses on a crucial American dilemma—the conflict between the statism widely embraced by America's elites and the American creed embodied in the Constitution and the writings of our Founders. And just as race was the all-important dilemma facing America seventy years ago, so power—who's got it: the Bigs or the people?—is the fateful dilemma confronting our country today.

Jim DeMint has some truly enlightening things to say about this issue. It is my hope that the arguments he makes, and the stories he tells, will reach the widest possible audience, will inspire a renewed appreciation of our little platoons, and will help assure the future of our beloved country.

Benjamin S. Carson Sr., MD,
Emeritus Professor of Neurosurgery,
Oncology, Plastic Surgery and Pediatrics,
The Johns Hopkins Medical Institutions

Falling in Love with America *Again*

To be attached to the subdivision, to love the little platoon we belong to in society, is the first principle (the germ as it were) of public affections. It is the first link in the series by which we proceed towards a love to our country, and to mankind.
　　　　　　　　—Edmund Burke,
　　　　　　　　　Reflections on the Revolution in France, 1790

Introduction

We can change America's course, but only if we understand what makes America exceptional.

I should have been the happiest of politicians. I was a respected U.S. senator from my home state of South Carolina. I had played a key role, through my political action committee, in bringing principled conservatives like Rand Paul, Ted Cruz, Marco Rubio, Mike Lee, and other new leaders to join me in the Senate. I was cheered when I addressed local and national rallies of the Tea Party, a dynamic new force in American politics. I was a frequent guest on television and radio, and quoted in leading newspapers and journals. I had challenged the Washington establishment and forced it to make major concessions on supposedly untouchable practices like earmarks.

By standing for fundamental American ideas like limited constitutional government and individual responsibility, and against politics as usual, I had made a difference in how Washington worked.

And yet I was deeply frustrated by how little Washington had really changed. We still have an ever-expanding federal government and an ever-mounting national debt—approaching $17 trillion as I write in mid-2013. As of 2013, the share of federal debt for every man, woman, and child in America is $53,000.

And despite all the trillions of dollars flowing from Washington, the official unemployment figure, as I write, hovers between 7 and 8 percent—and some Americans have dropped out of the labor force altogether. The real wages of the average American worker have not risen in thirty years. And we have a permanent underclass dependent upon government for everything from their food to their housing.

No matter how hard other conservatives in Congress and I tried to stop it, the federal government kept metastasizing, invading every aspect of the life of every American.

I started to wonder what kind of future my four grown children and four grandchildren face. There was a time when many of us believed that the American dream would endure forever because America was too big to fail. But the warning signs cannot be ignored. Economic weakness and cultural decay are all around us. I fear that many institutions in America, and especially government, may have gotten too big to succeed.

Yet despite the obvious threats to our future, we don't seem able to agree on what's wrong or what we as citizens can do to get America back on the right track. The question I hear most often as I travel around the country is an urgent one: "What can I do?"

Politics as Usual Is Not the Answer

Big-government politicians in Washington, D.C., are not going to solve our problems. Quite the opposite: If we don't stop them, they will turn our country into another bankrupt nation. Our politics have become intensely negative and even self-destructive.

Commonsense solutions like a balanced budget are ignored, and demagogues drown out the voices of reason and prudence.

We live in an age when instant communications and continuous polling, massively funded by special interests, have created a politics of misinformation and blatant pandering. Permanent campaigning has not only polarized politics, it has divided America. It has smothered our love of country and our love for one another.

I lived in this poisonous political environment for over fifteen years as a candidate, congressman, and senator. Then, in January 2013, I resigned from the Senate to join The Heritage Foundation as its president and CEO, convinced I could do more to help save the American dream for this generation and future generations from outside rather than inside the Washington establishment.

But saving the American dream is far beyond the power of any one person or institution. Every generation in its turn must fight for our country and sacrifice for the next generation. Now is *our* time. You and I, along with millions of other Americans, must join our hearts and minds to save the country we love.

I have talked with many discouraged Americans who believe that our problems are so big and intractable there is nothing anyone can do to save our country. *This is not true.* There is a way and only one way to start to change America's course, to turn back in a direction that will reunite our nation and preserve the blessings of liberty for us all: *We must fall in love with America—again.*

We must begin by recognizing the reason for the politics of deceit and distortion. Political consultants use negative campaigns to suppress voter turnout, especially among people who don't follow politics closely and who want little from government. The strategy works. If they successfully discourage Americans who don't look to government to solve their problems from going to the polls, that leaves the outcome of elections primarily in the hands of those who want more from government.

But if we can convince voters who want more freedom and opportunity—and *less* government intrusion into their lives—to register and vote, they can defeat the proponents of big government. This is what happened in the 2010 elections, when citizens inspired by the Tea Parties and their spontaneous grassroots activism turned out in force. It can happen again if we make clear to our fellow citizens how much is at stake, and provide the leadership to unite and inspire them.

Part of our challenge is to help our fellow Americans see that big government is not the solution to our problems; rather, it *causes* many of those problems, or makes them worse. Big government works hand in hand with big banks, big business, big labor, and big special interests, which are choking free markets and smothering the institutions of family, community, and church that built and sustained a strong, prosperous, and free United States of America through its first century and a half.

Now, big is not always bad—America is a land of big ideas, big dreams, and big accomplishments. But present-day big government is replacing self-government and what the British political philosopher Edmund Burke called the "little platoon."

The danger signs of a nation in deadly decline are all around us. State governments like those of Michigan and Illinois are edging toward bankruptcy. The city of Detroit became the largest U.S. city in history to file for bankruptcy. Young people are graduating from high school or college into a world of minimal job opportunities. Cohabitation is up and marriage is down. But the most serious casualty of big government and negative politics may be the loss of what Burke called "public affections."

"Public affections" means love of country, love of community, and love of our fellow man. It involves pride in our country and gratitude for our way of life. It is the source of patriotism and the fuel of responsible citizenship.

As Burke put it, "To be attached to the subdivision, to love the little platoon we belong to in society, is the first principle (the germ as it were) of public affections. It is the first link in the series by which we proceed towards a love to our country, and to mankind."[1] He is saying that the indispensable glue that holds a country together comes from our association with the people and institutions that are closest to us. I believe his insight is the most convincing explanation of America's exceptional success in the past and of our present decline.

The Founders of our Republic agreed with Burke about the importance of public affections to a united nation. In *Federalist* No. 46, James Madison, the father of the Constitution, challenged both state governments and the national government to rise above their parochial interests to "partake sufficiently of the spirit of both" state and national interests.

In his farewell address to the American people, President George Washington said that their new country "has a right to concentrate your affections." He reminded his fellow citizens that they had fought and triumphed together "in a common cause." "The independence and liberty you possess," he said, "are the work of joint counsels, and joint efforts of common dangers, sufferings, and successes."

In his first inaugural address, following a prolonged and bitter election campaign, Thomas Jefferson urged his fellow citizens to "unite with one heart and one mind." "Let us restore to social intercourse," he said, "that harmony and affection without which liberty and even life itself are but dreary things."

How, you may ask, is this possible? I think the only reasonable answer is through the kind of voluntary groups observed by French author Alexis de Tocqueville on his visit to America in the 1830s. He saw that within our states (there were twenty-four of them by then) were hundreds and hundreds of communities composed of individuals engaged in self-government. These communities were sustained by what he called "associations"—civic associations, religious and charitable organizations, business groups, local newspapers, and political parties. They built schools and hospitals and churches and in so doing deepened and widened the spirit of America.

Tocqueville identified two major factors that sustained that spirit—active local governments operating within a federal system, and the belief of the American people that they were masters of their own fate.

It is that American spirit—based on the first principles of the Founding but weakened by progressive big-government presidents from Wilson to Obama—that we must rejuvenate without delay.

Little Platoons—A Personal Perspective

When my children were in middle school, they played on the soccer and basketball teams at a small school sponsored by our church. My wife and I went to all the games and came to love our children's teammates and their families. This genuine love for the players and their families made us passionate fans of the teams and of the school. Our loyalty to the school led us to serve on the school board, drive on field trips, and participate in all parent activities.

Our involvement with the school also led us to become more active in the church and to build closer relationships with many families we met there. We taught Sunday school classes, participated in church socials, and volunteered to help whenever we could. The church became an integral part of our family life, and through other church members we became more involved with volunteer activities throughout our community.

I found myself serving on the United Way Campaign Committee, on the Chamber of Commerce Board, and in the Rotary Club—all as a result of my relationships with members of my church. We worked together to improve our local schools, health care, and roads, to help the needy, and to attract new businesses to our community. One of my fellow volunteers was a community banker who, with just a handshake as collateral, gave me a loan to start my own business, a market research firm. Some of the people I met through my volunteer activities helped my business grow by becoming clients.

I developed a deeper knowledge of my community and a genuine affection for it, and I had the satisfaction of making it a better place to live and work. My work at the community level brought me into contact with people throughout the state who were trying to improve the quality of life in their communities. We shared ideas and worked together in the effort to make our whole state the best place in the country to live and work. And whenever a large employer intending to build a new facility selected South Carolina instead of a competing state, we celebrated together.

Many of us also worked with volunteers in neighboring states to make our whole region more attractive to businesses from around the world. We worked with officials at the state and federal levels to overcome the bureaucratic obstacles that stood in the way of improved ports, highways, energy grids, schools, and other public services. I was a small part of all these activities, but I believed my participation was contributing to a better future for my family and our neighbors.

More important than my modest contribution to the improvement of my community, state, and nation was the impact that my involvement had on me. My attachment to my family, church, and school helped instill in me a real affection for my community, state, and nation. I became more personally attached to America because of my attachment to the little platoons of my life.

I learned that through voluntary participation and taking advantage of the small opportunities surrounding me, I could help shape the bigger worlds of my state and of America. I realized how lucky and blessed I was to live in a country that gave me the freedom and opportunity to make a difference.

This is how I fell in love with America—from the ground up. I love my country not because of what it has done for me, but because of what it has allowed me to do for myself, my family, my school, my church, my community, my state, and my nation. All these little platoons—and the big country that protects them and allows them to operate freely—have given me much more in return than I have ever given them.

Big versus Public Affections

I have also experienced the opposite of little platoons—the Bigs. Our children went from their small middle school to a big public high school. It had many good teachers and administrators, but the sheer size of the school created problems. The sports teams were all about winning, and even though our children were good athletes, there was no room for them on the soccer and basketball teams. Except for a few fund-raising events, it was difficult to find ways to get involved with other families at the school.

Unlike the elementary and middle schools our children attended, it was almost impossible to change anything at the big high school. The bureaucracy of teachers, administrators, the local school board, and state politicians, along with all the federal rules, discouraged parental involvement. And we couldn't choose another school unless we wanted to pay for a private school, which was far beyond our means and those of most of the parents in our community. So instead of working together to improve the school, we became disgruntled parents complaining about the things we didn't like.

Our family never developed much school spirit for this high school. We didn't get to know many families at the school except the ones we already knew from middle school. The whole experience created negative perceptions of the way our community and state operated our schools.

The high school was not my only local experience with Big. The community bank that had given me the loan to start my business was bought by a large national bank. The easy phone-call approvals for small loans for my business turned into a drawn-out multilevel paperwork process. I yearned for the days when I could talk to someone who could make a quick decision.

My charitable work with inner-city churches was often hindered by big federal agencies that resisted working with the religious organizations leading the effort to improve the quality of life for disadvantaged citizens. I know from personal experience that

African American churches that provided day care for the children of working single moms had to avoid any moral and religious teachings or risk losing the day-care subsidy provided by the state.

All of us have experienced the frustration of dealing with the complex billing systems and impersonal computerized customer service of big cell phone companies, cable operators, and monopoly utilities. As I said before, I am not arguing that all Big is bad and all little is good—you need a strong government when you go to war, to take the most obvious example. But there is an enormous difference between the government of power-hungry progressives and the constitutional government created by the Founders, based on the separation of powers and a balanced federalism.

It is very hard and frustrating to deal with a big, distant entity unless you have some personal connection with a smaller part of that entity. When Big is all there is, people are unlikely to hold genuine affection for the whole. Even when people are dependent on the services of Big—whether government or private organizations—they are likely to resent their dependency and lack of choices while disdaining the people who control them.

As a result, the core institutions of our freedom and democracy are now disliked and distrusted by many Americans because they are associated with Big. Capitalism, the free-market philosophy that made America the most prosperous country in the world, is now widely seen as greedy and unfair because it is associated with big corporations and big banks, which in turn are linked with big government.

Education and health care, once the most personal and close-to-home services, have lost much of the public's trust and confidence as their units have grown ever bigger and ever more under government control. Even charitable groups and some churches have lost public affection as they have grown big and impersonal.

Now, as I say, not all Big is bad, and Big doesn't have to mean disaffection and alienation. As a consultant for many large hospitals, colleges, and businesses, I was able to help improve attitudes and performance by reversing the emphasis of management from top-down to bottom-up. Yet even when the Bigs are decentralized and decision making is moved from the boardroom to the factory floor, the most they can do is complement the work of the little platoons. They can never replace them.

Washington: The Mother of Big

Americans have a tendency—and with good reason—to blame Washington for much of what's wrong with our country. In many ways and in many places, the federal government has overridden individual decision making and the little platoons that made America exceptional and inspired patriotism among our citizens. Turning away from the Constitution, the federal government has become a centralized, top-down power structure that is creating inefficiency in government, a weak economy, and a divided, dispirited citizenry.

Special-interest groups across the political spectrum are spending hundreds of millions of dollars on political campaigns hoping to win a 51 percent majority so they can gain control of this federal structure and force their ideas and policies on the other 49 percent. (Unfortunately, for reasons I will discuss later in this book, the Right cannot be exempted from this charge.) As a result, many Americans have grown suspicious and even contemptuous of one another and of their country.

In writing the Constitution (and the Declaration of Independence), the Founders were guided by certain first principles:

liberty and equality, the consent of the governed, private property, religious freedom, and the rule of law. All of these principles culminated in the idea of self-government—in the political sense of republican governance and the moral sense of governing ourselves.

That is how our federal government is *supposed* to operate. The original thirteen states came together to form a federal government to do those things they couldn't do separately. They signed a contract—our Constitution—that limited the federal government primarily to defense, the facilitation of interstate commerce, and a national system of justice. Just about everything else was left to "the States respectively, or to the people," as memorialized in the language of the Tenth Amendment, and adopted shortly after the original Constitution as part of the Bill of Rights.

Federalism—the constitutional concept of sovereign states united for common defense and cooperation—is a crucial component of our Republic and the infrastructure that makes our political liberty possible. But instead of honoring the contract with the states, power-seeking politicians and judges have continuously expanded the size and scope of the federal government. They endear themselves to many of their constituents with new programs and benefits, which require them to grow the government even more and increase the debt. And all the while, the American dream fades for more and more of our citizens.

Washington politicians have minimized resistance from the states to federal expansion by placating them with borrowed money. Unfortunately, besides increasing the national debt, federal money typically comes with expensive new mandates that require an increase in the size of state bureaucracy in turn. For just about every new federal program for education, roads, the environment—you name it—there is corresponding state government bureaucracy to administer it. And let us not forget: Every federal program comes with more federal rules and regulations that burden our liberty.

The end result has been the creation of an iron triangle of Washington politicians, federal bureaucrats, and state bureaucrats—a self-perpetuating arrangement that must be broken up if the American dream is to survive.

A Change in Direction

We can change America's course, but only if we understand what holds us together and what makes America exceptional. And I want to emphasize here that I am addressing *all* Americans—regardless of political party, race, creed, color, or ethnic origin.

Regardless of what political label we wear—Republican, Democrat, liberal, conservative, libertarian—we must remember that we're all Americans. Whether we are of African, Hispanic, Asian, Native American, European, or other descent, we must stand together to promote freedom, equality, and opportunity for everyone.

Falling in Love with America Again is about recognizing the little platoons that make America strong and prosperous and free. It is about recognizing how the Bigs threaten our way of life and the precious American dream.

This book will show how our big federal government and its big private-sector cronies are driving our country into a deeper and deeper hole. But the Bigs don't have to take us down with them, provided the little platoons are in place, ready once again to fulfill their historical role.

Tragically, many Americans don't appreciate the vital contribution the little platoons make to our well-being. That is why, with the help of my Heritage colleagues, I wrote this book. What makes it different, what makes it exceptional, is that it tells the stories of how all across America little platoons—families, communities, churches, schools, and volunteer organizations—are proving that decentralized, bottom-up efforts can work as well as ever. I showcase these successes and, using the best research and expert analysis available, demonstrate how such efforts can work for *all* Americans, not just those with a good job and money in the bank.

We will compare and contrast states that are helping their citizens to be successful with states that are collapsing under the weight of big government and bigger debt. We will document how some states are creating friendly environments, expanding job opportunities, and increasing their revenues without raising taxes. We will compare these successful states and their policies with states that are increasing government spending, chasing businesses and jobs away, and approaching bankruptcy.

Falling in Love with America Again will share inspiring stories of how Americans and their little platoons are growing local economies, improving schools, helping the poor and disadvantaged, making medical care more affordable, developing energy resources, and taking control of their lives. We will reveal how these successes create genuine affection between neighbors and a deep love for America, and how they contribute to restoring the federalism envisioned by the Founders.

I set out to write this book because I truly believe it is possible to rescue America before the federal government collapses under the weight of debt, irresponsible monetary policy, and bureaucratic dysfunction and takes the rest of us with it.

Friends of freedom, *our time is now!* We must all step forward to protect a fundamental idea of the American experiment: how the individual citizen, the states, and the federal government can work together to preserve our inalienable right to life, liberty, and the pursuit of happiness.

This is not a partisan idea: It is an American idea. And it is working in states and counties and communities and among the people all across our country. Please join us as we fall in love with America—again.

A Love Story

Everybody speaks for the poor, but nobody is talking to the poor.

—Bob Woodson

One of the heroes of my youth was the great fictional detective Sherlock Holmes. In *A Study in Scarlet*, Sherlock tells his good friend Dr. Watson about his unique profession. "I have a trade of my own," he explains. "I suppose I am the only one in the world. I'm a consulting detective, if you can understand what that is."

I recently had the great good fortune to spend some time with a modern-day Sherlock Holmes. His name is Bob Woodson, and like Sherlock Holmes he's an extraordinarily gifted man (among other things, he was awarded a MacArthur "genius" grant). He's also a detective of sorts. But unlike Sherlock, who specialized in identifying criminals, Bob specializes in identifying heroes—men and women who are making a difference in low-income communities throughout America. His Center for Neighborhood Enterprise (CNE), founded in 1981, seeks to provide these heroes with the recognition and support they need.

What's most remarkable about the people Bob works with is that their victories have taken place in some of our nation's most devastated neighborhoods, places that some might think were beyond hope. His success stories are found in neighborhoods where children duck quickly from the school bus into their apartments to stay out of the line of fire as warring gangs engage in drive-by shootings, and where drug addicts and alcoholics waste their lives away on street corners.

Bob is committed to supporting grassroots leaders who have transformed those neighborhoods, and he goes at his work with passion. "Everybody speaks *for* poor people, but nobody is talking *to* them," he declares. "The solutions can be found in the same neighborhoods that are experiencing the problems."

And he has no patience with the typical big government approach to poverty, where "experts" are hired to do what he calls "failure studies." In his words, "We believe in studying inventories of capacity because you learn nothing from studying failure except how to create it. We are visiting low-income communities all across America to find out what works and why."[1]

On another occasion, he explained how to go about it:

We should go into these low-income neighborhoods and begin to inquire as to how many people living in these communities are raising children who are not dropping out of school or using drugs and going to jail. We also must ask them how they are able to achieve in that environment. Any time we say, "60 percent of households are generating teen mothers," that means the other 40 percent are not. I do not see, however, scholars rushing in there to ask, "What is happening with the other 40 percent?" and "What are they doing that works?"[2]

Breaking the Bonds of Addiction

When it comes to the true experts, Bob knows that results trump credentials any day. "I don't care if you have a PhD after your name," he often says. "Some of the people I admire most have an 'ex' in front of theirs!"[3]

One of those people was an ex–heroin addict, Freddie Garcia, who in 1970, with his wife, Ninfa, launched the Victory Fellowship ministry, a faith-based program for hard-core drug addicts and alcoholics.[4]

To put it mildly, Victory Fellowship had unusual roots. Freddie had begun using drugs when he was just twelve and had his first fix of heroin when he was twenty-two. He first met Ninfa when she was driving the getaway car for a robbery. He describes in his autobiography the day he "hit bottom":

> I took our baby Josie along with me on burglaries and when I went to score. One hot humid morning, after scoring, I drove to the nearest gas station, took Josie into the men's restroom and put her down on the wet cement floor while I prepared my fix. I was tense and in pain. The sweat ran into my eyes and burned, blurring my vision. Nothing went right. Josie started to cry. Someone banged at the door, wanting to use the restroom. I pierced my arm over and over, missing the vein. I felt like screaming at my four-month-old baby—but then the needle hit a vein.

At once, every muscle in my body relaxed. I felt good, but glancing in the mirror, I saw myself—hollow cheeked and unshaven. I hadn't bathed for several days and the odor of my own body nauseated me. I bent down to pick up my little girl from her "bed" of dirty toilet paper. The foul stench tore at my nostrils, but she was smiling at me, her big eyes brimming with tears, her hands reaching up. "Man, how did I get this low?" I whispered as I held her close. "I never wanted it this way, my little baby."[5]

After trying—and failing—to become free of addiction by committing himself to a hospital for addicts and going through psychiatric care, counseling, and group therapy, Freddie headed for Los Angeles, thinking if he got out of his old environment he might be able to quit heroin. Within a month Ninfa and baby Josie arrived to be with him. But soon, once again, Freddie fell into looking for a fix when, unexpectedly, he encountered a faith-based outreach program that changed his life. After an arduous withdrawal, but with the support of the ministry, Freddie broke the bonds of his addiction.

Freddie and Ninfa went back to San Antonio and, determined to reach out to the addicts they had known, launched Victory Fellowship (known today as Outcry in the Barrio). The ministry had very humble beginnings. Freddie and Ninfa simply moved their furniture out of their small house to the yard to provide floor space for the addicts and alcoholics they invited to move in with them.

Since it was launched more than forty years ago, the ministry has expanded to one hundred sites in five countries, including a $3.6 million rehabilitation center in its home base of San Antonio, and has empowered thousands of men and women to reclaim and renew their lives. As Woodson points out, "Victory Fellowship only accepts people that everyone else has given up on."[6]

After Freddie succumbed to kidney disease in 2009, his son Jubal took over the ministry. In 2012, he attended an antipoverty conference hosted by The Heritage Foundation. Although the ministry has grown in scope and scale, Jubal explained, the essential principles guiding its strategy remain the same. As addicts and alcoholics begin the painful process of recovery, they are immersed in the supportive, understanding environment of a group home with house parents who, like the Garcias, provide unconditional love and consistent care. But that parental love is coupled with guidance, limits, discipline, and an expectation of personal responsibility.

A key element is the role played by recovering addicts, who provide support for others who are taking their first steps toward freedom from addiction. In Jubal's words, "We always stay with them day and night for the first three days because that's when they're very vulnerable. And we always have ex–heroin addicts take care of the heroin addicts, because they remember what they went through, and they are loving and compassionate with the guys."

The end of addiction is followed by a slow and laborious process of development in which old habits are broken and new qualities of character begin to form. "That is where the hard work is," said Jubal. "Addiction can be broken in an instant, but it is harder to live in freedom than in bondage, so there is that tendency to go back. Freedom is more difficult because bondage does not involve responsibility."

Jubal summarizes his ministry with a twinkle in the eye that is reminiscent of his father: "We disagree with government agencies on only two issues: what causes people to become addicted and what the solution is."[7]

In spite of its amazing success in changing the lives of addicts, in 1992 Victory Fellowship was nearly snuffed out by the heavy hand of the Texas Commission on Alcohol and Drug Abuse (TCADA) because the ministry's counselors were not certified. Freddie turned to Bob Woodson, who brought the issue to the attention of the media. When syndicated columnist Bill Raspberry wrote a column titled, "A License? To Save Lives?" and others in the media began to probe the issue, the TCADA withdrew from its position.

In 1995, when the TCADA threatened to shut down another faith-based program for addicts and alcoholics in San Antonio, Teen Challenge, Freddie went once again to Bob Woodson for help. "I know about drug addicts," he told Woodson, "but I don't know anything about politics."

Woodson sprang into action. He engaged the Institute for Justice, a public-interest law firm, to file for an injunction on Freddie's behalf. Bob helped Freddie organize a demonstration on behalf of Teen Challenge at the Alamo, which Marvin Olasky, editor of *World Magazine*, featured on the magazine's cover.

Eventually even the mainstream media were compelled to carry the story of how Texas bureaucrats were trying to put the faith-based groups out of business. And when Woodson was granted an interview with Texas's then governor, George W. Bush, he used the opportunity to inform Bush about how his own commission was undermining the work of one of Texas's most effective faith-based institutions.

Not surprisingly, the TCADA once again backed down.

Injury with Government's Helping Hand

Woodson understands the importance of groups like Victory Fellowship because he grew up surrounded by strong and supportive little platoons. He describes the strength of the community structures in the South Philadelphia neighborhood of his childhood in the 1940s—an era when community structures often stayed strong despite poverty and racial injustice. Although his father died when Bob was just nine years old, throwing the family into financial hardship, Bob grew up enveloped by a wealth of community support. Nearly all his friends lived in families headed by both a mother and a father, and he often spent time in their homes. He describes the important support that community groups such as black fraternal organizations provided for his family:

> We were surrounded by members of a number of black fraternal organizations who afforded my mother what social life she enjoyed and provided activities and events for us children to attend. These men in the neighborhood would always be available for father and son dinners. Sometimes, entire trains were leased by the O. V. Catto Black Elks Lodge, which would take hundreds of black families to Canada for conventions, or black-owned bus companies such as the Jackson and Gray Company were hired for outings at the seashore. Blacks owned large meeting halls with auditoriums, gyms, lounges and bars.
>
> On a rare occasion, I would even be treated to an outing at the professional baseball field where thousands of black fans would cheer on the likes of Jackie Robinson,

Satchel Paige, and other stars of the Negro National League. The men and women who continually put their arms around our family—those caring and generous folks with their fancy aprons, red fezzes, and other ornate trappings—were not doctors, lawyers, or other professionals but butlers, maids, carpenters, hairdressers, and laborers. They were people who were my mother's friends and all were anchored in the black church.[8]

Woodson shows how the foundation of low-income neighborhoods has been a casualty of the War on Poverty, as big government attempted to take on the roles that had once been filled by families, churches, and community groups. In his words, even the government agencies that are not overtly hostile to grassroots outreach (as the TCADA was) have inflicted "injury with the helping hand" with their regulations and restrictions.

By their very nature, needs-based public assistance programs tend to discourage work and marriage—which are the stepping-stones to upward mobility and the foundation of civil society, since in most cases marriage or increased work leads to a reduction in benefits. It should come as no surprise, then, that since the mid-1960s the greatest surge in out-of-wedlock births and the greatest disintegration of the family has occurred within our nation's poorest communities. Today, more than 70 percent of black children are born outside of marriage, a complete reversal from the 75 percent of black births within wedlock fifty years ago.

When families fragment, government services are often woefully inadequate to provide a secure environment for children. Consider the case with foster care. Today, half a million children are trapped in the system, and nearly 30,000 foster children "age out" each year at eighteen, never having experienced life in a stable family.

Compare that with the success of faith-based efforts to find adoptive families for children. In New Jersey, for example, the Harvest of Hope project launched by Pastor DeForest "Buster" Soaries and his congregation of the First Baptist Church of Lincoln Gardens has partnered with other churches in an effort to find foster homes and permanent families for children. To date, the initiative has recruited 455 African American families to serve as licensed foster care homes, and helped place more than 255 children with adoptive families.[9]

Please don't misunderstand me. I'm not suggesting that African Americans were better off in the 1940s or the 1960s than they are today. On the contrary, I think they are better off—especially since the enactment of the Civil Rights Act in 1964. But because of big government and the deterioration of civil society, they're not as well off as they should be.

Grassroots Initiatives and America's Founding Values

The approach of the grassroots leaders within the network of Bob Woodson's Center for Neighborhood Enterprise stands in sharp contrast to large government programs that typically view low-income Americans as dependent victims. CNE's community leaders recognize and build on the capacities of the poor. The essential goal of their outreach is not continued dependency, but a steady rise to self-sufficiency.

An emphasis on giving something back in return for benefits received is a common element of virtually all the neighborhood groups that Bob Woodson works with. As one former drug addict who is now helping to reach others declared at a conference cosponsored by Heritage and CNE, "Compassion without expectation is enablement."[10]

Step 13

Among the first grassroots organizers whom CNE worked with was Bob Coté, whose Denver-based residential program, Step 13, has turned around the lives of hundreds of hard-core addicts and alcoholics. In speaking to participants in a CNE What Works and Why forum, Coté told of one drunk he took in on a winter night; the man's face was frozen to the sidewalk in his own vomit when Coté found him. Men like that one, who entered Step 13 when their lives were seemingly beyond hope, have gone on to be responsible husbands and fathers, dependable employees, and successful entrepreneurs.[11]

Key elements of Coté's program are reciprocity, rewards for taking on increasing levels of responsibility, and, in his words, "constructive envy." All Step 13 residents work, whether it is at an outside job, performing tasks at the facility, or in one of the program's in-house companies (which include a car detailing service, the restoration of donated vehicles, a graphic design business launched by a resident, and a rent-a-worker program that provides everything from lawn care to restaurant staff). Some of the addicts who come to the program spend some time initially at a hospital or detox center to get off drugs. Those who live at Step 13 are screened for drugs and alcohol, and they attend weekly meetings.

All new residents start out sleeping in a military-style dorm. As they become more responsible, they progress to a single room, and then to an apartment. "When the guys see others who are working, saving, and buying a car or a computer, it shows them their life doesn't have to be the way it is," Coté said. "It's positive reinforcement that comes from their own."

Coté told the stories of Adam and Martin, who gave that sort of positive reinforcement to their counterparts at Step 13. Both were addicted to meth when they came to the program—Adam for ten years and Martin for fourteen. Because the drug notoriously attacks calcium, both first went to a dental clinic to fix their teeth and then received training for a job. Within two years, Martin had saved $34,000 and bought a home. Adam saved more than $20,000, bought a home, and continues to work with Step 13 as a steam cleaner in its auto business. "When the guys see these two men who were about as low as you can go and have now purchased a house and a car and have a good job, they know they can't give any excuses for themselves," Coté said. "I show them that homeless does not mean helpless."

With its in-house enterprises, Step 13 is 70 percent self-sufficient; in addition, it receives support from private donors, but no city, state, or federal funding. Coté decried typical homeless programs, which he calls "bunks for drunks"—they give alcoholics and addicts a "cot at night and a doughnut in the morning" before sending them back out onto the streets.

Having once been addicted to alcohol himself, Coté understood the psychology of the streets, and he knew how counterproductive are government programs that dole out checks and benefits, which enable addicts to, as he put it, "commit suicide on an installment plan." These include one city program that gives each participant an apartment and $720 a month. After paying $110 for rent, the individual can spend the rest of that money however he wants, including on alcohol. In Coté's words, "You have five hundred people with a master's in sociology dealing with two thousand street people with a doctorate in 'streetology,' so you know who is going to win!" He called the "experts'" approach "compassion without logic."

In sum, Coté put his strategy simply:

> Work Works. It pays for food, it pays for shelter, and it does something even more important: It gives the man the kind of self-esteem he needs to be a healthy, productive member of society.... What most homeless people need is help breaking an addiction and a way to build their self-respect. Blind compassion does nothing to promote their self-esteem and self-respect. Handing a dollar to a drunk just helps him stay drunk, and any program that takes responsibility away from a capable person dehumanizes that person.... At Step 13, we nurture in each resident independence, individual responsibility, self-sufficiency, and industriousness. We give a guy as long as he needs to turn his life around.[12]

Sadly, Bob Coté passed away on September 27, 2013, while I was still writing this book. Any tribute I could give pales in comparison to the legacy of saved lives he left behind, so I'll just say this: We need more like him.

House of Help, City of Hope

I could go on citing one inspiring success story after another, but I'll limit myself to one more.

In the shadow of the Capitol building in Washington,

Woodson discovered Bishop Shirley Holloway, of Mt. Olive Kingdom Fellowship International. In 1997, Bishop Holloway launched House of Help, City of Hope, a two-phase program that addresses homelessness, drug addiction, and alcoholism. Like Step 13, House of Help has some form of work requirement for all participants.

The first stage of Holloway's ministry, the House of Help, helps participants turn away from self-destructive behavior, attitudes, and relationships. They may also need immediate dental or medical care, counseling, and possibly medication to deal with the effects of years of addiction. When they are ready to move on to the second stage, the City of Hope part of the ministry helps each person to develop a plan for his or her life.

"We deal with the whole substance of a person," says Holloway. "You may stay at one stage for two years, but you don't leave until that's finished. Then you're ready to move to the next place. For example, do you need to go to school to get a high school diploma or a college degree?" Holloway has forged many partnerships throughout Washington, D.C., to offer work skills training, job placement, and entrepreneurial opportunities.[13]

Among the graduates of Holloway's program is Dawn, a third-generation welfare dependent who left the rolls by providing cleaning services. She has even gone on to launch her own small janitorial business, Early Morning Dawn.

Holloway's ministry to homeless men, women, and families has expanded from its initial location in an abandoned building to three refurbished facilities in D.C. and the surrounding area. She describes her work as providing "individuals that society has cast aside" with the "building blocks" to restore their lives.

One crucial building block is providing men and women with guidance in forming strong marriages. To date, dozens of couples have married through Holloway's ministry—and all but a handful of them have stayed married.

Little Platoons Throughout the Nation

In his efforts to identify neighborhood leaders who are changing lives and communities, Bob Woodson has followed the same strategy throughout the decades. He goes into barbershops, hairdressing salons, and lunch counters and asks the people there, "If you were in a time of crisis, who would you turn to?" It's not a high-tech method, but it is highly successful. In virtually every city he has visited, Bob has identified people who are selflessly serving to meet the needs of their neighbors.[14]

Since CNE was launched more than thirty years ago, Woodson has identified, supported, and provided training and technical assistance for thousands of grassroots leaders in dozens of states.[15] In 2013, Bob identified more than twenty groups in Milwaukee alone for policymakers who wanted to see, as he puts it, "what works, and why." Woodson compares the center's function to that of a metal detector that locates precious ores in the most unlikely places.

Woodson refers to these little platoons in low-income communities as America's "Josephs," after the young Israelite whose guidance revitalized Egypt at a time of crisis. He points out that Pharaoh was willing to go beyond his court counselors, who, like many of today's credentialed "experts," could offer no solution, and he says what today's Josephs need is to be linked to counterparts of "the Pharaoh," who can provide recognition, support, and resources for their efforts. He writes:

The answers to many problems America faces can be found in our own modern-day Josephs. Many of these community healers have come out of our prisons. They have experienced what it is to live in drug-infested, crime-ridden neighborhoods. Many have themselves fallen but have been able to recover through their faith in God. Their authority is attested to, not by their position and prestige in society, but by the thousands of lives they have been able to reach and change.... They embrace the worst cases and they work with meager resources, yet their effectiveness eclipses that of conventional professional remedies.[16]

And just as Woodson's little platoons have won victories in communities that face the greatest odds, they have counterparts who are leading the charge on every issue—from health care to education to welfare—that is critical to the well-being of our society. These modest men and women—not the arrogant know-it-alls who infest Washington's government agencies and bureaus—are America's real agents of change. They bring to life the relationships and allegiances that federal programs more often than not destroy—relationships that can turn lives around. They make our society glow with those "public affections" without which there can be no true patriots.

Too Big to Love

As big government has grown larger and ever more intrusive, we are in danger of falling out of love with our country.

B ob Woodson and his network of little platoons have very valuable lessons to teach the rest of us. Let me summarize what I learned from my meeting with Bob, and from studying his remarkable record of achievement:

• We need to remember, when we're talking about homelessness or drug addiction or juvenile delinquency, that we're not simply addressing abstract "problems." We're dealing with human beings—and humans are spiritual as well as physical beings. (That may sound corny and hopelessly old-fashioned, but it's true.) You can throw all the money in the world at their physical needs, but unless you find a way of breaking through to their spiritual core, you won't accomplish anything lasting.

• We need to be a little more humble and recognize our intellectual limitations. Human beings are complicated, and they have complicated problems. Comprehensive "solutions," developed at long distance by Washington bureaucrats—even well-meaning bureaucrats equipped with advanced academic degrees—are unlikely to improve matters, and might well end up hurting the very people they're supposed to help.

• We need to realize that our nation is blessed with Good Samaritans who really do love their neighbors, understand their problems, and are eager to help. We should look to these men and women for guidance, even if some of them never finished high school. We should try to create the conditions in which they, and the little platoons they lead, can effectively carry on their work. Above all, we should not undercut them.

Unfortunately, for decades Washington policymakers have ignored these lessons.

• Instead of empowering our little platoons, they have sidelined them.

• Instead of encouraging experimentation and innovation, they have developed one-size-fits-all programs that ignore local conditions and treat human beings as if they were interchangeable cogs in some vast social machine.

• Instead of measuring the success of social programs by the number of lives they turn around, they have measured success by the number of dollars they spend.

Under these circumstances, is it any wonder that we haven't had much success in helping the most vulnerable among us, despite huge expenditures of taxpayers' money? And what bothers me even more than the trillions of the tax dollars Washington has wasted is the impact this is having on America's spirit.

Once upon a time, we Americans were known for two characteristics that might seem contradictory: our intense love of our country, and our equally intense skepticism about the people who govern it. But as big government has grown ever larger and more intrusive, and as the little platoons that are the seedbeds of patriotism have been reduced to shadows of their former selves, we Americans—for the first time in our history—are in danger of falling out of love with our country.

This must not be allowed to happen.

Bob Woodson's story, and those of the courageous men and women with whom he has worked, are inspiring reminders of how regular people can change the world around them. Their stories provide vivid examples of how timeless principles and institutions such as personal responsibility, volunteerism, marriage, family, and work can rescue individuals and rebuild communities. Woodson's impact is truly a success story from the ground up, built on individuals and the little platoons that support them. Multiply Woodson's story millions of times over and you have the American success story.

I will share many more of these inspiring stories in later chapters. But it is important at the outset for every American to understand the main enemy of these successes—Big. Especially big government.

The greatest difference between the America of today and the America of a hundred years ago is that we have been changed from a bottom-up, decentralized team of little platoons to a top-down, centrally controlled conglomeration of Bigs. Progressive politicians have misled Americans into thinking that a better society can be achieved only through a strong central government with the power to institute "reforms" like Obamacare and No Child Left Behind. Once we understand the problems with Big, we can work together to restore the ideas and principles that work for all Americans.

Too Big to Trust

On June 17, 2013, Gallup released its annual national opinion survey about public confidence in major American institutions.[1] Of the sixteen institutions asked about in the poll, only three enjoyed the confidence of a majority of Americans: the military, small business, and the police. A fourth, organized religion, had the confidence of nearly half, 48 percent. And as you can see below, the other twelve had confidence ratings—the proportion of people who said they had either "a great deal" or "quite a lot" of confidence in them—of less than 40 percent.

Institution	Percent "a Great Deal" or "Quite a Lot" of Confidence
The presidency	36
The medical system	35
The U.S. Supreme Court	34
The public schools	32
The criminal justice system	28
Banks	26
Television news	23
Newspapers	23
Big business	22
Organized labor	20
Health maintenance organizations (HMOs)	19
Congress	10

I don't suppose you're surprised to see Congress bringing up the rear. After six years in the House of Representatives and eight in the Senate, I'm much more surprised about the 10 percent of the country that *does* have confidence in Congress than I am about the 90 percent that doesn't.

Confidence in these institutions is not only low, it's falling. Since Gallup's 2002 poll, public confidence in the presidency has fallen 22 percentage points; in banks, 21 points; and in Congress, 19 points. Newspapers and television news have both lost 12 points. Organized labor and public schools have both lost 6. Of these twelve institutions, only three have gained: HMOs by 6 points, big business by 2 points, and the criminal justice system by 1 point.

These specific numbers reflect a broader mood around the country, reflected in pollsters' well-known "Right Track/Wrong Track" question, which asks Americans about their view of the direction of the country. As I write, according to Real-ClearPolitics' "poll of polls," which averages the results of several national surveys, 59.1 percent of Americans believe the country is on the wrong track, and less than one-third—31.1 percent—believe we're on the right track. Across generational, regional, class, and party lines, Americans are anxious, frustrated, and confused about why the country doesn't seem to be working the way it once did.

In an excellent story, "In Nothing We Trust," *National Journal* reporters Ron Fournier and Sophie Quinton delved into these numbers and some real-life situations behind them to try to explain this broad collapse of public trust in the institutions that used to define—and invigorate—the American way of life. As they put it:

Government, politics, corporations, the media, organized religion, organized labor, banks, businesses, and other mainstays of a healthy society are failing. It's not just that the institutions are corrupt or broken; those clichés oversimplify an existential problem: With few notable exceptions, the nation's onetime social pillars are ill-equipped for the 21st century. Most critically, they are failing to adapt quickly enough for a population buffeted by wrenching economic, technological, and demographic change.[2]

All of this rings true. But *why?* What *happened?*

America has certainly changed a lot in the last ten, twenty, and forty years—but America has *always* changed a lot. Our openness to change, our innovativeness, our seemingly bottomless capacity to adapt is one of our nation's defining characteristics. There have been technological transformations and economic dislocations in recent years, but we've had those before too. We went from being subjects to being citizens, from having an agricultural economy to having an industrial one. We went from a rural to an urban to a suburban society. We've fought wars, absorbed immigrants, generated enormous social movements, and come out on the other side of all these changes *stronger* than when we went in.

What is different this time? Why is the national mood so anxious and public confidence in our institutions cratering *now?*

I believe the beginnings of an answer to this question can be found in the parts of that Gallup survey that received less attention: data about the institutions that *are* still trusted.

Take another look at the four top-scoring institutions in Gallup's 2013 public-confidence survey:

Institution	Percent "a Great Deal" or "Quite a Lot" of Confidence
The military	76
Small business	65
The police	57
The church or organized religion	48

What traits do these institutions have in common that other institutions seem not to share? The first thing that comes to mind, strictly as a practical consideration, is the competence or effectiveness of these institutions. At a basic level, they tend to do what they say they'll do. In most Americans' experience, servicemen, entrepreneurs, cops, pastors, and rabbis are good at their jobs.

Confidence in our military is almost universal among those who know even a single American soldier, sailor, airman, or marine. Today—although this hasn't always been the case—everyone in uniform is there by choice, to serve and protect. Ours is the finest fighting force in the world, the most professional, the most efficient, and the most moral and humane. America's warriors are our best and brightest, and we admire them for it. And again, at that most basic level of competence, the military does its job well: It keeps us safe, and wins our wars. Even the rare case of gross misconduct in the ranks stands out because we hold our servicemen to a high standard and demand that wrongdoing not be tolerated.

The police put criminals in jail and keep us and our property safe. There is the occasional case of police corruption, but these are dealt with firmly. Whatever your opinion about various criminal justice *policies*, there is no question that as a nation, we've rarely been safer from criminal violence.

What about religion? Does it deliver on what it offers to believers? Truth, answers, comfort, direction, motivation, strength, love, dignity, happiness? To the faithful, myself included, it absolutely does.

Finally, there is small business, which ranks *second* in this poll of public confidence, behind only the military. This may seem strange—entrepreneurs ahead of cops or pastors?—but remember that the poll doesn't ask people whom they *love*, but whom they *trust*: who they are confident will make good on their promises.

And making good on their promises is the only way small businesses survive. The money a grocery store or bicycle repair shop receives is given voluntarily, in exchange for something the customer regards as being of value. When there is a problem—a stained shirt, say, or a leaky faucet—the small business *fixes* it, or it doesn't get paid, and it loses customers.

In economic terms, these four trusted institutions *add value* to our lives. Individually and collectively, we are better off for our soldiers, cops, pastors, and entrepreneurs. Each in their own way, these people do right by us. They look out for our interests. They have our backs.

If I had to list the traits shared by these institutions that make them trustworthy, I would say a clear mission, honesty, accountability, responsiveness, and fairness.

Now, would you use those same words to describe the institutions listed in Gallup's survey that have *lost* the public's confidence? Prudent Wall Street banks? Honest politicians? Responsive health care bureaucrats? Would you call the media honest, or public schools accountable?

Seen from this perspective, I think that the *National Journal* article missed a key point in its analysis. Or rather, what the article *didn't* focus on might be just as important as what it did. It does say there are some "notable exceptions" to its indictment. I would identify these exceptions as the institutions that *do* still enjoy the trust of the American people. And on examination it's not hard to see why: They have earned it.

By contrast, the institutions that have *lost* the American people's confidence have deserved to lose it. I don't think this is a mystery at all. They're not trusted because they're not trustworthy.

The Bigs

As you might have noticed, they are also very big—or part of an institution, the federal government, that is very *very* big.

Look again at the four institutions that still have the public's confidence—the military, the police, small business, and organized religion. As I said earlier, big isn't always bad. What's bad is big and *impersonal*. And with the four trusted institutions, even if the overall organization is very big—as is the case with the U.S. military and with some religious denominations—the way we experience them in our lives is on a human scale: small, local, and personal.

The average size of an American police department is about twenty-five sworn officers. The vast majority of small businesses have only a handful of employees, if that. The median American church has seventy-five regular participants in its weekly congregation—just a few dozen families' worth.[3]

Even the U.S. military, one of the largest organizations in the world, is an exception that really does prove the rule.

Consider, first, that every branch of our armed services is broken down into close, tight-knit units that are in fact small—in the army, for example, a platoon has three or four squads, and a squad has only four to ten soldiers. Second, military personnel voluntarily subject themselves not only to the formal Uniform Code of Military Justice, which insists on much more individual discipline and subordination than any business's employee handbook, but also to the military's informal culture of honor, which does more to encourage individual virtue than would any threat of years in Leavenworth.

These factors distinguish our armed forces from other large organizations, and protect them from the problems associated with organizational bigness. The military looks big, but acts small.

On the other hand, the institutions that have *lost* the confidence of the American people tend to be the opposite of the small, responsive, accountable institutions that have kept it. They are (or constitute a proxy for) large, imperious, impersonal, and seemingly indifferent entities: the three branches of the federal government, the health care system, the criminal justice system, the media, the public education system, big business, and big labor.

Up and down the list, the problems of these institutions are problems of institutional bigness.

They are inflexible and slow to respond to the ever-changing needs and preferences of individuals in the modern world. They are complacent, satisfied, and heavily invested in a status quo that has given them their size, wealth, and influence, and therefore they are suspicious of—even hostile to—anything that threatens the status quo.

Like everyone else, people in these institutions have their own personal interests. They want to keep their jobs and increase their power and compensation. But people in these distrusted institutions don't have to earn their success in quite the same way as people in the trusted institutions.

Cops, small business owners, pastors and rabbis, and military personnel advance in their professions only if they add value to the lives of others. And that goes not just for the individuals, but also for the smaller organizations that make up the broader institutions. To succeed, police departments, military units, small businesses, churches, and synagogues have to *deliver*. People in the large, untrusted institutions don't.

In the economist Arthur Brooks's formulation, the difference between these two groups of people is the difference between "makers," those who have to produce to survive and earn their success, and "takers," the people and institutions that get along just fine despite failure, even repeated and catastrophic failure.

Evidence for this reality is easy to come by.

During the Great Recession of 2008–2009, thousands of innocent small businesses were caught in the crunch, couldn't pay their bills, and went under. Meanwhile, many of the giant corporations that had facilitated and profited from the financial mischief that led to the Wall Street crash got bailed out at taxpayer expense.

Lost Trust

The interesting story that emerges from the public-confidence survey isn't the doom-and-gloom, America-is-broken story the mainstream media give us (newspapers and television news earned their low confidence ratings in the Gallup poll too!), but the clear and revealing dividing line between the institutions Americans *do* trust and the ones we *don't*.

For all their apparent diversity of agendas, America's big institutions actually have much more in common with one another than with the people belonging to smaller institutions outside their exclusive circle. The distrusted Bigs not only have power over people in ways that smaller, trusted institutions do not, but they are also seemingly immune from the consequences of their mistakes. Smaller institutions—to say nothing of regular people—are not.

The result has been a loss of trust and public affection for America's large institutions and even for America itself.

The Crucial Difference

You can boil down the difference between the trusted and distrusted institutions, between Arthur Brooks's "makers" and "takers," to a single word: *service*.

The military, the police, small businesses, and religious institutions serve. They serve *us*, both as individuals and as the broader community. Their success—indeed, their very survival—depends on putting others ahead of themselves. A soldier and a police officer put their lives on the line for the rest of us. A small businessman provides us with the goods and services we need. And religious leaders, especially in the West's Judeo-Christian tradition, measure themselves against a standard of humble, charitable, self-sacrificial love.

Every soldier, cop, entrepreneur, pastor, and rabbi is human, of course, and falls short of his or her service ideals all the time. But the ideal exists, and adherence to it is the rule, rather than the exception, in America's trusted institutions.

This is one of the great moral triumphs of individual liberty. When individual success is based on service—as it is in a barracks, a storefront, a police station, a church, and a synagogue—people choose to serve. But the flip side of this story is one of the great moral cancers of entitlement. When people *can* succeed despite looking out only for themselves and ignoring everyone else, history and human nature tell us that many of them will choose *not* to serve.

Even the distrusted institutions have individual members who earn our trust. And our perceptions will depend on whether we're looking at those individuals or at the institution as a whole. "The medical system," for instance, can be seen two ways—as compassionate individual care providers or as a faceless, soulless bureaucracy. The same goes for the public schools, the criminal justice system, and the media institutions. People might have high regard for a hardworking and caring teacher, a wise judge, and a trusted newscaster or newspaper columnist, but they distrust the broader institution. Even banks, I bet, if Gallup for the purposes of the poll had divided them into big banks and community banks, would show a huge disparity—as in the experiences I recounted in the introduction to this book.

Even the Supreme Court and the presidency fit this pattern up to a point. There is nothing impersonal about the nine-member judicial body and the solitary chief executive. We know their names, and—whether we want to or not—we know quite a bit about those individuals. And yet they represent an enormous entity, the federal government, that seems ever more unresponsive to the American people.

And then at the bottom of the list are institutions that carry lack of responsiveness to extraordinary lengths—labor unions, big business, HMOs, and Congress.

Indeed, those four institutions seem almost defined these days by how much they are *not* looking out for us. They have their own agendas, interests, and incentives, which don't mesh with ours, and may be opposed or even hostile to ours.

That wasn't always the case. To find out how Americans came to so distrust our largest institutions, we have to first understand how and why Americans trusted them in the first place.

For there was a time when the federal government, large businesses like the automobile manufacturers, labor unions that helped their members achieve the American dream, and the big three TV channels seemed to make good on their promises. Whether that perception was ever as accurate as we remember is up for debate, but the fact is that today even the perception no longer exists. So what happened?

Big Connections

Consider again the lists of trusted and distrusted institutions in America today, and you'll notice another revealing pattern:

Trusted Institutions	Distrusted Institutions
The military	The presidency
Small business	The medical system
The police	The U.S. Supreme Court
The church or organized religion	The public schools
	The criminal justice system
	Banks
	Television news

(continued)

Trusted Institutions	Distrusted Institutions
	Newspapers
	Big business
	Organized labor
	Health maintenance organizations (HMOs)
	Congress

Do you notice that there seems to be a strong correlation between the public's distrust of an institution and the closeness of its bonds with the federal government?

Of the twelve institutions on the right-hand side:

• **three** are actually branches of the federal government (the Supreme Court, the presidency, and Congress);

• **two** are theoretically state or local government systems (criminal justice and the public schools), but Washington is exerting more control over them than ever;

• **three** are institutions that were already heavily regulated and that now have been all but taken over by the federal government (the medical system, HMOs, and banks); and

• **two** have been propped up by the federal government's recent forays into cronyism (big business and organized labor).

In fact, the only two distrusted institutions not tied to Washington, newspapers and television news, are losing customers, money, and credibility so quickly that calls have already been heard from those who revere the Age of Big for them to be rescued by—you guessed it—the federal government!

In other words, the distrusted institutions either are part of or inextricably bound up with the federal government, or are going broke.

What about the trusted institutions?

As a rule, small businesses not only have almost nothing to do with the federal government, but are famous for opposing and resenting federal regulations, favoritism, and taxes.

As for religion, we tried to protect it from our government with our First Amendment prohibition on government establishment of religion or interference with free exercise of religion. Unfortunately, the federal government is now threatening the freedom of religion by forcing faith-based organizations to provide coverage of abortion-inducing drugs they believe are wrong and by eroding the religious liberty of military personnel, to name just two examples.

The term "police" refers to state and local law enforcement. No one hears "police" and thinks "FBI." And though the federal government now sends more money to state and local police departments than ever before, Washington does not yet set policy for them. Local police work, as an institution, has almost nothing to do with Washington.

And then there is "the military," the most trusted of our nation's institutions, while at the same time an arm of the federal government. Does this fact contradict the trend? Not really. The military—with its culture of honor, code of conduct, legally enforced subordination, and social separation from the broader society—is distinct from what we normally mean when we say "the federal government."

Let me put it another way. Do you think of the secretary of defense as part of the federal government? Probably. But do you think of the secretary of defense when you imagine "the military"? Probably not. By contrast, the sailor or infantryman or fighter pilot you *do* think about when you hear "the military"—do you really associate him with Washington or "the federal government"? I didn't think so.

So now we have three emerging lines dividing trusted from distrusted institutions in America today.

Trusted institutions are either small or organized as a collection of small units; they succeed only through serving others; and they have little or no connection to the federal government. Distrusted institutions, by contrast, are large, can succeed despite indifference to others, and are part of, inextricably linked to, or propped up by the federal government.

I think it is this last dividing line—dependence on Washington—that is the most important.

After all, independent institutions that do not serve others fail. They are supposed to. Fast-food joints that don't cook their burgers the way customers ordered them, dry cleaners that send clothes back with stains still on them, charitable foundations that spend all their contributors' money on overhead—they are all likely to start losing customers or donors very quickly. Even wildly successful corporations that succumb to complacency and begin taking their customers for granted find themselves overtaken by smaller, hungrier competitors.

A free market, controlled by customer demand, *eliminates* complacent institutions. As soon as a business takes its customers for granted, or a nonprofit group takes advantage of its contributors, markets punish them for it and force them to either reform or close. Only government can guarantee survival to an institution, even when it fails in its core mission.

Why? Because government in the civilized world has the ultimate monopoly power: a monopoly on force. In many ways, a monopoly on force is *what government is.* This is true whether you're talking about a democratically accountable government, subject to the rule of law and popular consent, such as the U.S. government, or a brutal dictatorship like Hitler's Germany or Saddam Hussein's Iraq. As Jonah Goldberg puts it in his *Tyranny of Clichés,* "If you defy the government, eventually men with guns will come to your home and force you to either pay up or go to jail. If you resist, it is likely they will hit you or shoot you."

Pointing this out shouldn't be considered an attack on government. There are plenty of things about government to complain about, but its monopolization of force is not necessarily one of them. The monopolization of the *legitimate* use of force by government was a giant leap forward for humanity. Handing the mechanics of public order and national defense over to a group of people trained for the task of managing it gave everyone else the freedom to work at what *they* were best at.

But that monopoly is also what makes government power so perilous—so attractive to the kinds of people who should not have it, and dangerous in the hands of anyone unaccountable to the public. It's the ultimate power, the power to force rather than persuade. And it's the power that large institutions—that is, those with the most to lose in the unpredictable contest of competitive markets and voluntary exchanges—try to enlist to their ends.

If you take a look at one of the Bigs in contemporary America—actual monopolies or businesses or industries that act with a monopolist's indifference to consumer demand, customer service, quality, or innovation—you'll find high walls and deep moats of government policies protecting them from competition.

The secret to the failure of our big institutions is the failure of the biggest institution of them all. As obnoxious as the various Bigs may be—big banks, big business, big labor, big insurers, and so on—behind every one of them is the federal government, the Mother of Big.

The Mother of Big

Compared to the federal government, the largest corporation in America is a mom-and-pop store.

I f you think I am exaggerating, please consider these words, written by Thomas Jefferson, the author of the Declaration of Independence: "Experience hath shewn that even under the best form [of government] those entrusted with power have, in time, and by slow operations, perverted it into tyranny."[1]

Jefferson was right. There is nothing inherently corrupt about America's distrusted institutions. Labor unions, big businesses, the media, and the rest have done great things for our society. But when "perverted" by "those entrusted with power," these institutions take on the worst traits of government, especially the decoupling of service from success.

This decoupling occurs when an institution becomes so large as to be insulated from the negative effects it has upon the people it purports to serve. A Big is an organization that has reached such a size that its continued existence—its success—is no longer contingent upon its quality of service. This dubious distinction finds its highest manifestation in our bloated government.

Consider the relationship of the federal government to three great pillars of the American dream: owning a home, sending one's children to college, and retiring in comfort.

The desire for these things is almost universal. Everybody wants them, almost everybody is willing to work for them, and everybody who achieves them merits the respect of his friends and neighbors. People who retire with financial security, who own their own home, and have put their kids through school really can be said to have lived the American dream. These aspirations are pure, true, and good.

They're also hard to achieve—ask anyone who's done it, or is trying to do it.

Politicians know this. And so they ask themselves, "Wouldn't it be great if we could use government to make home ownership, college, and retirement security just a little bit easier—a little more accessible for people struggling to make it?"

Many—indeed *most*—citizens agree with this. And so Washington got to work.

The federal government created Social Security to protect Americans from poverty in their golden years, and Medicare to guarantee them health insurance.

To increase access to mortgages, the federal government created the Federal Housing Administration. And it created Fannie Mae and Freddie Mac as GSEs (government-sponsored enterprises) to lower the cost of mortgages so that more and more people could own their own homes.

And to increase access to higher education, the federal government plays a major role in providing subsidies, loans, and grants to students.

Again, noble aspirations, overwhelming public support, purity of intention on the part of all concerned. And what do we have to show for this "help"?

Own your own home . . .

Federal housing programs and subprime loan marketing enlarged the housing bubble of the 2000s. When the bubble burst, it helped to fuel the financial crisis that threw the U.S. economy into recession and spread across the planet.

. . . send your kids to college . . .

Federal intervention in the student loan industry is still in the process of inflating *its* bubble. Because government loans are not connected to either the performance or the price of a college, they allow schools to jack up tuition rates because students can borrow the money to pay the higher rates. Over the last thirty years, median family income has stagnated[2] while the cost of college tuition and fees has increased 439 percent—four times the rate of inflation.[3]

Yet, just as with the subprime mortgage bubble, many of the student borrowers will not be in a position to pay back their loans. Many of them don't stay in school, and even the ones who do graduate may get degrees that aren't worth very much in the job market. So chances are good that this bubble too will burst, and taxpayers will once again be on the hook for a trillion-dollar bailout.

. . . and retire in comfort.

Social Security's long-term shortfall is more than $12 trillion and rising. According to a 2010 Gallup poll, 76 percent of Americans aged eighteen to thirty-four do not believe the system will be there for them when they retire. Its so-called trust fund has no real assets, just IOUs from the U.S. Treasury.

As for Medicare's trust fund, it is operating at a cash flow deficit; that is, it sends out more money every year than it takes in. If it keeps on at this rate, Medicare's trustees have reported, it will be empty as soon as 2026.[4] They note that Medicare's long-term shortfall is more than $34 trillion and rising—although other economists peg it to be far worse.[5] And according to a 2011 Gallup poll, 67 percent of Americans believe Social Security and Medicare either are already in crisis or will be within ten years.[6]

The politicians who created these systems weren't stupid. They were motivated by compassion and all sorts of other positive emotions. They thought they were doing good. And these programs have *absolutely* helped *some* people *some* of the time. But they are government monopolies. And even though government monopolies don't go out of business, they do *fail*. They fail to live up to their promises, they fail to do right by their "customers" (citizens like you and me), and they fail to hold down costs—*all because they fail to serve.*

Unlike a business in the private sector, a government monopoly is never replaced. A chain bookstore such as Borders could replace independent bookstores, and Amazon.com could replace Borders. But no competitor can drive Medicare or Fannie Mae out of business, because government monopolies, subsidies, and regulations prevent competition. And because of their protected status, they don't have to break even to survive.

Indeed, when government programs do fail, politicians more often than not chalk the problems up to lack of funding, and throw good money after bad. So in the field of government-provided services, the only law we know for certain will work is the law of unintended consequences.

This is how government grows and grows and grows. Government's attempts to solve a problem, even when successful, unintentionally create two or three more problems. In time, those problems grow big enough to catch the politicians' attention, spurring them to create two or three more "solutions," which of course in time create six or nine new problems. And on and on.

In a free market, entrepreneurs figure out creative new ways to solve problems, producing ever better results at ever lower prices. Entrepreneurs do this because it's the only way for them to beat their competitors, win customers, and make a profit. Otherwise they fail, and other entrepreneurs learn from their failure. Government doesn't have to make a profit, so it doesn't have to solve problems, or improve quality, or lower its prices.

No one in government has been fired for the Social Security and Medicare crises. No government agency went under because of the subprime mortgage crisis. Congress considers itself wholly unaccountable for the financial crisis that will inevitably occur because of its massive increases in federal subsidies for student loans, even though a majority of its members have intentionally ignored the laws of mathematics as well as the law of unintended consequences in order to appeal to young voters and their parents.

The Three Problems of Big

There are three basic problems with these big, failed, but surviving monopolies run or supported by the federal government: the economic problem, the political problem, and the moral problem.

The Economic Problem

The economic problem is that these Bigs distort markets by giving politicians control over what rightly belongs to the people. In a free market, as we have seen, over time the better providers succeed and the worse providers fail. This is good for hundreds of reasons, but I'll name just two.

First of all, competition forces each competitor to serve us, his customers. In a competitive market, very few customers are taken advantage of or ignored.

Second, because markets reward only those companies and nonprofits that are good at their jobs—providing high quality for reasonable prices—the money that *isn't* spent on failing competitors in those markets gets redirected to more useful purposes. If a town has three plumbers, and has only enough business for two, the worst of the three is forced to get better at plumbing, sell his services for a lower price, or go into another line of work his community needs more of (teaching, perhaps, or landscaping, or accounting). Either way, both he and the town ultimately benefit—he by making a better living, and the town by getting higher-quality services one way or another.

Government intervention distorts all this by rewarding special interests for reasons that have nothing to do with improving quality, lowering price, or delivering what we want. When noncompetitive characteristics are rewarded, we get more of them: Prices rise, quality suffers, and the economy sags.

The Political Problem

Just as the Bigs distort our economy, they also distort our politics. As they turn their attention away from their customers and toward politicians, the Bigs simultaneously turn politicians' attention away from the national interest and toward special interests.

As soon as the first Big is told yes by Congress or the president or a regulatory body, that encourages other Bigs to ask for their own special favors.

Meanwhile, having created massive, unaffordable programs like Social Security and Medicare that, despite their flaws, are extremely popular, Congress lacks the political will to undertake the huge task of reforming them. Instead, lawmakers focus their energy and attention on small-bore gifts to their preferred Bigs.

This is how thousands of parochial special-interest earmarks work their way into almost every spending bill. This is one big reason why the Internal Revenue Code has swelled to tens of thousands of pages. Every little provision was lobbied for by some business or association or by a state or local government, which got a congressman or senator to insert it into some piece of legislation. While every American has the constitutional right to petition government for redress of grievances, when a Big petitions for a benefit that helps it at the expense of the rest of us, government should say no.

I can personally attest that Congress spends too much time hearing requests for special favors, working to include them in legislation, and collecting campaign contributions both from the parties who get the favors and those who want them in the future—and it spends almost no serious time on real matters of national consequence.

So the Bigs look out for the politicians, the politicians look out for the Bigs, and no one looks out for the people, who eventually sour on the obvious special dealing and double standards, and disengage from what they see as an unfair political system rigged against them.

The Moral Problem

They're right. This is the great *moral* problem of the Bigs: The special dealing they encourage is fundamentally unfair.

Our free-market system—with individual liberty, equality of opportunity, and personal accountability—is not perfect. But it *is* fair. It is fair that success is based on hard work and skill, and that it is earned in open, transparent competition, through voluntary transactions.

It is *not* fair for government to tip the scales of that competition for our dollars and take away our decision-making power and our freedom. It is *not* fair for Washington to rescue GM and Chrysler, which had lost fair and square to Ford, Toyota, and Honda.

Contrary to politicians' rhetoric, our current federal policies don't protect us from large, powerful institutions—they protect the large, powerful institutions from *us*. They protect some failing businesses from deserved bankruptcy. They protect failing labor unions from workers' choices. They protect large health insurers from the need to deal with actual customers. They protect big banks from their investment losses.

The result is that Washington forces the people who work hard, play by the rules, and live within their means to bail out the people who don't. It's not "the system"—the Republic established by the Founders and the free markets it protects—that's doing this. It's the federal government, including lawmakers and judges, that is slicing Americans into groups, some of which have to pay their hard-earned money *into* the system—while surrendering ever more of their freedom—so that other people and businesses can take it *out*. That is the key moral problem of this era of "too big to fail."

What has it wrought? A sagging economy, a fractured political system, and a society divided by government into competing special interests, all looking out for themselves at the expense of everyone else. And the worst casualty of all: our love for our wonderful country.

Too Big to Manage

To recap: Americans distrust some of the nation's largest institutions because those institutions are untrustworthy, and their untrustworthiness can be traced back to their unhealthy connection to America's biggest institution of all, the federal government.

So we have to fix the federal government.

But what if we can't? What if the reason no one can figure out how to reform the federal government is that it simply can't be reformed?

Take a look at our national politics and federal policymaking since 1981.

In the thirty-two years since Ronald Reagan was inaugurated, Republicans have held the White House for twenty years: eight under the conservative Reagan, four under the more moderate George H. W. Bush, and eight under George W. Bush, who seemed at times to be the most right-leaning *and* left-leaning of the three. Democrats have held the presidency for twelve of those years: eight under Bill Clinton, who governed as a liberal for two years and as a moderate Democrat for six; and four-plus, as I write, under the aggressively liberal and progressive Barack Obama.

The House of Representatives was held by the Democrats from 1981 until the Republicans won it in 1994. The GOP then held the House from 1995 until the 2006 elections, when the

Democrats took it back and held it for four years. The Republicans took it back again in 2010.

Meanwhile, the Republicans held the Senate from 1981 until 1987, the Democrats for eight years after that, then the Republicans for six, then it was tied, then the Democrats took it back for a while, then the Republicans did, then the Democrats did, and they still hold it at this writing, in mid-2013.

So I ask you. Set aside your partisanship: Which party is *really* to blame for the dysfunctional mess that is the federal government today? After all, the Democrats controlled Congress for most of Reagan's and Bush 41's terms, and the Republicans controlled it for most of Bill Clinton's. Can you really look at some social or economic problem and seriously argue that it's entirely Ronald Reagan's or Bill Clinton's or Newt Gingrich's or Nancy Pelosi's fault?

I'm not saying that there's no difference between the parties, or that federal elections don't matter. Instead, I'm saying that maybe the root cause of the dysfunction of the federal government isn't its transient political leadership, but something else entirely.

Think of it this way. In 2013 the federal government will spend about $3.5 trillion. A large chunk of that money will not achieve its intended purpose. Some of it will be wasted or stolen; some of it will disappear into the abyss of rampantly bad government accounting. And there will be pork-barrel spending and special-interest kickbacks and cronyism and all the rest.

But at the end of the day, the president is not a pilot flying an airplane, with all the controls in front of him in the cockpit. As far as the administration of the federal bureaucracy goes, the president is really just a manager. And no manager in the history of mankind has ever efficiently managed a $3.5 trillion organization with 4.5

million employees, let alone the $5.8 trillion government President Obama's official budget envisions for fiscal year 2022.

It is especially hard for anyone to manage efficiently a giant governmental organization that was not designed to operate efficiently. The framers of our Constitution intentionally designed it to be inefficient—dividing power between states and a central government and separating power among the three branches of government. Their purpose was not efficiency, but the preservation of liberty.

So this is not a criticism of Barack Obama, who before his inauguration as president had never managed *anything*. Nor is it a criticism of George W. Bush, who before his election as president had run, with varying degrees of success, a state, a major-league baseball team, and an oil company. What I'm saying is that efficiently managing a $3.5 trillion organization is humanly impossible—beyond the wit of man, as they say.

Does that sound like an exaggeration? Look at it this way.

The number one company in the Fortune 500 for 2013 is Wal-Mart, which in 2012 took in total revenues of about $470 *billion*, and which employs 2.1 million people. If it were part of the government, Wal-Mart would not even be the *second* biggest federal program. Both Social Security ($779 billion in 2012) and Medicare ($491 billion) are bigger.

Put it another way. In 2010, Medicare *fraud* was estimated to be $60 billion, or about seven times as much money as the combined profits of the nation's ten largest insurance companies. Compared to the federal government, the largest corporation in America is a mom-and-pop store.

Keep in mind, the CEOs of massive corporations are

handpicked from among the very best business managers on earth. They are the pinnacle of the pinnacle, chosen from an elite whose specific skills make them among the few people in the world capable of doing what they do.

The president of the United States, on the other hand, gets his job on the basis of political, public relations, and social factors that have nothing—*literally nothing*—to do with his executive, managerial competence. This is true of Republican and Democratic presidents alike. And it's not meant as a criticism of either party's candidates, or of our constitutional process of presidential elections. But there is no reason to believe that even the most inspiring national leader has any idea how to run a $3.5 trillion organization.

In fact, there is no reason to think that the most brilliant CEOs in corporate America could do much better than our recent presidents on this score.

Just look at Wall Street in 2008. That year, the five largest financial institutions in the United States—Citi, Bank of America, JPMorgan Chase, Goldman Sachs, and Morgan Stanley—had *combined* total revenues of less than $600 billion. These companies' senior executives were counted among the most brilliant, savvy, and sharp-eyed businessmen in the world. They were paid tens of millions of dollars for their managerial genius.

And by the end of the year, it had become clear that their companies were hopelessly entangled in a global financial crisis that destroyed trillions of dollars of wealth, and they didn't know what to do about it.

Think about that. Some of the most brilliant and best-trained executive minds on earth, running entities that were comparatively small (compared to the federal government, that is), were overwhelmed by their problems.

I don't mean to cherry-pick evidence or make any kind of case against talent and intelligence—the world could use a lot more of both. For every high-flying disaster in a corporate corner office, there are many equally brilliant managers who are prudent and wise. And I certainly don't believe that we should choose our presidents the way corporations choose their CEOs, or that we should elect only successful business managers to public office.

What I'm saying is that even the best business minds in the world have sometimes proven incapable of running businesses that, however huge they are in the corporate world, would only amount to a rounding error in the federal budget. Maybe the federal government has gotten so big, its problems grown so pervasive, that they can't be fixed.

It's not as if no one has ever tried.

After all, every president since Jimmy Carter has promised the American people a gimlet-eyed investigation of the federal bureaucracy to identify and weed out inefficiencies.

Ronald Reagan brought with him to the Oval Office The Heritage Foundation's groundbreaking *Mandate for Leadership* policy handbook, which laid out steps for reforming just about every agency, office, and bureau in the federal government. Reagan led a successful turnaround of our economy and our national self-esteem. But he did not succeed in dismantling a single cabinet-level department.

George H. W. Bush tasked Vice President Dan Quayle and his Council on Competitiveness with revamping and reforming federal regulations.

Bill Clinton set *his* vice president, Al Gore, to leading his administration's Reinventing Government initiative.

George W. Bush promised to bring his MBA private-sector

management style to bear on the bureaucracy. Bush's PART initiative reviewed every government program, but its recommendations were ignored by Congress.

Barack Obama claims his own efforts to reform the internal functions of government have been "unprecedented."

And yet the federal budget has only grown, grown, grown under all of the above. The only thing unprecedented about President Obama's fiscal discipline is its absence.

An objective observer might conclude that such efforts were cynical window dressing—lip service to limited government, but never meant to accomplish anything except make politicians look busy.

Maybe, but remember that all these initiatives were launched early in the new presidents' terms, when they were presumably at their most idealistic and confident of their capacity to realize their goals.

Mission Impossible?

Maybe I'm naïve, but isn't it at least as likely that these presidents simply discovered, in the course of their good-faith efforts to "reform" (however defined) the federal government, that the job was simply impossible?

Again, the federal government is one of the largest organizations in the history of the world, probably exceeded only by the massive state apparatuses of the Soviet Union and Communist China. Many of its employees are almost impossible to fire or even really discipline. It can never go out of business, at least not in the way a failing business can, and so there's no incentive to "beat" any competitor or "win" new customers. Meanwhile, the senior executives are mostly short-term appointees, while the workforce enjoys near-lifetime tenure.

If you're still doubtful, take a few moments and compare the president's situation with your own.

Imagine you were promoted to be senior manager of your office—henceforth, everyone will report ultimately to you. Now multiply the number of your company's employees—your coworkers—by, say, ten. Now try to work out in your mind how you could make such an organization work efficiently, both in day-to-day operations and in meeting long-term goals. It's a daunting task, but you probably already have a few ideas. But let's add a few presidential wrinkles.

First, imagine that you can't fire unproductive workers, and that all employees are in fact guaranteed raises every year regardless of how well or badly they do their jobs. Now imagine that you don't control your own budget either. Two committees—one of which has 100 members and the other 435, and approximately half of both not only oppose but sincerely hate your ideas—tell you how and where you can spend most of the money. The job I've described is only a fraction as difficult as the job of reforming the federal government, and it's already almost impossible.

Every four years, every presidential candidate promises voters that he will finally succeed where others have failed. And every four years, whichever one the voters choose, they will be disappointed.

Individual presidents, cabinet secretaries, and congressional committee chairmen can make improvements at the margins, but the federal government is simply too large to *fix* in anything like its current form.

Consider the path of someone tenacious and crazy enough to try to follow through on the job.

Let's say a brilliant, dedicated, one-of-a-kind cabinet member dives into the deadening morass of his department's bureaucracy, congressional oversight, and the authorizing and appropriating processes and figures out a way to save the American taxpayers the incredible amount of $300 billion.

Well, thanks, but $300 billion is about as much money as the federal government spends in a month. It's about as much as the federal government nowadays *borrows* every five months—that is, in less time than it would take the brilliant department head to get his money-saving scheme through Congress and enacted into law.

Furthermore, the most modest attempt to reduce government spending produces something akin to mass hysteria among the Washington establishment.

If you'll remember, in the spring of 2011, President Obama's congressional Democrats and the opposing Republicans almost shut down the government—and, according to some, brought the economy to the brink of chaos—over proposed budget cuts of slightly more than *one-tenth* of our cabinet member's cuts, a mere $38 billion, or about as much as Washington spends over a long weekend. Uncle Sam continued to operate as usual.

Let's not forget the sequestration "crisis" in the fall of 2012. Progressives on Capitol Hill and in the media predicted that the government would stall and the nation would be brought to its knees if federal spending was reduced by the required $85.3 billion. As I write, we are deep into 2013, and the world has not ended. Government agencies are operating and government checks are going out the door.

In point of fact, the sequester cuts only about 6 percent off the *growth* of government spending. Some programs will experience actual reductions, but most programs, including the very largest, will just grow more slowly. Federal spending will still rise by about 70 percent over the next decade.

More, much more, needs to be done to rein in big government, starting with the thinking of those who run Washington. They think government can do anything, and they think they have the answer for everything. That is what Nobel laureate Friedrich Hayek called "the fatal conceit."

For example, as many of America's largest institutions have in recent years neared collapse, the federal government—the Mother of Big—has stepped in to rescue them because politicians considered them "too big to fail."

I think this assessment is exactly backwards. The problem with big business, big labor, big education, big health care, big banks, and big government especially is not that they are too big to fail, but that they have not been allowed to fail.

4

The Rule of Big

When buying and selling are controlled by legislation,
the first things to be bought and sold are the legislators.
—P. J. O'Rourke

There are many reasons why America is such an exceptional nation, and one of the most important is the opportunity it offers ordinary men and women to make the most of their God-given talents. But an opportunity is not a guarantee: It takes hard work—*lots* of hard work—to realize the American dream.

No one understood this better than Frederick Douglass. A former slave who escaped from bondage to become one of America's leading abolitionists, Douglass honored and respected *free* labor as fervently as he hated and opposed *slave* labor. As he said in 1872, "America is said, and not without reason, to be preeminently the home and patron of self-made men.... Search where you will, there is no country on the globe where labor is so respected and the laborer so honored, as in this country."[1]

At the heart of the American dream is the idea that success must be earned. Just think of any successful person you know. Success is built on talent, hustle, concentration, discipline, honesty, and resourcefulness. Sam Walton, the founder of Wal-Mart Stores and the most successful merchant of his time, was at work every day at 4:30 in the morning and put in long days in his cramped office in Bentonville, Arkansas. "Mr. Sam" was the embodiment of the entrepreneurial spirit.

But let's be honest, the pursuit of success according to Mr. Sam's strict code is a grind. Trying to be good *all the time?* Bearing responsibility for your mistakes, knowing that a single one could throw your life off the rails? Outhustling your competitors, knowing that as soon as you do, your competitors will try to outhustle you by imitating and improving on everything you do?

The desire for life to be a little bit easier is universal—who wouldn't want to tilt the playing field a little bit, instead of having to work so hard for everything? There are, of course, two ways to make life come easier. The first is to work even harder for now, so that you can set aside some extra money to invest for the future, while delaying gratification in hopes of reaping even greater rewards down the line. As golfing great Arnold Palmer once said, "The more I practice, the luckier I get." This is the honorable path, taken by just about everyone you've ever respected in your life.

The second way to make life come easier is, well, to cheat—to break the rules of the game, whatever that game may be.

What does all this have to do with the present crisis of Big? Simply this: So long as there are only two ways to get ahead—the legitimate way, which leads to earned success, and the illegitimate way, which leads to unearned success or, if things go wrong, to jail—the system of freedom and responsibility we call democratic capitalism works very well.

As a rule, people who make good choices (who work hard, play by the rules, and live within their means) succeed, and people who make bad choices (who don't work hard, don't play by the rules, and live beyond their means) fail.

This goes for institutions large and small, and for people powerful and weak. The rules for all of us start with the law and, ultimately, the U.S. Constitution.

One of the problems of Big is that it creates a third option: neither obeying the rules nor breaking the rules, but *changing* the rules as you go. That's what happens in cronyism, which is in effect legal cheating. Emphasis on "legal."

That is one of the most frustrating aspects of the crisis of Big: Most of the time there is no *crime* to prosecute. The institutions that want to make life easier for themselves get the government to change the rules, so that what would have been cheating, and what many people *see* as cheating, is actually blessed by the state. The transactions of crony capitalism—campaign contributions on the one side, policy changes on the other—are all perfectly legal.

This is why so much of the criticism of special interests as such is incomplete, or even misdirected. Attacking special interests for accepting government favors is like criticizing a four-year-old for eating ice cream for breakfast. The proper targets of criticism are not the beneficiaries of the bad policy, but those in charge who acquiesce to their requests—the government agencies that provide the favors; the parents who allow their kids to eat whatever they want.

When government officials change policies to benefit special interests, the responsibility for the "cheating" lies with the officials, not the special interests. They, after all, are only playing by the rules the government sets. As long as politicians effectively put the rules of the game up for sale, it's hard to fault people for trying to buy or rent them. As P. J. O'Rourke once put it, "When buying and selling are controlled by legislation, the first things to be bought and sold are the legislators."[2]

And so, in this chapter about specific Bigs and their political mischief, keep in mind that in every single case their special pleading was successful only on the say-so of politicians and bureaucrats who are supposed to say no to them. In and of itself, it's not all that harmful to society for an oil company to try—to *try*—to influence energy policy or for a Wall Street bank to try to influence financial-services legislation. After all, they have a constitutional right to petition the government. What's harmful is when government officials say yes. However obnoxious it is that special interests spend so much time and money trying to get benefits from government, they're not the ones who took an oath to defend the Constitution.

The Founders did not create a government of limited powers because of some esoteric political or philosophical theory, but because of their practical observation that people are self-interested, and that people with power have a tendency to use their power selfishly.

And so, as the saying goes, "The only way to get rid of corruption in high places is to get rid of the high places." If you want to limit the power of special-interest lobbying, you have to limit the size, scope, and power of the government being lobbied.

Again, people are people. That goes for the special interests and the public officials they influence. Together, they have the power to make each other's lives easier, and, being people, they take the opportunity to do so. If this is at everyone else's expense, that doesn't especially matter to them because, again, the power of the state protects them from accountability to the public or the market.

And so they help each other . . . to our money.

Here are some examples.

Big Banks

As you may remember, the liberals who won the elections in 2008, in large part because of public anger about the financial crisis, responded to the subprime mortgage mess by crafting sweeping new regulations that would supposedly prevent anything like it from ever happening again. Liberals insisted that government regulators simply needed more power to prevent greedy bankers—"banksters"—from destroying the economy again.

The chairmen of the banking committees in the U.S. Senate, Chris Dodd (D–CT), and House of Representatives, Barney Frank (D–MA), set about writing their bill, which became known as Dodd-Frank.

What did Dodd-Frank do? Among other things, it created—and continues to create—thousands of new rules and regulations that will cost banks billions of dollars to comply with.

But only a handful of banks in the world can afford to spend that much money on regulatory compliance, so even the smartest, most competitive small and medium-sized banks today are permanently locked out of the top. They don't have extra hundreds of millions lying around to spend on lobbyists and lawyers to comply with endless new regulations.

What Dodd-Frank essentially accomplished was make sure that today's biggest banks will retain their dominance.

If you don't believe me, just ask the big bankers.

Jamie Dimon, CEO of JPMorgan Chase (the largest bank in the United States, with $1.8 trillion in deposits and $18 billion in annual profits), who is seen as Dodd-Frank's leading critic on Wall Street, has said at various times that he supports "75 percent" or "80 percent" of Dodd-Frank.[3]

Vikram Pandit, the CEO of Citigroup at the time, was the subject of a *New York Times* article headlined "Citigroup's Pandit Shows Love for Dodd-Frank," in which he is quoted as saying he supports "a lot" of Dodd-Frank.[4]

And Lloyd Blankfein, the CEO of Goldman Sachs, the world's largest investment bank, told Congress in 2010, "The biggest beneficiary of reform is Wall Street itself.... *The biggest risk is risk financial institutions have with each other*" (my emphasis).[5]

Read that last point again: The big banks aren't worried about regulation; they're worried about competition. And because government regulations eliminate much of the competition, big banks *love* big government.

Big Business

Of course, big banks are not the only ones who love big government. Almost all big corporations benefit from, advocate for, and downright like big government.

Consider the case of big tobacco. You would think that Altria, the parent company of Philip Morris, the largest tobacco company in America, would have bitterly opposed the Family Smoking Prevention and Tobacco Control Act of 2009, which for the first time placed tobacco products under the regulatory control of the notoriously heavy-handed Food and Drug Administration.

But while smaller tobacco companies *opposed* the Family Smoking Prevention and Tobacco Control Act, Altria *supported* it.[6] Why? Because when the FDA jumps into the market and changes the rules, those smaller tobacco growers and marketers would find themselves in a minefield without a map. On the other hand, not only would Altria, because of its standing in the industry, be able to hire all the lawyers it needs to navigate the new regulatory geography, but in all likelihood its lobbyists would have been working hand in glove with the FDA to craft the regulations in the first place.

This is a recurring theme; it's standard operating procedure for *most* federal regulation of the economy. Just like the biggest banks, the biggest tobacco company will take a hit from government regulations—in terms of regulatory compliance costs, legal fees, the need to hire more lobbyists, and so on—but because it's the biggest player in its industry, it can best absorb the hit. In fact, increased regulatory costs *help* industry-leading corporations stay on top, because the increased costs hamstring the smaller competitors. It would take years and millions of dollars to get an innovative, healthier product on the market—dollars a small tobacco company doesn't have.

In short, a Big sometimes welcomes more government regulation (especially if it gets to help write the regulations) because it gains an advantage over its competitors.

That's why H&R Block and Jackson Hewitt, the nation's largest tax preparation companies, supported new IRS regulations for tax preparers—while smaller tax-preparing companies and independent accountants opposed them.[7]

That's why leading food producers and their trade association, the Grocery Manufacturers of America, lobbied for stricter federal food regulation—while small and organic farmers and food processors opposed it.[8]

And that's why the nation's largest toy companies, Mattel and

Hasbro, lobbied *in favor* of strict new federal regulations on toys;[9] that's why General Electric, Philips, and Osram Sylvania lobbied *in favor* of stricter federal standards on lightbulbs;[10] and that's why the American Trucking Association *supported* new and stricter Environmental Protection Agency rules regulating the trucking industry.[11]

Of course, there are any number of examples of successful businesses that sincerely want to stay out of politics and cronyism and focus solely on their products and customers—but are pulled into the game by the politicians and bureaucrats.

Veteran Washington journalist Michael Kinsley, who was hired by Microsoft in 1995 to start its online magazine, *Slate*, wrote of the transformation Microsoft undertook in the wake of the federal Justice Department's antitrust lawsuit against the software giant:[12]

> For many years before the lawsuit, Microsoft had virtually no Washington "presence." It had a large office in the suburbs, mainly concerned with selling software to the government. Bill Gates resisted the notion that a software company needed to hire a lot of lobbyists and lawyers. He didn't want anything special from the government, except the freedom to build and sell software. If the government would leave him alone, he would leave the government alone.

This was typical of the high-technology industry that flowered on the West Coast in the 1980s and 1990s. The industry was so hypercompetitive, and the pace of innovation so breakneck, that companies and executives literally didn't have the time to take an eye off their business to focus on politicians. Kinsley continues:

At first this was regarded (at least in Washington) as naïve. Grown-up companies hire lobbyists. What's this guy's problem? Then it was regarded as foolish. This was not a game. There were big issues at stake. Next it came to be seen as arrogant: Who the hell does Microsoft think it is? Does it think it's too good to do what every other company of its size in the world is doing?

Ultimately, there even was a feeling that, in refusing to play the Washington game, Microsoft was being downright unpatriotic. Look, buddy, there is an American way of doing things, and that American way includes hiring lobbyists, paying lawyers vast sums by the hour, throwing lavish parties for politicians, aides, journalists, and so on. So get with the program.

To its credit, Microsoft resisted. But soon enough, the lawsuit came. It cost Microsoft millions of dollars in legal fees, tarnished its reputation, and, of course, forced it into "the game":

[Microsoft] moved its government affairs office out of distant Chevy Chase, Md., and into the downtown K Street corridor. It bulked up on lawyers and hired the best-connected lobbyists. Soon Microsoft was coming under criticism for being heavy-handed in its attempts to buy influence.

What's worse, as Kinsley notes, is that the rising generation of technology companies have learned from Microsoft's "mistake":

Google learned from Microsoft. It did not diss Washington. It has had a Washington lobbying operation almost from the very beginning of the company, way back in 2003. In 2008, Google opened a glamorous new D.C. office, described by Google's senior manager of global communications and public affairs as "a showcase of the company and what it means."

Please remember this the next time you hear someone complain about the corrupting influence of big business on government. Very often, it's the government that initiates the "dance." And very often, it's not a dance at all—it's a shakedown.

If you're angry about this, join the club. But whether you're a Tea Party conservative or an Occupy Wall Street liberal, understand that this is a bipartisan problem. Republicans attack Democrats for their support of green energy companies that eventually go belly up. And Democrats attack Republicans for their support of subsidies to oil and gas companies and coal companies.

The fact is, they're both right. But rather than working to get rid of federal help for both traditional and alternative sources of energy and leave the energy market in the hands of energy consumers, Republicans and Democrats instead agree to subsidies for *both*. That way, Republican and Democratic politicians get what they want—and the campaign contributions they *really* want—so everybody wins.

Everybody, that is, except the consumers and the taxpayers.

Bigonomics

How did Big take over so much of America? As so often in life, most of the explanation comes down to incentives.

Career bureaucrats and even high-ranking political appointees in the federal government tend to make somewhere between $75,000 and $200,000 a year. That's a very nice income, especially when you add in the government's ironclad job security and outrageously generous benefits. Nevertheless, the lobbyists for the institutions those officials regulate typically make two or three times that. High-ranking executives of those institutions make even more. In Washington, it's a rule of thumb that government staffers charged with overseeing an industry want to go to work for that industry one day, for a huge raise. "Cashing in," it's called, or "moving to K Street" (the downtown Washington artery that's synonymous with the lobbying business).

So, before the first meeting takes place and the work of drafting a new regulation gets started, there is built into every regulatory relationship in Washington a powerful incentive for the government overseers to "work with" the regulated industry, rather than antagonize it and burn future employment bridges. This is a good thing to get angry about, but judge not, lest ye be judged. Again, people are people. And the impulses and incentives built into this system are entirely human.

That's the truth behind the old joke that idealists go to Washington to do good, but stay to do very, very well.

The constitutional antidote to the unavoidable temptations of self-interest among regulators is to subject federal bureaucrats to intense congressional oversight. Congress creates the regulatory agencies, after all, and so it's Congress's job to make sure those agencies toe the line and don't get co-opted by big business.

But as soon as we say that, we're facing two more problems.

First, as I've pointed out before, the federal government is a $3.5 trillion organization. If its agencies and bureaus were divided up evenly among the 435 members of the House of Representatives and the 100 senators, each would be responsible for more than $6.5 billion worth of bureaucracy. Even assuming that all 535 members spent every hour of every day on bureaucratic oversight, focused like a laser beam on this boring, thankless work, they could hardly master more than a fraction of the bureaucracy in their domains. And this would all be to the exclusion of legislative priorities, committee assignments, constituent services, and the demands of today's endless reelection campaigns.

Furthermore, we would have to assume that each member of Congress is *competent* to understand and reform a $6.5 billion bureaucracy—a slice of the federal government that, if it were a private-sector company, would rank in the 380s in the Fortune 500 listings. As much as I like and respect my former colleagues, if they could competently manage $6.5 billion companies, they'd be doing it.

And even if these two far-fetched assumptions could be realized, you'd run into problem number two: Politicians have even stronger personal incentives to "partner" with the special interests than bureaucrats do. Unlike bureaucrats, congressmen and senators have to run for reelection every two or six years, and so their self-interest always pulls them toward the big special interests, which have all that money to give away.

So almost *everyone* in Washington has an incentive to grow government, scratch each other's back, and increase the "partnership" between government and special interests.

Today, there are so many bureaus, agencies, commissions, and government-sponsored enterprises (GSEs) that it's literally impossible for 535 congressmen and senators to keep track of them. The federal government is not only too big to succeed, it's too big to oversee and too big to control. There is nothing in the incentive structure to lead a member of Congress to spend a lot of time and energy watchdogging an anonymous regulatory office in an anonymous federal agency, keeping tabs on its decisions and expenses to make sure it's acting in the interests of the taxpayers and consumers.

So the dance goes on.

Big Labor

But big banks and big business aren't alone in loving big government. Their nominal antagonist, big labor—especially public-sector unions—loves big government too.

One of the most powerful and colorful leaders of the American labor movement was George Meany, who served as president of the AFL-CIO from 1955 to 1979. Meany started out as a plumber, and is responsible for one of my favorite quotes: "Anybody who has doubts about the ingenuity and resourcefulness of a plumber never got a bill from one."

Today, I'd change that quote to read, "Anybody who has doubts about the ingenuity and resourcefulness of big labor doesn't know how it's come to dominate the Democratic Party."

The magnitude of union influence in Democratic politics is truly astounding. The *Wall Street Journal* unearthed documents showing that the unions have actually spent *four times* as much on lobbying and election activities as was previously believed:[13]

The usual measure of unions' clout encompasses chiefly what they spend supporting federal candidates through their political-action committees, which are funded with voluntary contributions, and lobbying Washington, which is a cost borne by the unions' own coffers. These kinds of spending, which unions report to the Federal Election Commission and to Congress, totaled $1.1 billion from 2005 through 2011, according to the nonpartisan Center for Responsive Politics.

The unions' reports to the Labor Department capture an additional $3.3 billion that unions spent over the same period on political activity.

That adds up to $4.4 billion in just six years. That buys you a lot of favors. So do the boots on the ground that unions provide Democrats on election day:

The hours spent by union employees working on political matters were equivalent in 2010 to a shadow army much larger than President Barack Obama's current re-election staff, data analyzed by the *Journal* show.

The unions' "shadow army" in the 2010 *midterm* elections was larger than the president's 2012 reelection staff?

Even in Washington, $4.4 billion is a lot of money. It's not a stretch to say that without big labor, hundreds of state legislative seats, many governorships, and dozens of House and Senate seats would be out of the Left's reach. And without organized labor, progressives would have a hard time *ever* winning a presidential election.

As a strong advocate of the First Amendment and political free speech, I don't have any problem with labor unions engaging in politics, even to this enormous extent. As with any other market, the market for political speech should remain essentially free of government intervention. Rich or poor, conservative or liberal, individual or group, America belongs to all Americans, so all Americans should be free to get involved. Unfortunately, union membership is often coerced, with dues taken out of paychecks and used for political purposes without workers' permission. This is not free speech.

And what does big labor get for its enormous, invaluable political contributions to liberals? The same thing other Bigs get: direct subsidies, quasi-monopoly powers, bailouts, regulatory favoritism. Lots of things, as we'll see, but they all really boil down to one thing: money.

Automaker Bailouts

The most transparent political payoffs to big labor in recent years were the federal bailouts that rescued General Motors and Chrysler from bankruptcy. When the financial crisis hit in 2008, GM and Chrysler were among the many American companies that were simply not going to survive the storm. Neither company was remotely profitable; each had been losing billions of dollars in the years leading up to the financial crisis. They were failing businesses, on their way to bankruptcy.

But why was Washington in such a rush to bail out the automakers? Because their employees are union workers, and bankruptcy would have meant restructured contracts with the unions. These companies were not just hitting hard times—GM and Chrysler were *never* going to be able to sell enough cars to meet their retiree obligations. At the time of the bailout, General Motors had 96,000 employees, but supported more than a million retirees. The union contract allowed workers to retire in early middle age, at nearly full salary and benefits, and to keep collecting that pension for the rest of their lives. And so if the companies had been reorganized under a normal bankruptcy process, union benefits would have been the first in line to take a haircut. Wages for current workers would probably have been lowered, and the unsustainably high pension and health care benefits for retired workers would have been cut back.

But the federal government intervened. First under President George W. Bush, then continuing under President Obama, Washington shoveled billions to GM and Chrysler, stretching the TARP law, which was intended for financial institutions, to its limits.

The money didn't save GM or Chrysler from bankruptcy. But the federal cash put the Obama White House in a position to call the shots as the two firms were reorganized. The overwhelming beneficiaries of this infusion of taxpayer money were the unions, which were given unprecedented priority over other creditors of the bankrupt firms. In the GM bankruptcy alone, this was worth over $26 billion, more than the total net loss to taxpayers of the GM bailout. In other words, if it hadn't been for this union payoff, taxpayers would not have lost money on the GM bailout.[14]

Another underreported story was the tragedy of Delphi, a company that made parts for GM cars. One feature of the bailout was a fund of $1 billion to "top off" depleted pensions. Delphi, which had once been part of GM, had an agreement with GM that the former parent company would make good on its pension debts to the new company's employees. According to 2009 e-mails obtained by the *Daily Caller*, Treasury Secretary Timothy Geithner led the move within the Obama administration to make sure the "top-off" funds went only to *union* workers' pensions.[15] Delphi has both union and nonunion workers; its union workers, therefore, were bailed out, while its nonunion employees lost a good part of their pensions.

Every decision made in the auto bailouts was political. The more compensation GM and Chrysler employees receive, the more compulsory dues they pay to the union bosses, and the more the union bosses can spend to elect and reelect Democrats. In 2008 and 2009, big labor and big government got together, not to help the economy or the auto industry, but simply to help each other.

This shameless symbiotic relationship is not an anomaly. It happens every day in Washington, D.C.

In the spring of 2011, the National Labor Relations Board took legal action against the Boeing Company, based in Washington State, demanding that the airplane manufacturer shut down its brand-new $2 billion plant in my home state of South Carolina. South Carolina, you see, is a right-to-work state, where workers do not have to join a union as a condition of employment. But the machinist unions that control Boeing's Washington factories and plants felt those South Carolina jobs belonged to them. The Obama administration agreed, and tried to kill thousands of South Carolina jobs to appease its union clients.

Never mind that the union's contract with Boeing gave the company total freedom to build new factories wherever it wanted, and that the South Carolina jobs were all *new*—all the existing union jobs in Washington continued.

The NLRB's complaint was eventually settled—the union agreed to drop the complaint as part of its contract renegotiations with Boeing—but you can be sure that President Obama's NLRB has not given up its position that businesses should be able to locate only where the labor unions and the federal government say they can.

Public-Sector Unions

Private-sector unions such as the autoworkers and Teamsters are often corrupt and overly cozy with big government, but at least they have a basic claim to moral and economic legitimacy. That cannot be said of government-employee unions.

The rationale for organized labor goes something like this: Because the workers at a given company help create that company's profits, they are morally entitled to a fair share of the wealth. If, by organizing and bargaining collectively, they can negotiate more favorable employment terms, extracting from the company higher compensation and better work conditions than they might negotiate individually, they have the right to do so. Especially when the union movement started, more than a century ago, and workers had less geographical mobility than they do now, they were seen as particularly vulnerable to exploitation by the richer, better-connected, and more powerful business owners.

But with public-sector workers, the moral logic of collective bargaining is not only inapplicable, it has been turned completely on its head. Again, in a private business, employers and employees are both responsible for the company's profitability. Employees are free to negotiate for more money. But if labor costs go too high, forcing the company to raise the price of its products, customers will go elsewhere, and both the employer and the employees will suffer.

But government doesn't work that way. Its "customers"—a.k.a. taxpayers—can't go elsewhere. Rising costs are simply paid for with higher taxes or more debt. There is nothing keeping employees from demanding more, and not much reason for government managers to say no.

In fact, the system gives them every reason to say yes not just to higher salaries, but to more government employees. The more the government spends, the more government workers it hires, which means more government union members, more government union dues, and more money to spend electing big-spending politicians. Wash, rinse, repeat.

The result? In states and municipalities around the country, government unions so dominate local politics that their labor contracts are *literally* bankrupting whole communities—not just headline-grabbing Detroit, but also places like Boise County, Idaho, Central Falls, Rhode Island, and Stockton, California.

To see how wrong the current situation is, think back to your grade-school history classes. Most of us were taught that the unions arose to protect poorly educated laborers toiling in dangerous factories and sooty mills. And there is a lot of truth to that. But today, the majority of union members aren't manual laborers. They are bureaucrats with undergraduate and often graduate degrees working at computers in air-conditioned offices.

What's more, unlike private-sector union members, government union members tend to make more money than the people who pay them—the taxpayers. The average federal employee today earns, in salary and benefits, about twice as much as the national average for the whole workforce. That is, the average public-sector employee makes twice as much in salary and benefits as the average American.[16] Government union members don't produce anything, but still earn twice as much money as their bosses—the American public—who do.

The original justification for unions was that they protected the vulnerable from exploitation at the hands of an unaccountable economic elite. But today it is the public-sector unions that are doing the exploiting and the taxpayers who need protecting.

Ironically, the very idea of collective bargaining by government employees was anathema to liberals, and even labor leaders, of an earlier era.

Franklin Roosevelt wrote in 1937, "The process of collective bargaining, as usually understood, cannot be transplanted into the public service." He went on, "A strike of public employees manifests nothing less than an intent on their part to prevent or obstruct the operations of Government."[17] George Meany agreed with FDR. "It is impossible to bargain collectively with the government," he said in 1955.[18]

Roosevelt, Meany, and other liberals until roughly the 1960s understood that the labor movement in the United States was part of the productive private economy that created the nation's wealth. They understood that there was something deeply undemocratic and un-American about a special class of workers pitting their personal interests against those of the American people, as if there should be an inherently adversarial relationship between public servants and the public.

Yet that is exactly where things stand in jurisdictions across the country—to the detriment of taxpayers, communities, individual freedom, and fundamental justice. As always, the question arises: How do they get away with it? And as I hope you've guessed by now, the answer is: *big government*.

Public-sector unions spend enormous amounts of money electing big-government politicians. Those politicians are then the ones who negotiate and approve compensation and benefits for public employees. The politicians' reelections and personal ambitions depend in large part on the continued support of the unions, and so they have every incentive to offer them more, more, and more: higher pay, more generous benefits, greater job security. Both sides in the negotiations have a direct incentive to jack up the taxpayers' obligations to the unions, and no one stands up for the taxpayers.

And just as with the other Bigs, public-sector unions get plenty of indirect assistance from government to go along with the cold hard cash.

Teachers' unions are perhaps the most powerful government unions. They have become such a powerful force, especially in the Democratic Party, that they almost completely control education policy in Washington, D.C., as well as in many states and school districts around the country. And while there are many dedicated teachers in K–12 schools throughout America, there's little doubt that teachers' unions put the interests of their members ahead of the interests of students and parents—with catastrophic results. (I'll have much more to say about them later on, when I discuss education policy.)

And it's not just the teachers' unions.

In Minnesota in 2004, government-employed bus drivers in the Twin Cities struck, leaving the transportation system in chaos, to protest reforms insisted upon by then governor Tim Pawlenty. In the end, Pawlenty won his reforms and saved his taxpayers millions of dollars.[19]

When Wisconsin governor Scott Walker and Republicans in the legislature tried in 2011 to modify state-employee collective bargaining rights, government employees marched on the capitol in Madison. Democrats in the legislature, lacking the votes to stop the measure, fled the state to prevent the state senate from voting on the budget. The unions eventually lost. Then they sued.

Then they spent millions of dollars trying to recall Walker. And they failed, at least in part because Walker's opponent in the recall election had used the collective bargaining reforms to balance his county's budget![20]

In California, cities and towns like Stockton, San Bernardino, and Mammoth Lakes are declaring bankruptcy because their employee retirement costs are destroying their budgets. Other cities are taking preventive measures to reform employee benefits. The very night Walker won his recall election, voters in San Diego and San Jose overwhelmingly endorsed such reforms.

In sum, from California to Rhode Island to Wisconsin to New York, reformers are trying to get their budgets out from under the crushing weight of decades of union contracts made possible by decades of cronyism.

Big Problems

I hope it is clear by now that despite all the promises you hear from politicians, big government does not really help the little guy. Big government fosters big business, big unions, and big costs to taxpayers. Big government and its big partners rob individuals and our nation of freedom, opportunity, and prosperity. Even worse, the Bigs have put America and the world on a catastrophic economic course.

We've heard a lot about the bankruptcy of Greece and the economic decline of other European countries. This is a result of big government, big public employee unions, big taxes, big cradle-to-grave welfare entitlements, and socialistic policies that have destroyed the private sector. And now the stories of big debt and bankruptcies are coming from right here at home.

Look at the city of Detroit, which has been controlled by liberal/progressive lawmakers and big unions for more than half a century. Four months before the city filed for bankruptcy, the Republican governor of Michigan, Rick Snyder, acting under state law, made the unprecedented move of taking all decisions about the city's finances away from elected local politicians and putting them in the hands of a professional manager.

Other major U.S. cities and many states, such as California and Illinois, are following Detroit and Europe into the abyss created by big government and big labor.

The U.S. national debt is now larger than our economy and increasing by hundreds of billions every year. State and local debt exceeds $3 trillion, with another $3 trillion in unfunded pension obligations. The numbers are too big to imagine. And that's my point. Big government leads to big problems while replacing the little platoons that really work.

There is still time to turn our country around. In the following chapters, we will see how the little platoons are making a difference day in and day out in every part of America. But first we need to take a look at an institution our Founders bequeathed us that's as vital to the little platoons as oxygen is to humans: Madisonian federalism.

Federalism: Our Founders' Priceless Legacy

We need to rediscover true federalism so as to revitalize the little platoons of family, church, and community.

You may wonder why I am devoting an entire chapter to federalism, which may sound like something only a political scientist would care about. Well, the reason is simple: Federalism provides our nation's little platoons with the space they need to grow and flourish. And if we want to overturn the stifling rule of the Bigs, the little platoons are our best hope. So, no federalism, no little platoons. The connection is that fundamental.

Please bear with me as I explain the key role of federalism in helping all of us to love America again.

Since the founding of the Republic more than two hundred years ago, there have been many different ideas about federalism. Political scientists have coined many phrases—"creative" federalism, "fiscal" federalism, "new" federalism, "competitive" federalism, "cooperative" federalism—to describe different ways of answering the question of what is the proper relationship between the states and the national government.

And then there is the original federalism of James Madison and the other Founders, who constructed what they believed was a balanced relationship between the national government and the states. Because their main concern was a too strong central government—King George III was still very much on their minds—they created an elaborate system of checks and balances between the three branches of the federal government and between the federal government and state governments. The structural separation and division of powers was the Founders' design for preserving our liberty.

Summarizing what the Founders had in mind, Madison wrote in *Federalist* No. 45, "The powers delegated by the proposed Constitution to the federal government are few and defined. Those which are to remain in the State governments are numerous and indefinite." You can tell which government Madison considered more important—he capitalized the word "State" but not the word "federal."

Madisonian federalism recognized a legitimate national authority while protecting state autonomy, local self-government, and, as constitutional scholar Matthew Spalding put it, "a vast realm of [personal] liberty."[1] A half century later, the French political thinker Alexis de Tocqueville observed that the result was "a great open space" for an amazing civil society where character-forming institutions like families, schools, and churches—Tocqueville's version of Burke's little platoons—were free to cultivate the virtues required for self-government. However, he warned, an ever-expanding central government could seriously weaken and even wipe out such voluntary associations.

In the Founders' view, the states were essential to the new polity they were establishing. As the constitutional scholar Eugene W. Hickok has written, the men who gathered in Philadelphia for the Constitutional Convention of 1787 came as delegates from their states. The Constitution, once drafted and accepted by the Constitutional Convention, was debated and had to be ratified by state conventions. The central debate in Philadelphia and in the later state conventions revolved around the relationship between the proposed central government and the governments of the several states.[2]

When you think about it, federalism has been at the heart of many of America's most heated controversies. Americans think of the Civil War as being about abolishing slavery, and in large part it was. But it was also, and importantly, over the relationship between the central government and the states. The New Deal became possible only after the Supreme Court decided to allow President Franklin Roosevelt's unprecedented expansion of federal power. Present-day issues such as abortion and gay marriage are partly federalist issues.

And yet federalism is frequently misapplied and misinterpreted. For example, constitutional federalism is not "states' rights." As Hickok puts it, "Individuals have rights. Governments at all levels have various powers but not rights." To merge federalism with states' rights "tends to confuse the meaning of both." Too often, says Hickok, the idea of states' rights is used to appeal to old passions and calls up images of racism and discrimination.

We need to rediscover *true* federalism so as to revitalize the little platoons of family, church, and community.

It won't be easy, because the progressivism initiated in the early twentieth century, advanced by Woodrow Wilson, expanded by Franklin Roosevelt and Lyndon Johnson, and expanded yet again by Barack Obama, has brought profound changes at all levels of government. Progressives believe passionately in the efficiency and the necessity of centralized planning. They think big government is the solution, although most Americans know it's the problem. Progressives from Wilson to Obama never met a problem they didn't believe the federal government could solve.

The birth of big government came with the dawn of the twentieth century, when Congress established federal control of the banking system, strengthened antitrust laws, began shrinking our economic liberty, and started regulating workplace conditions. The most sweeping change came in 1913 with the ratification of the Sixteenth Amendment, which gave Washington the authority to establish a national income tax. "The income tax," Hickok writes, "established forever the political advantage the national government would have over the states." As the use of this authority developed through the twentieth century, it enabled the federal government to make billion-dollar grants to the states for national programs, largely transforming once-independent states into administrative arms of the national government.[3]

That same year of 1913, the Seventeenth Amendment authorized the direct election of U.S. senators, doing away with the principle that the Senate should reflect state interests, not popular interests. Congress was turned into a wholly national institution, and, just like that, the federalism envisioned by the Founders was almost gone.

With the New Deal as his primary instrument, President Franklin D. Roosevelt expanded the federal government into every economic nook and social cranny of America. The New Deal has been rightly called a constitutional revolution. The once-accepted understanding of the Constitution as having permanent principles was replaced by the notion of a "living" Constitution whose meaning could change depending upon the political winds and the disposition of the Supreme Court justices. As Chief Justice Charles Evans Hughes once put it, "The Constitution is what the judges say it is."[4]

Under progressive federalism, the states were allowed to retain authority over some issues within their borders—like public schools and law enforcement—but in other areas accepted a secondary role as administrators of national programs enacted in Washington, underwritten by federal tax dollars, and carried out at the state and local levels. Regrettably, states got in the habit of taking money from Washington and accepting Washington's conditions on how to administer the money, thereby becoming administrative branches of the federal government. Inevitably, the influence of the little platoons sharply declined as citizens accepted an ever-increasing presence of government in their lives.

Sad to say, Americans became clients of the government rather than the masters of it—straying far from the original intention of the Founders. Public assistance became entitlements, and more than 45 million Americans now receive food stamps. Uncle Sam turned into Big Brother, who seemingly had bottomless pockets, which of course were really the pockets of the taxpayers. At least bottomless pockets are what many thought we had until the Great Recession that began in 2008.

That recession sparked a great awakening of a different kind for the American people, expressed most dramatically in the emergence of the Tea Party, which rose up and scored stunning political successes in 2010.

Which brings us to today and two questions:

Is it possible for America to return to the original federalism of the Founders?

Is it possible to redress the current imbalance between the federal government and the states?

These are not simply academic questions. I am convinced that if we do not bring back the original federalism, *true* federalism, our nation is headed for a future very different from what you and I dreamed of when we were starting out.

Why is federalism so important? Let me turn again to Alexis de Tocqueville, one of the most perceptive observers ever to visit our shores. As I said in the Introduction, he saw that within our states were hundreds and hundreds of communities made up of individuals engaged in self-government. These communities were sustained by civic associations, religious and charitable organizations, business groups, local newspapers, and political parties. They built schools and hospitals and roads and churches, and in so doing deepened and widened and enriched the spirit of America.

Tocqueville identified two major factors that sustained that spirit: active local governments operating within a federal system, and a belief held by the American people that they were the masters of their own fate.[5] That belief was weakened and then turned upside down under progressive presidents from Wilson and FDR to Harry Truman and Lyndon Johnson.

Big government continued to see the American people not as independent citizens who can provide for themselves and help their fellow citizens but, in the words of my predecessor at Heritage, Ed Feulner, as "subjects whom it must tax and on whom it must spend." Government, Feulner went on, must be built on respect for the virtues of a civil society—especially freedom and faith—"or it will ultimately destroy civil society."[6] Citizens need not only a government that supports freedom but a balanced federalism that makes freedom possible.

The Heritage Foundation has highlighted areas where changes in the relationship between the federal government and the state governments should be undertaken:

- **Education**: States should be able to direct their own education funds without being restricted by federal plans and mandates.
- **Transportation**: Each state should be able to control and assign priorities for its own highway/transportation programs, in addition to being allowed to retain all the federal fuel tax revenues raised within the state.
- **Homeland security**: Replace complicated grants with cooperative agreements, and get the federal government out of every "natural disaster" relief project.
- **Overcriminalization**: We are in danger of becoming a nation under arrest. Congress should require proof of a guilty state of mind for federal criminal offenses and punish only those who are blameworthy.[7]

Despite what you may have heard, I can report that the American spirit has not faded away and that a faithful version of the original federalism is making a strong comeback in our states, cities, towns, and communities.

Here, for example, is what several of our more entrepreneurial governors are doing:

During his two terms as Indiana governor, from 2005 to 2013, Mitch Daniels cut the number of state employees by 18 percent; trimmed and capped state property taxes; balanced the state budget by holding spending to less than the inflation rate; enacted a statewide school voucher program; and adopted the first right-to-work legislation among the states in a decade. He also took on social issues, signing bills that toughened drug enforcement, regulated abortion, and defended traditional marriage. [8]

As a result, Daniels received kudos left and right, including the 2010 Herman Kahn Award from the Hudson Institute and a 2013 Bradley Prize from the Lynde and Harry Bradley Foundation. The *Economist* praised the governor for his "restraint and efficiency" and said he was "the kind of man who relishes fixing a broken state—or country."[9] Urged to seek the 2012 Republican presidential nomination, Daniels ultimately decided instead to accept the post of president of Purdue University, no small responsibility. The current state of higher education is one of America's most pressing problems.

Governor Bobby Jindal, elected to his first term in 2007, implemented an unprecedented purge of Louisiana's historically corrupt government, raising the state from number forty-six in integrity (as rated by the Better Government Association) to number five. He has cut state taxes six times and returned $1.1 billion to the taxpayers.[10] He continues to press for eliminating the state income tax and shifting to a sales tax, as Texas did years ago. Although fiercely condemned by teachers' unions and harassed by the U.S. Department of Justice, Jindal has worked to defend the school voucher program he expanded to improve education in Louisiana.

One month after taking office in 2011, Governor Scott Walker of Wisconsin, at great political risk, supported legislation requiring state public employees to increase their contribution to their pension and health plans and eliminating many of their collective bargaining rights. FDR—who, as we saw in chapter 5, believed public employee unions were a contradiction in terms—would have warmly endorsed Walker's initiative. Walker survived a walkout of Democrats from the state legislature and a recall election—proving that Wisconsin voters endorsed his reforms, which dramatically shifted state spending, from a $3.6 billion deficit to a half-billion-dollar surplus.[11]

Declaring in 2012, his second year in office, that he had a plan to "reinvent" Michigan, Governor Rick Snyder shook up the state's liberal establishment by reducing spending by $1.8 billion and abolishing the state's business tax. As part of his plan to attract business and jobs to the state, Snyder also signed landmark legislation making Michigan the twenty-fourth right-to-work state. Big labor is still in a state of shock.[12]

Recognizing the reality of a global economy, the Michigan governor led trade missions to Europe, Asia, and other regions, seeking to improve business relations with foreign countries and open up research and development possibilities with foreign universities.

Oklahoma governor Mary Fallin took office in 2011 and immediately set to work. She cut the state income tax, provided relief to working families, and spurred economic growth in the private sector. Her first year in office, Oklahoma achieved a net increase of about 41,000 jobs and kept the unemployment rate among the lowest in the country. The state ranked first in the nation in growth of manufacturing jobs in 2011; Oklahoma's manufacturing workforce that year grew five times faster than the national average.[13]

Daniels, Jindal, Walker, Snyder, and Fallin represent a new breed of governor, committed to fiscal prudence, cooperation between the private and public sectors, unapologetic compassion for the disadvantaged, and the forging of a new and more balanced relationship with the federal government.

Now, they haven't had to do it all on their own. They are fortunate in that they can call on a close-by resource to help them, in the form of the flourishing network of conservative state think tanks stretching from Bangor, Maine, to Sacramento, California.

The origins of the state think tanks can be traced to a September 1973 meeting among Henry Hyde, at that time still an Illinois state representative; future Illinois state senator Mark Rhoads; conservative activist Paul Weyrich, founder of the Free Congress Foundation and a cofounder of The Heritage Foundation; and Lou Barnett, who had worked on Ronald Reagan's 1968 presidential campaign and would later head Reagan's political action committee, Citizens for the Republic. At this meeting, they launched the American Legislative Exchange Council (ALEC), which for forty years has been promoting limited government, free markets, federalism, and individual liberty in state legislatures.[14]

In 1981, ALEC was inspired by President Reagan's formation of a national Task Force on Federalism to develop task forces on health care, education, civil justice, and other issues, seeking to decentralize government and move authority from the federal to the state level.

By the time President Reagan left office in 1989, ALEC had begun encouraging the formation of freestanding think tanks and writing model legislation for the state legislatures. Today, about a thousand bills based at least in part on ALEC research are introduced every year in the states. On average, about 20 percent are enacted, among them laws establishing the testing of teacher competency, pension reform, and enterprise zones in the inner cities.

ALEC's success caught the attention of South Carolina

businessman Thomas A. Roe, a longtime Heritage trustee, who in 1986 had expressed a concern to President Reagan about his "New Federalism." Roe pointed out that Reagan's program transferred powers and resources to state-level bureaucrats, who "weren't necessarily better" than their federal counterparts. The states, Roe said, needed something like The Heritage Foundation. Reagan replied, "Do something about it." Tom Roe did, leading the establishment of the South Carolina Policy Council and then, in 1992, the State Policy Network. "I'm a grassroots person," Roe explained.[15]

I am proud to say that Heritage has always been a strong supporter of state think tanks. For example, John Andrews, founder of the Independence Institute in Golden, Colorado, says that his organization "nursed at Heritage's breast."[16]

The State Policy Network says that the most important step in policy work is defining your end goal. What will create lasting policy change? Whom do we educate? Should we use digital or old media? Should you depend on grassroots outreach or personal lobbying? Success, says SPN, "takes the heart of a social worker and the brains of a military strategist."[17]

Right here, I must utter a note of caution about expecting too much from federalism. One commentator has declared, "Federalism is simply the best political system ever conceived of for maximizing human happiness."[18] Tell that to the inhabitants of the "progressive" state of California, which has so taxed and regulated its people that they are moving by the thousands to Texas, Nevada, and—who knows?—perhaps even Canada in pursuit of freedom. The truth is that there are good state governments and bad state governments, good governors and bad governors. People can stay and help fix their state governments or "vote with their feet" and move to states with better governments.

The American Enterprise Institute's Michael Greve has pointed out two problems with what he calls "excessive decentralization," one regulatory, the other fiscal. Suppose you want to run a national enterprise that sells things on the Internet, produces lifesaving drugs, or provides flood insurance. You immediately face legislatures, courts, attorneys general, and regulators from fifty states, all "united in a desire to have a piece of you and your business."[19]

Some states have declared they have a right to conduct their own global warming policy and have signed what purport to be greenhouse treaties with foreign nations. In many ways, state overreach has paralleled federal overreach.

Fiscally, the problem is that federal transfer programs are as irresistible to some governors and state legislatures as catnip is to a cat. Medicaid is growing by leaps and bounds in large measure because some states are willing to expand it to get federal matching funds. Apparently they are willing to spend to the brink of bankruptcy because they believe they will be saved by a federal bailout. I can hear them saying, "If Washington rescued General Motors, why not rescue Illinois?" Greve says that trusting states to preserve federalism is like trusting the Fortune 500 to defend free markets.

The question therefore is not, "How much federalism should we have?" but "What kind of federalism should we have?"

The right kind of federalism is one that places the people first, not the federal government and not even the state governments. It is guided by the words of James Madison, father of the Constitution, who wrote, "The public good, the real welfare of the great body of the people, is the supreme object to be pursued; and no form of government whatever has any other value than as it may be fitted for the attainment of this object."[20] Remember always that the purpose of federalism—dividing powers among different levels of government—was to help preserve the liberty of the people.

Madisonian federalism, based on the Constitution and on competition among the states, also will best promote the welfare of the people by encouraging the little platoons of society.

We have tried the centralization of power in the federal government for the last eighty years, and it has not worked—just the reverse. The costs of the federal government have grown dangerously high, and the goods and services it provides are mediocre or unwanted at best. The time is now to redefine the proper roles and responsibilities of the federal, state, and local governments. The answer is not the elimination of federal power but the return to the states of their proper power as reserved by the Constitution.

No better example of the importance of the right sort of federalism can be found than our children's education. No one disputes that far too many of America's children lack proficiency in reading and math. Government bureaucrats insist that more money and another 100,000 teachers will solve the problem. But although we have seen inflation-adjusted federal per-pupil expenditures nearly triple since the 1970s, reading achievement has remained stagnant, achievement gaps persist, graduation rates for disadvantaged children have been unchanged, and American students still lag far behind students in many other advanced countries.[21] The solution? *Less* governmental intervention, more choice, and true involvement by the leaders of the most important little platoon—parents.

Or take the case of the National Labor Relations Board's attempt to stop Boeing, whose home base is in unionized Washington State, from building a factory in right-to-work South Carolina. That is federal overreach to the *n*th degree and a gross violation of constitutional federalism.

*   *   *

I want to end this chapter by looking at one of the oldest and most effective conservative state think tanks—the Mackinac Center in Midland, Michigan, which does so much on an annual $5 million budget. That judgment is confirmed by the liberal publication the *American Prospect*, which concluded that Mackinac "played a central role in passing right to work" in Michigan.[22] Liberals are in awe of the long-term strategy of free-market organizations like the Mackinac Center.

To people outside Michigan, says the center's president, Joseph Lehman, it seemed as if Michigan became a right-to-work state in just seven days. Governor Rick Snyder called for worker freedom on a Tuesday, state lawmakers introduced legislation on Thursday, and the governor signed it into law the following Tuesday. But those seven days, declares Lehman, were the last seven yards of a ninety-nine-yard touchdown drive planned twenty years before by the Mackinac Center.[23] "We took on all comers," he says, talking to anybody and everybody about the economic effects of right-to-work, at a time "when lawmakers didn't want to touch the subject." As the *American Prospect* put it, Mackinac focused on right-to-work when "it wasn't safe to talk about it."[24]

The talking began on April 20, 1992, when adjunct scholar George C. Leef called for right-to-work for federal employees and greater freedom for all union members, including a Michigan law that would make voluntary the portion of union dues used for political purposes.[25]

Two years later, Mackinac's then president, Lawrence Reed, and its then senior vice president, Joseph Overton, called for right-to-work in the state. In March 1997, the center's former director of labor policy, Robert Hunter, predicted that Michigan would become a right-to-work state "within a decade."

In April 2001, State Senator Glen Stell introduced the first legislation to make Michigan a right-to-work state. A year later, a Mackinac poll showed substantial public support for labor reform, including among union members. In February 2006, senior economist David Littmann told the Michigan House Tax Committee on Restructuring that the state must adopt a right-to-work law.

In August 2008, Mackinac's incoming president, Joseph Lehman, kept up the pressure, writing in the *Detroit Free Press* that a right-to-work measure ought to be put on the ballot. UAW member and Ford worker Terry Bowman shocked union leaders by forming Union Conservatives for union members who support right-to-work.

On November 6, 2012, Michigan voters decisively rejected Proposal 2, which would have banned a right-to-work law. Union leaders had overplayed their hand, and on December 11, 2012, twenty years after a Mackinac scholar first proposed it, Governor Rick Snyder signed right-to-work legislation. Workers no longer had to pay union dues to get and hold a job.

"The right to work victory," says Joseph Lehman, "shows the power an idea can have when it is pursued with principle and perseverance."[26]

The center has been equally persistent about education policy, arguing in the early 1990s for charter schools and for the privatization of such services as transportation, custodial work, and provision of food.

An in-depth study by Stanford researchers released in January 2013 shows that Michigan charter schools far outperform conventional public schools in math and reading. In Detroit, charter schools did better than conventional schools by 49 percent in math and 47 percent in reading.

Michigan is unique among the states in the number of charter schools it authorizes and the autonomy it gives them. By any reasonable standard, Michigan's twenty-year experiment in charter schools is working, thanks to boards, principals, teachers, and parents, all aided by the continuing research of the Mackinac Center.

The center's first paper calling for privatization of public school services was published in 1993. It took a while, but by 2001, 31 percent of school districts in Michigan were contracting out at least one of the services mentioned above—food, custodial, or transportation. In 2012, a Mackinac survey found that 61 percent of school districts were outsourcing at least one service, for state-wide savings of $12.8 million.

In education, jobs, taxes, and other areas, the Mackinac Center has always striven to create a more dynamic civil society, which Mackinac scholar Michael LaFaive defined as "that network of private groups, community associations, religious organizations, families, friends, co-workers, and their heartfelt interactions." I like that word "heartfelt," because it touches on the central question of this book: How do we go about falling in love with America again?

Lindsey Dodge, the brilliant young editor of Mackinac's publications, recalls a telling scene in the TV series *Mad Men*. Following a family picnic, the mom shakes out the picnic blanket, scattering the trash everywhere, and the family happily departs, leaving someone else to clean up their mess. As Lindsey points out, that is disrespectful of other picnickers, bad for the environment, and a mighty poor example for the children in the family. This also seems to be how much policy is made nowadays: without regard for the welfare of future generations.[27]

How do we counter such careless, selfish behavior? Mackinac's Joe Lehman suggests that we can begin by praising those who are rarely praised. Not the famous and the powerful but:

The working mom and dad who must figure out what the family will have to sacrifice to pay for the latest tax hike, because politicians refused to "sacrifice any government spending."

The business owner who looks to government to enforce the rules fairly, "not as a conduit for subsidies or cronyism."

The young union leader who realizes the age of compulsory unionism has passed, and who quietly commits to renewing the union on "the cornerstones of voluntary cooperation and valued service to workers."

The parents and grandparents who foster in their offspring a deep respect for liberty, limited government, self-reliance, and generosity.

The pastor, priest, or rabbi who teaches, encourages, and exhorts his flock to strengthen the moral underpinnings of civil society, "without which no people can be free."

The citizen who won't let his elected officials get away with saying one thing and doing another.

Those willing to risk their own lives, fortunes, and sacred honor "in defense of others' lives, liberties, and pursuit of happiness."[28]

Let us all praise such Americans. Let us resolve to follow their example. And let us see how these people, organized in little platoons, are changing the face of our country.

Love Begins at Home

The love that we first experience as a family is the foundation for the love of neighbor that can ultimately extend to America as a whole.

If you're at all like me, the word "family" conjures up a host of powerful, positive images: the warmth of a kitchen where parents and other relatives swap stories and share laughter; the thrill of a summer night when siblings and cousins compete to catch the most lightning bugs in their Mason jars; your dad cheering you on as you take your position at home plate; your mom buying you that Easter dress your heart was set on. Such treasured times are more than isolated moments in your life. They have a lasting impact on how it unfolds.

Decades of academic research have confirmed what any grandmother sitting on her front porch could have always told you: Growing up with the loving care, guidance, and support of a mother and father helps children to thrive, and affects virtually every aspect of their adult lives. That's why I consider the family the most important of America's little platoons.

Children living with both parents enjoy a range of benefits

with regard to how well they do in school and how far they go in their education. In their preschool days, they tend to show higher levels of verbal and reasoning skills, and in their teen years, they are more likely to graduate from high school and go on to college.[1] Teens whose parents are involved in their lives and activities are less likely to use drugs or alcohol or become sexually active.[2]

Likewise, teens whose parents talk with them about their concerns and encourage their interests are less likely to exhibit behavioral problems or engage in acts of violence. In fact, something as simple as having frequent family dinners is related to less likelihood that adolescents will use drugs or alcohol.[3]

Studies have also shown that a mom's and dad's involvement is linked to the emotional well-being of their children. Teens whose parents spend time with them after school, at dinner, and in the evening are less likely to experience emotional distress, and those who say their parents are responsible and involved tend to have higher self-esteem and are less susceptible to peer pressure.[4]

Then there are the economic benefits to a strong family's foundation, which have been well documented by scholars and policy analysts. Heritage senior research fellow Robert Rector, for example, found that marriage could decrease the odds of child poverty by about 80 percent. As he wrote, "Being married has roughly the same effect in reducing poverty that adding five to six years to a parent's education has. Interestingly, on average, high school dropouts who are married have a far lower poverty rate than do single parents with one or two years of college."[5]

In sum, the family is the front line of defense, the "first responder," and the source of sustenance for children.

Parents, of course, don't need academic studies to understand this. They know it intuitively. In fact, even when they have fallen short, their love for their children can call them to change their ways. This was the case with Rodrick Yarborough, a drug dealer who at one point controlled nearly 70 percent of the drug traffic in his low-income neighborhood of Bonton in Dallas.[6]

Yarborough commanded respect on the streets, but he came face-to-face with the dismal reality of his life when he walked into his living room late one evening to find his little three-year-old son rolling a piece of paper like a joint, as the boy had seen his dad do so many times. Yarborough recalls that that incident brought a powerful message home: "I need to change." But changing was not easy. In addition to the lucrative drug trade he commanded, Rodrick lived in government-subsidized housing with his girl-friend, Alisha.

The flow of government aid helped perpetuate a cycle of dependency in Yarborough's entire neighborhood and created a culture devoid of marriage and stable families. As Rodrick explained, kids in the neighborhood quickly learned the system: "They're thinking, 'When I get older, I have a couple of kids, I get assisted housing and food, and I have a couple hundred dollars to do whatever I want to do.' It's an ongoing cycle."

Rodrick's life changed when two volunteers from a local ministry called H.I.S. BridgeBuilders—an older married couple named Ron and Cheryl Murff—befriended him and challenged him to reevaluate his relationship with God and his family. With the Murffs' mentorship and support, Rodrick eventually gave his life to Christ and married Alisha. They were able to move with their four children into a Habitat for Humanity home that Ron Murff's company sponsored. Rodrick's children now look up to a father who has shown personal responsibility in his relationships and community.[7]

The benefits of growing up in a stable family with two loving, committed parents will affect children's prospects for the future. Imagine what a difference it would make if the transformation in Roderick and Alisha's lives could be achieved in households throughout their neighborhood.

And the benefits that accrue to children in a loving two-parent home have a ripple effect throughout society. Parents not only provide the necessities of nourishing meals, care, and treatment in times of sickness or injury, and the invisible sustenance of love and support that is necessary for their children to thrive, but they also provide moral and spiritual guidance and teach basic principles of citizenship and care for their neighbors. In this nurturing environment, children grow up to be the kind of citizens who make society flourish—individuals who hold down jobs, contribute to their communities, and have the confidence to express their creativity in ways that can benefit society.

Since children tend to follow the marital trajectory of their parents, those who grew up surrounded with the comfort and support of their mother and father are more likely to have healthy, stable marriages and intact families of their own.[8] The family is the first school of love, and the lessons it teaches last a lifetime and extend in relationships throughout society.

The Decline of Marriage

Researchers across the ideological spectrum have acknowledged that children are indeed most likely to thrive in a family with both a mother and a father.[9] Yet since the 1960s, this little platoon that is the bedrock of America's civil society has been eroded—by a self-oriented culture that is focused on individual fulfillment;[10] by the rise of a movement that dismisses the unique value of the father and of men in general;[11] by a popular culture that is inundated with television shows and films that do not recognize the value of the traditional family; and by government overreach that has undermined the roles of parents.

One wave eroding family security began in 1969 with the introduction of no-fault divorce in California, making it possible for either spouse to dissolve a marriage for any (or no) reason, shattering the essential stabilizing values of marital commitment and faithfulness to the wedding vow.[12] Over the next fifteen years, virtually every other state followed California's lead. As a result, from 1960 to 1980 the divorce rate in our nation doubled, and nearly one-half of the couples who wed in the 1970s divorced before reaching their twenty-fifth wedding anniversary.[13] Though the divorce rate is decreasing today, it still remains high.[14]

Needless to say, the epidemic of divorce has left its scars on the generation of children who suffered through the ordeal of parental separation. These young people tend to have lower academic performance and experience more psychological and emotional challenges than children in intact, married families.[15]

One daughter of married parents who divorced, now an adult, describes what the dissolution of the family meant to her and other children in her neighborhood. In vivid detail, Susan Gregory Thomas writes:

> When my dad left in the spring of 1981 and moved five states away with his executive assistant and her four kids, the world as I had known it came to an end.... Growing up, my brother and I were often left to our own devices, members of the giant flock of migrant latchkey kids in the

1970s and '80s. Our suburb was littered with sad-eyed, bruised nomads, who wandered back and forth between used-record shops to the sheds behind the train station where they got high and then trudged off, back and forth from their mothers' houses during the week to their fathers' apartments every other weekend.[16]

To her surprise, many divorced mothers who later e-mailed her about her article said that she was right and that they had not given enough thought to how their divorce would affect their children.[17]

The era of divorce was followed by current trends that reveal a skittishness about marriage among the current generation of young adults. Through the last six decades, marriage rates have steadily fallen, and only a little over half of Americans are currently married, compared to nearly 70 percent in the 1950s.[18] Even couples who do walk down the aisle do so at a later age. The average age of first marriage for women in the United States is nearly twenty-seven, and for men it's nearly twenty-nine.[19] In fact, the average age of first marriage is now higher than the average age of first childbearing, and more than 40 percent of births today are outside marriage.[20]

Many young adults who experienced the pain of parental divorce in their childhood now consider cohabitation as a way to "test drive" their relationships. Today, nearly 12 percent of couples living together are unmarried—a tenfold increase since 1960.[21] Though many of these couples thought that they were ensuring that their own subsequent marriages would last, the sad truth is that both cohabiting relationships and marriages that are preceded by cohabitation are more likely to end in a breakup.[22]

And once again, the greatest impact of this experiment is on the children. Children born into households headed by a cohabiting couple are more likely to suffer from a range of emotional, social, and behavioral problems, and are less likely to succeed academically.

Worse yet is that all these cultural phenomena are taking their greatest toll among our nation's most vulnerable population: those with the lowest incomes, education, and prospects for the future.

More than 60 percent of unwed births occur to women in their twenties, while only a little over 20 percent of children born outside of marriage are to mothers under nineteen years old.[23] It is women in their twenties and thirties who are forgoing the commitment and relative stability of marriage by putting cradles before wedding bands. The vast majority of women giving birth outside of marriage also tend to have only received a high school diploma, making the already difficult road of single parenthood much more daunting.[24]

For many low-income women, the concepts of marriage and childbearing have become disconnected; among high school dropouts, an astonishing 83 percent of first births are outside marriage.[25] And this creates a negative economic and cultural "feedback loop": Without the benefits of an intact family, their children are far more likely to live in poverty and as teens to engage in high-risk or antisocial behavior. And in turn, they are likely to pass these pathologies on to the following generation.

As researchers Kathryn Edin and Maria Kefalas explain in their book *Promises I Can Keep: Why Poor Women Put Motherhood Before Marriage*, the low-income unmarried mothers they interviewed "saw marriage as a luxury, something they aspired to but feared they might never achieve, [but] they judged children to be a necessity, an absolutely essential part of a young woman's life, the chief source of identity and meaning."[26]

Consider their interview with Nikki, an eighteen-year-old mother of a newborn, who said, "The vows tell you everything. You have to be there for that person till death do you part. To love, honor, and obey. When you get to a marriage you have to understand that it's a *big step* that you are taking and that is the person that you have chosen to be with for the rest of your *life*. If you really know the words 'the rest of your life' and you start getting that voice in the back of your head, 'Oh, that's a long time!' Maybe you shouldn't get married."[27]

Likewise, twenty-four-year-old Linda, a mother of two preschoolers, proudly told the authors that she is a person who takes marriage very seriously and not merely as "a piece of paper," adding, "I been with my boyfriend for six years and we have two kids and *I'm* not ready yet for marriage."[28]

At the same time, nearly all the mothers interviewed by Edin and Kefalas said that their children brought far more benefits to their lives than burdens. In the words of a twenty-one-year-old mother of a five-month-old, "I'd have no direction [if I didn't have a child]."[29] A nineteen-year-old, who had a three-year-old and a toddler and was now pregnant again, put it much the same way: "It's what gets me going.... It's like a burst of energy."[30] Many of the unmarried low-income mothers describe their children as a source of love. In the words of a twenty-three-year-old legally blind mother of a preschooler and an infant, "I never imagined that there was any kind of love like that out there, never imagined it."[31]

Similarly, many inner-city young men whose children were born outside of marriage say that becoming a father was a big event in their lives. For example, when asked if being a father made a difference in his life, a twenty-four-year-old community college student said that if it had not been for his daughter, "I'd be dead, because of the simple fact that it wasn't until Brianna was born that I actually started to chill out."[32]

In fact, even in the midst of the most devastated, drug-infested, crime-ridden neighborhoods, many young unmarried parents still uphold the ideal of the stable, secure two-parent family. For example, Will, a former drug dealer who had done time in prison, left the mother of his four children, who was a heroin addict, but he still believes that a two-parent family with the father as breadwinner would be the best thing for his kids. In his words, "I don't think I take *good* care of my kids. But I do take care of them to the best of my ability.... I should be able to provide a *family* for them. Like, with their mother. Instead of leaving her, I should have just tried to work it out, put her in a program and stayed with her."[33]

Asked what type of father he would like to be, Will immediately responded, "Ward Cleaver [the dad in the 1950s sitcom *Leave It to Beaver*], because he is, like, the ideal dad." (His own father disappeared from his life when Will was just an infant.)

When a young man like Will keeps this vision of the intact family alive, in the midst of an environment virtually devoid of such role models, it is nothing short of a cry for help.

You would think that the leaders would do everything in their capacity to answer that cry. Tragically, however, for nearly fifty years big government has been tone-deaf to the real situation of the poor and its dynamics. Rather than supporting the little platoon that is the bulwark and foundation of civil society, government departments and agencies have stepped into the role of the father, supplying monthly checks, subsidizing groceries and housing, and meeting other needs of mothers and their children through the bureaucracies of more than seventy programs in a massive and growing welfare system.

Nevertheless, marriage, far from being unappreciated by the young and disadvantaged, is still considered important. It is the all-encompassing government social net that has made it optional, rather than an economic necessity, for raising children. Thus there are more broken homes, and the cycle continues: Government programs have flooded into communities to fill the void left by never-formed families.[34] Of the roughly $450 billion in means-tested welfare spent by federal and state governments in 2011 on families with children, roughly three-quarters went to single-parent families.

But big government's agenda for the poor actually undermines their prospects for rising up. It discourages both work and marriage, because in most cases marriage or increased work leads to a reduction in benefits. Under the current structure of welfare programs such as food stamps, public housing, Medicaid, and Temporary Assistance for Needy Families, a mother will receive far more assistance if she is single than if she marries an employed man—never mind the profound personal, social, and economic benefits of marriage to the most vulnerable Americans.[35]

Moreover, big government's antimarriage policies extend to other economic sectors of society—for example, the "marriage penalty" in the Internal Revenue Code. For decades, many middle-income Americans filing joint tax returns were forced to pay a greater share of their hard-earned income to the federal government than their single counterparts.

In the early 2000s, Congress passed and President Bush signed tax reform legislation that provided some relief. In fact, the Joint

Committee on Taxation estimated that 35 million couples would have paid an average of $595 more in income taxes in 2011 had the marriage penalty relief not been extended.[36] While Congress made the Bush-era reductions of the marriage penalty permanent in 2013, other marriage penalties remain, such as the way the Earned Income Tax Credit is structured. I'm glad to say The Heritage Foundation advocates a flat tax plan that would eliminate marriage penalties altogether.

Obamacare will also take a toll on families. To offset some of the increased costs of a one-size-fits-all government health care scheme, Obamacare will give tax credits based on an individual's or a married couple's income to purchase a health plan on the government-run insurance market.

However, the way the tax credits are structured, many middle-income married couples will receive $1,500 to $10,000 less per year in premium support than cohabitating couples with the same combined income. This penalty creates a strong disincentive for men and women to marry, and actually encourages some who are already married to divorce and cohabit.[37]

In addition, over the past several decades the federal courts have helped to create a climate of opinion that weakens the family. Take the Supreme Court's 1973 decision in *Roe v. Wade* that legalized abortion-on-demand. I agree with the late Judge Robert H. Bork, who called *Roe v. Wade* "a radical deformation of the Constitution."[38] But apart from constitutional issues, *Roe* has disturbing cultural implications. Legalizing abortion-on-demand has further entrenched the devaluing of the family and denigrated motherhood.

Then there is the effort, which has been going on for decades, to use the "separation of church and state" to eliminate all references to religion in any government-sponsored activity. Set aside for the moment the fact that the words "separation of church and state" are nowhere to be found in the Constitution. Just ask yourself whether it's really possible for the federal government to wage a relentless war against such public manifestations of religious faith as public school prayer (outlawed by the Supreme Court in 1962), without simultaneously undermining private manifestations as well?

I sincerely doubt it. Children aren't well versed in the fine points of constitutional law, and if they see school authorities eliminating the invocation at graduation ceremonies, banning Bible study groups from campus, and excising the words "under God" from the Pledge of Allegiance, they're likely to conclude that there's something inherently bad about religion—which is precisely the conclusion that militant secularists want them to draw. And once you undermine religious faith, you're also undermining the family—because faith is one of the strongest bonds holding families together.

And then, of course, there's the ceaseless assault on the traditional idea of marriage. The most recent foray is the effort to equate same-sex marriage and heterosexual marriage—but this is merely the culmination of trends that have been going on for a very long time now. As my Heritage colleague Ryan T. Anderson has written, "Long before there was a debate about same-sex anything, far too many heterosexuals bought into a liberal ideology about sexuality that makes a mess of marriage: cohabitation, no-fault divorce, extra-marital sex, non-marital childbearing, massive consumption of pornography, and the hook-up culture all contributed to the breakup of our marriage culture."[39]

Of course, recent actions by the Obama administration and the decisions of the Supreme Court on the Defense of Marriage Act and California's Proposition 8 have opened the threshold for further erosion of the institutions of marriage and the family through the redefinition of these pillars of civil society that have served to protect and nurture children for thousands of years.

Protecting Marriage from Redefinition

While we work to restore an appreciation and respect for the many benefits of the institution of marriage and the family, we must also face the most significant challenge to marriage yet—the effort to fundamentally redefine it.

Marriage predates government and is the fundamental building block of all human civilization. At its most basic function, the institution of marriage exists to bring a man and woman together in commitment to one another and to any children that they produce.

How we define marriage deeply matters for public policy. Government recognizes the unique and irreplaceable benefits that marriage produces for adults and children. Marriage is the best institution in society to ensure the well-being of children, and the government's recognition of marriage encourages moms and dads not only to commit to each other, but also to take responsibility for their children by providing them a stable, loving home.

As Ryan Anderson explains, government can treat people equally while recognizing the truth of marriage:

> While respecting everyone's liberty, government rightly recognizes, protects, and promotes marriage as the ideal institution for childbearing and childrearing. Adults are free to make choices about their relationships without redefining marriage and do not need government sanction

or license to do so.... All Americans have the freedom to live as they choose, but they do not have the right to redefine marriage for everyone else.[40]

Redefinition would fundamentally alter the institution of marriage by denying the basic biological fact that it takes a man and a woman to make a child and that a child deserves both a mom and a dad. Redefining marriage would make the institution about whatever adult, emotional bonds the government says it is—without concern for the children those emotional bonds may produce.

We've already seen what happens when the desires of adults are placed before the needs of children through the advent of policies like no-fault divorce and the rise in unwed childbearing: More children live without the stability, commitment, and love of a married mom and dad, more kids experience the pains of economic and social challenges of single-parent households. Of course, we salute brave mothers and fathers grappling with the challenges of single parenting; but these individuals deserve our respect precisely because they're making the best of a bad situation.

When a culture of marriage breaks down, the state is often left to pick up the pieces. Big-government welfare programs rush in, but never fill the void left by a broken family.

Worse, redefining marriage is a threat to religious freedom that marginalizes those who affirm marriage as the union of a man and a woman. Already, in Washington, D.C., Illinois, and Massachusetts, we've seen the consequences of government recognition of same-sex relationships for religious freedom. Faith-based adoption and foster care organizations in those localities were forced to give up the good work they were doing on behalf of vulnerable children because the government would have forced them to place children with same-sex couples—even in violation of their principles.[41]

The Supreme Court's recent decisions on marriage left all fifty states free to define marriage as the union of a man and a woman, as citizens and their elected representatives in the vast majority of states continue to do. We all have a profoundly important role to play in the wake of the Supreme Court's decisions: to continue to proclaim the truth about marriage in our culture, policy, and conversations. We need to teach the next generation about the importance of marriage, model successful marriages for our own children, and engage our culture through entertainment media with why marriage matters to society.

Public policy must continue to tell the truth about marriage as the union of a man and a woman and maintain the freedom of Americans to continue believing, teaching, and living out that truth. And we all need to be prepared to defend the institution of marriage— what it is, why it matters, and the consequences of redefining it—in our conversations at work, at church, and around the dinner table.

Reviving Our Most Important Little Platoon

Without any government support, and indeed despite stumbling blocks created by big government, little platoons within civil society have come forward to defend and revitalize the family in America.

In 1997, Hamilton County, Tennessee, had a serious problem. Thirty-three percent of adults living in the county had experienced divorce (compared to a 22 percent national divorce rate at the time), and the county's largest city, Chattanooga, had one of the highest rates of out-of-wedlock births in the country.

Recognizing the human toll of such social breakdown, Julie Baumgardner and a handful of other community leaders started First Things First, an award-winning grassroots organization that empowers teens and couples with research-driven techniques to start and sustain lifelong marriages and healthy families.

"Through vehicles such as conflict resolution, mediation, pre-marital education and communication skills, couples are learning what it takes to have a healthy, long-lasting marriage," Mrs. Baumgardner explains. "What research is showing is that while marriage is a covenant entered into between two adults it is not just for their benefit; it benefits children and society as a whole."[42]

First Things First works to prepare young people for marriage and to strengthen existing marriages by providing educational resources on issues facing dating teenagers, single adults, newlyweds, married couples, new parents, and empty-nesters. Through efforts including websites targeting teens and young adults looking for a lifelong partner, marital enrichment classes, new-dad boot camps, and a dozen other events and resources, First Things First has gone a long way toward educating Chattanooga citizens about marriage. Since the group's inception in 1997, Hamilton County's divorce rate has decreased by 27 percent and the pregnancy rate among unwed teenagers has decreased 44 percent.[43]

Even in the nation's most impoverished neighborhoods, committed grassroots leaders have stepped forward to promote marriage and the family as essential to individual and community revitalization. In chapter 1, I told about the dynamic and impassioned Bishop Shirley Holloway, whose House of Help, City of Hope ministry has helped thousands of seemingly hopeless drug addicts and alcoholics to reclaim their lives and establish stable, healthy familial relationships.

These grassroots initiatives are both effective and inspiring. Nonetheless, I believe that successfully challenging a popular culture that denigrates the family and marriage will require a lot more from all of us.

Our religious institutions should lead a campaign to highlight the benefits of marriage and to revitalize a culture in which the married, intact family is revered and thrives. That will take religious leaders willing to dedicate time and resources to marriage counseling and education and religious organizations dedicated to building thriving families.

Our celebrities should extol the beauty of marriage and the family, our philanthropists should use their influence to support marriage education efforts, and national media campaigns should expand public awareness of the family's role as America's leading first responder.[44]

Meanwhile, policymakers should encourage family formation and stability by removing marriage penalties from the tax code and other federal programs.[45] That includes reducing or eliminating marriage penalties in means-tested welfare programs, in order to encourage low-income couples to make the commitment of marriage.[46] Public policy that affirms, supports, and promotes marriage and the family is based on a commonsense truth: Children deserve every chance to experience the social, economic, and personal benefits of being raised by a mother and a father who are committed to each other and their children in lifelong, married love.

The love that we first experience, learn, and cherish in the family can extend to virtually all the other little platoons we encounter throughout our lives, and ultimately to our great nation as a whole.

Faith: Learning to Love

For millions of Americans, how we practice our faith is at the core of our identity.

On August 17, 1790, President George Washington sailed from New York City (then our nation's capital) to Newport, Rhode Island. He took along with him his secretary of state, Thomas Jefferson, and the governor of New York, George Clinton. On the morning of August 18, he was feted by Newport's leading dignitaries, among them Moses Seixas, the warden of Newport's tiny Hebrew congregation. Seixas thanked Washington for his extraordinary leadership and expressed the hope that the United States would extend respect and tolerance to all its citizens, regardless of their background or religious beliefs.

On August 21, President Washington responded to Seixas. In my opinion, Washington's letter to the Hebrew congregation of Newport is one of the gems of American literature:

> It is now no more that toleration is spoken of as if it were the indulgence of one class of people that another enjoyed the exercise of their inherent natural rights, for happily,

the Government of the United States, which gives to bigotry no sanction, to persecution no assistance, requires only that they who live under its protection should demean themselves as good citizens in giving it on all occasions their effectual support....

May the children of the stock of Abraham who dwell in this land continue to merit and enjoy the good will of the other inhabitants—while every one shall sit in safety under his own vine and fig tree and there shall be none to make him afraid.[1]

Washington's letter is a classic statement of our cherished "First Freedom." Religious freedom is central to our identity as Americans, and because we give "to bigotry no sanction, to persecution no assistance," the United States has always been—and remains to this day—a beacon of hope to oppressed men and women everywhere.

A Shining City upon a Hill

Long before "under God" was inserted into the Pledge of Allegiance in 1954, the religious character of the American people was a clear fact—woven into our founding documents, enmeshed in our history from the very beginning.

When the first settlers voyaged across the ocean in the seventeenth century, many of them had religious freedom in mind and in their hearts as they journeyed westward. President Reagan would call upon John Winthrop, one of the first pilgrims who settled in Massachusetts, in his farewell address as he left the White House in 1989.

In closing out his presidency, Reagan struck a religious chord to capture what's at the center of America:

The past few days when I've been at that window upstairs, I've thought a bit of the "shining city upon a hill." The phrase comes from John Winthrop, who wrote it to describe the America he imagined. What he imagined was important because he was an early Pilgrim, an early freedom man. He journeyed here on what today we'd call a little wooden boat; and like the other Pilgrims, he was looking for a home that would be free.

I've spoken of the shining city all my political life, but I don't know if I ever quite communicated what I saw when I said it. But in my mind it was a tall, proud city built on rocks stronger than oceans, wind-swept, God-blessed, and teeming with people of all kinds living in harmony and peace; a city with free ports that hummed with commerce and creativity.[2]

Because religious freedom is such a crucial component of our self-definition as Americans, most of us would be horrified to be told that religious freedom was under assault here at home. Religious persecution, we all know, is something that takes place in other, less enlightened lands; but not in America—never here!

Yet in fact, religious liberty really is challenged here at home. And if you'll stop and think about it, you'll understand why. As the reach of big government grows ever longer, as it encompasses more and more areas of life, it is bound to encroach on matters that individuals used to decide for themselves, consulting only their conscience and their faith.

Consider, for example, the impact of Obamacare on religious freedom.

Today, Americans in many faith communities find themselves embroiled in conflict over what is known as the "HHS mandate." In interpreting the "preventive services" provision of the so-called Patient Protection and Affordable Care Act, the Department of Health and Human Services mandated that employers provide their employees health care coverage of contraception, abortion-inducing drugs, and sterilization regardless of the employers' religious or moral objections.

The HHS mandate allows only formal houses of worship to opt out of the policy. Countless other institutions run by religious organizations (including schools, hospitals, and social service providers), other nonprofits, and businesses of all sorts are still forced to comply with the mandate or face devastating fines. The administration has attempted to "accommodate" certain religious employers, but as of the summer of 2013 the administration's rhetoric is turning out to be just that—empty rhetoric.

When people who run a business want to do so in accordance with the principles and values of their faith, the HHS mandate puts a barrier in their way. If they choose not to comply, they'll face fines of up to $100 *per day* per employee. If they drop insurance altogether to avoid the conscience conflict, they'll still face fines of about $2,000 per year per employee.

Take, for example, the Green family, which owns the Hobby Lobby, a nationwide chain of stores selling arts-and-crafts supplies. These hardworking, job-creating entrepreneurs are devout evangelical Christians. As a testament to their faith, all Hobby Lobby stores are closed on Sunday, and the company invests in communities through partnerships with numerous Christian ministries. Employing more than thirteen thousand workers in five hundred stores across forty-one states, the Greens want to provide employee health insurance in accordance with their faith-bound conscience.

Under the HHS mandate, this would be impossible. The Greens would be forced to violate their faith by providing health care that covers abortion-inducing drugs that they believe are immoral, or else face penalties of $1.3 million *per day* for refusing to comply. You read that right: $1.3 *million per day*.

The Greens weren't looking for a showdown with the government. They just want to be free to run their business according to their religious convictions, as they always have. But now they have to take a stand in order to do that. Demonstrating genuine moral courage, the Greens, with legal help from the Becket Fund for Religious Liberty, are challenging the Obama administration's HHS mandate in court.

As David Green, the founder and CEO of Hobby Lobby, put it:

[O]ur faith is being challenged by the federal government. The Health and Human Services "preventative services" mandate forces businesses to provide the "morning-after" and the "week-after" pills in our health insurance plans. These abortion-causing drugs go against our faith, and our family is now being forced to choose between following the laws of the land that we love or maintaining the religious beliefs that have made our business successful and have supported our family and thousands of our employees and their families. We simply cannot abandon our religious beliefs to comply with this mandate.[3]

The Greens are not alone. Today, people of faith are standing strong across the country, remaining bravely and passionately opposed to obeying this government mandate that violates their faith. There are now more than eighty cases involving over two hundred plaintiffs challenging Obamacare's HHS mandate. The outcry has been such that the Obama administration has finally announced an eighteen-month delay in implementing the employer mandate. But this is still only a delay—putting off the pain for another day.[4]

The HHS mandate is just one example of how big government's expansion into more and more areas of the economy is undermining religious liberty. Another example concerns Barronelle Stutzman, a Washington State florist. The state's attorney general brought a lawsuit against her. Why? Because she refused to arrange flowers for a same-sex wedding, since her "relationship with Jesus Christ" forbids her to have anything to do with such ceremonies. Never mind that she has openly gay customers, and that there are plenty of other florists who would have been glad to provide the flowers for this wedding. The court is threatening her with a $2,000 fine and seeking an injunction under the state's consumer protection law in order to force her to violate her beliefs by actively contributing to something that is against her conscience.

And then there's the case of Illinois religious adoption agencies: the Evangelical Child and Family Agency in Wheaton and Catholic Charities of the Rockford Diocese. In 2011, the Illinois legislature passed a civil union bill. Historically, these agencies placed children only with married couples. The civil union law would force them to place children with unmarried, cohabitating couples—whether homosexual or heterosexual—practices that violate their teaching on marriage and family. The day after the civil union bill passed, the Evangelical Child and Family Agency confirmed that Illinois refused to renew their contract.[5] Faced with the choice of violating its conscience or staying true to the tenets of its faith, Catholic Charities ended its $7.5 million contract with the state of Illinois.

Confronted by this pattern of assaults on religious liberty, religious leaders are speaking out. Testifying before a subcommittee of the House Judiciary Committee, Catholic bishop William E. Lori offered a frank assessment of the times we're living in. Lori pointed out that the Bill of Rights and the Declaration of Independence require government "to acknowledge and protect religious liberty as fundamental, no matter the moral and political trends of the moment." But in recent days, Lori said, "the bishops of the United States have watched with increasing alarm as this great national legacy of religious liberty, so profoundly in harmony with our own teachings, has been subject to ever more frequent assault and ever more rapid erosion."[6]

When a leading American religious figure goes before Congress and charges that religious liberty is under assault in this country, all of us, regardless of what faith we profess, need to sit up and pay very, very close attention.

What Is Religious Liberty?

Big government policies often water down our Founders' conception of religious liberty to a mere freedom to worship: As long as faith is expressed within a house of worship, deeply held beliefs are respected. Step outside those four walls, however, and protection of your religious freedom ends.

But this is confusing religious liberty with freedom of worship.

Religious liberty is not limited to what the faithful do on Fridays, Saturdays, or Sundays. Religious liberty is the freedom to live out deeply held beliefs every day of the week.

Our nation's Founders, however, never conceived of a nation where the deepest truths about the human condition would be confined to the house of worship. This is made clear in the First Amendment of the Constitution:

> Congress shall make no law respecting an establishment of religion, or prohibiting the free exercise thereof; or abridging the freedom of speech, or of the press; or the right of the people peaceably to assemble, and to petition the Government for a redress of grievances.

New York Times columnist Ross Douthat made a very astute observation about the contents of the First Amendment. Notice what that amendment says and does *not* say:

> The words "freedom of belief" do not appear in the First Amendment. Nor do the words "freedom of worship." Instead, the Bill of Rights guarantees Americans something that its authors called "the free exercise" of religion.
>
> It's a significant choice of words, because it suggests a recognition that religious faith cannot be reduced to a purely private or individual affair. Most religious communities conceive of themselves as peoples or families, and the requirements of most faiths extend well beyond attendance at a Sabbath service—encompassing charity and activism, education and missionary efforts, and other "exercises" that any guarantee of religious freedom must protect.[7]

Douthat's observation accurately captures what lies at the heart of our Founders' view of religion. America's founding documents were designed to protect religion by allowing individuals to *freely exercise* their faith without government interference.

While debate continues on the specific religious beliefs of many of our Founders, none of them could be accused of advocating what the late Richard John Neuhaus called the "naked public square"—the idea that religious appeals are somehow off-limits in public discourse. On the contrary, the Founders had a vision of public life that allowed religious faith and religious conviction to flourish for the good of society. According to Benjamin Rush, "the only foundation for a useful education in a republic is to be laid in religion. Without this there can be no virtue, and without virtue there can be no liberty, and liberty is the object and life of all republican governments."[8]

But why did the Founders so value religious freedom that they made it the subject of the first clause of the First Amendment? Because the freedom to one's own conscience and the freedom to obey and believe is, as Pastor Rick Warren said, "the fundamental right on which all others are built; because if I don't have the right to believe and practice what I believe, the freedom of speech, the freedom of assembly, those are worthless. It all starts with: do I have the right to make conscious moral decisions?"[9]

I believe the Founders of our nation would have nodded in agreement when Pastor Warren said these words. He gets it right: Religion isn't just about personal piety or attending reverent services one day a week. As the Constitution underscores, religion has as its core feature the right to be *exercised*; faith requires action. For millions of Americans like me, how we practice our faith is at the core of our identity.

In all the confusion over church, state, religion, and politics, it's important to keep in mind that while our constitutional order keeps *church* and *state* distinct (which is good), it doesn't seek to keep *religion* and *politics* separate. Why? Because the former informs the latter. Religion and politics are inseparable because the values of our faith *should* inform what we value in our politics. They both seek to answer questions about the good life.

Religious Practice and the Common Good

Religious communities in America have birthed some of the greatest social movements in our nation's history and have been on the forefront of social reform movements. In today's pro-life movement, which sees younger Americans becoming increasingly pro-life, people of all faiths have banded together to protect human dignity and unborn life. More than eleven hundred faith-based crisis pregnancy centers provide an alternative for mothers seeking an abortion—free ultrasounds, diapers, food, and clothing. As a testament to the entrepreneurial power of faith, there are now more pregnancy care centers in America than abortion facilities!

In the civil rights movement of the 1960s, Dr. Martin Luther King Jr. stirred Americans with his resounding sermons, emphasizing God's love for all people and tearing down racial barriers. Speaking of the church's relationship to the state, Dr. King said:

> The church must be reminded that it is not the master or the servant of the state, but rather the conscience of the state. It must be the guide and the critic of the state, and never its tool. If the church does not recapture its prophetic

zeal it will become an irrelevant social club without moral or spiritual authority.[10]

Dr. King's words capture the spirit of America's religious roots—fiercely independent, but present in the public square in order to advance the cause of human dignity in America. We are all beneficiaries of the dream that Dr. King saw from afar.

The late Chuck Colson, known as President Nixon's "hatchet man," experienced a radical conversion as he was awaiting trial for his role in the Watergate cover-up. From his time in prison, Colson gained an acute understanding of the importance of dignity for the incarcerated. After his release from prison, he founded Prison Fellowship, a ministry aimed at preventing prisoners from becoming repeat offenders. Animated by an evangelical faith, Prison Fellowship supports prisoners and their families in hopes of seeing ex-prisoners become devoted family men and hard workers.[11]

Ministering to over 200,000 prisoners across the nation, Prison Fellowship has seen great success through its various programs. Participants in prison Bible study sessions have shown a sharp decrease in repeat offenses. And its Angel Tree program delivers donated gifts and the Gospel message to the children of prisoners.

One such prisoner was Chris Cleveland, who entered Albuquerque's Metropolitan Detention Center in 2002. Chris left behind an eight-year-old son, Christopher, whom he loved dearly, but with whom he almost never spoke. One day, a Prison Fellowship volunteer slipped an Angel Tree pamphlet through the food-tray slot in Chris's cell door, and Chris registered his son to receive a basketball "from Dad." That gift broke the ice. Thanks to Angel Tree, father and son were able to connect every Christmas.

Meanwhile Chris grew closer to God, and was baptized in

2005. Released from prison in 2006, Chris has Christopher living with him today, and while their relationship hasn't always been easy, Chris is a good dad and a regular churchgoer, and is raising his son in Christ.[12]

Another remarkable faith-based program is Focus on the Family's Wait No More. Launched in 2008, it works with churches to help families adopt children out of the foster care system. Holding recruitment events at churches throughout the United States, Wait No More representatives coach families about how to adopt, and provide them resources and networking opportunities to facilitate the process. Within months, Wait No More helped reduce the number of children in the Colorado foster care system by half.[13]

"I'm stunned by the number of kids we've moved off the waiting list," Focus on the Family president and chief executive Jim Daly told the *Denver Post*. "I was one of those kids—a kid that doesn't have a mom and dad. I was never adopted, but I was very appreciative of the people who came along to mentor me."

Daly points to the Bible's strong emphasis on caring for the widow and the orphan. "This country has something like 300,000 churches and 130,000 orphans. The math is pretty simple."

Consider how the First Baptist Church of Leesburg, Florida, is transforming lives and healing broken people. Organizing what they call a "Christian Care Center," members of the congregation have surrounded themselves with people struggling with alcohol, drug addiction, homelessness, or even unplanned pregnancy. If there's a problem or emergency in someone's life, First Baptist Leesburg is there to help.

Catherine Parman, one of the center's assistants, is clear as to what motivates them: "That's the whole thing of Christian Care Center: Matthew 25. We feed them, we clothe them, and we help them when they're sick, we give them shelter, and if they're in jail, we visit them."

Dr. Charles Roesel, the pastor emeritus of the church, speaks movingly about the care center: "The question is often asked, 'Why are you involved in ministry? Isn't it the old social gospel that was all social and no gospel?' That's the reason I do not call it the social gospel—I call it 'ministry evangelism.' Every ministry we have is for the purpose of meeting the total needs of the individual. And the greatest need they have is to have a personal relationship with Jesus Christ. What the ministry does is open the door where they're willing to hear what we say because they see what we do. They see that we care about them as a person, not as a prospect."[14]

City government also noticed something powerful happening, something that brings delight to Dr. Roesel. "I want you to know when we started ministry evangelism in the church, the local government said you can't do it because that's not the work of the church. Well," said Roesel, "I had to let them know it *is* the work of the church. They said, 'This is not what churches do! You are to meet on Sunday, you are to sing, you are to preach, but you can't be involved in all these ministries you're talking about!' Now, they're thrilled."

Today, thousands of churches, mobilizing hundreds of thousands of volunteers, provide a wide array of services to Americans in need, proving that Alexis de Tocqueville was right when he wrote, nearly two hundred years ago, that religion is "the first of America's political institutions" because although it "never mixes directly in the government of society," it determines "the habits of the heart of all Americans."[15]

Even a massive religious organization like the Knights of Columbus thrives not by the centralized power of a few, but by the beating of thousands of hearts in thousands of chapters. That's what made it one of the most successful service organizations in America: Through the work of its own little platoons, tightly tied to their respective communities and each with an independent command structure, the Knights have provided a whopping 644 *million* man-hours and $1.44 *billion* to charitable causes in the last decade alone.[16] Not just to Catholics, but to everyone.

Not only does religion serve the common good, but a substantial body of research suggests that it makes a real difference in the everyday lives of individuals, families, and communities:

- Religious individuals tend to give more to charity. The so-called charity gap between those who practice their faith and those of no faith was studied by American Enterprise Institute president Arthur Brooks. He found that 94 percent of people who attend weekly services are likely to give to charity, compared to only 73 percent of people who do not attend weekly services.[17]

- According to Brooks, religious people are "far more likely to donate blood than secularists, to give food or money to a homeless person, to return change mistakenly given them by a cashier, and to express empathy for less fortunate people."[18]

- Those who attend religious services are more likely to volunteer in their community.[19]

- Religious individuals tend to live longer lives and tend to be healthier.[20]

- Religious individuals are likely to say that they are very happy with their lives and optimistic about the future.[21]

- Religious people are less likely to exhibit depression, anxiety disorder, and phobias. They are less likely to become addicted to alcohol or drugs, and less likely to commit suicide.[22]

• Noted sociologist Byron Johnson's book *More God, Less Crime: Why Faith Matters and How It Could Matter More* convincingly shows that higher rates of religious practice typically mean less crime.[23]

• Numerous studies indicate a correlation between religious practice and a decrease in divorce. This led the late David Larson, a psychiatrist and professor at Duke, to draw the conclusion that attendance at religious services is the most important predictor of marital stability.[24]

• According to sociologist Brad Wilcox of the University of Virginia, a father's frequency of religious attendance is an indicator of parental involvement. The more a father attends religious services, the greater the likelihood he will be involved in his children's lives.[25]

These are just a few of the scientific measurements that show religion's importance to social well-being. When religious believers are free to exercise their faith, all of us are better off. Thus both the religiously faithful and those who do not have a faith have a strong interest in preserving and protecting religious liberty.

But as big government continues to expand, the ability of religious believers to freely exercise their faith—already under threat—is bound to diminish even further. We need to be good stewards of religious freedom and work against the drive to push religion out of the public square altogether, hemming it in with an impenetrable web of bureaucratic mandates, rules, and regulations.

We also need to repeal the policies forcing small business owners like the Greens to pay for practices they abhor, that compel religious agencies to abandon their adoption and foster care services, and that bring the wrath of the state down on someone like flower arranger Barronelle Stutzman.

After all, it's hard to love a country that routinely forces its citizens to violate their faiths.

Let Doctors Be Doctors

Substituting regulation for free markets and innovation is the reactionary way of thinking.

I t has been said that insanity can be defined as "doing the same thing over and over and expecting different results."

While I don't think most of my former Senate colleagues could be certified as crazy, there were times when I thought they needed their heads checked.

Despite the fact that history is packed with examples of how the free market works and big government doesn't, the Senate in 2010 passed the so-called Patient Protection and Affordable Care Act (a.k.a. Obamacare), which aims to put big government in charge of our families' health care.

I believe the passage of Obamacare marked the triumph of ideology over imagination. The ideology, of course, is statism—the belief that Big Brother can solve our problems. Like other ideologies, statism closes our minds to the alternatives before us and prevents us from imagining new, creative solutions to our challenges—in this case, our health care challenges.

Health Care Sharing Ministries

What kind of solutions? Take, for example, group self-insurance. Indeed, to use one important illustration, imagine a form of coverage where the people who pay your bills also pray for you. It sounds too good to be true—but it exists and in fact is thriving in America. In groups called "health care sharing ministries," members take turns paying one another's medical expenses, and as part of the benefit package the ministry also promotes responsibility, good health, and family values.

The premise behind the health care sharing ministry is simple. Say that the Smith family participates in a ministry in which each family is committed to paying $300 per month. If one of the Smiths incurs a $1,500 medical expense, the family will submit the bill to the ministry. The Smiths themselves will pay $300 toward the bill, and the ministry will divide up the remaining $1,200 among four other families, who will pay $300 each. That way, the $1,500 will be covered, and no one's checking account will be hit by a sudden jolt.

In months when the Smith family has no significant medical expenses, they will pay a portion of other families' medical bills, just as the other families did for them. As its name suggests, the ministry focuses on sharing the burden of health care expenses among the community—without any intervention from big government or big insurance companies.

What makes health care sharing so special is the values that imbue these ministries. They focus on the communitarian ideal of service to neighbor and service to the Lord. As Tony Meggs, the CEO of Christian Care Ministry, said, "I don't think it would work without the faith element. I don't think that ultimately it would work outside of this collective moral agreement with each other, that commandment in Galatians that we're required to carry each other['s] burdens."[1]

And by carrying each other's burdens, participants in sharing ministries prevent that burden from falling to the government. According to a Samaritan Ministries executive, about half of its members have incomes below 200 percent of the federal poverty line, and many of them could qualify for government aid.[2]

Most of these ministries are explicitly Christian and accept as members only people who adhere to Christian belief structures. They emphasize spiritual health and personal responsibility and, as strong supporters of marriage as the foundation of the family, they do not cover unmarried cohabiting couples (though they do accept singles, with the membership priced accordingly). Participants must also abstain from using tobacco and illegal drugs.[3]

And while sharing ministries help pay for catastrophic medical expenses like treatment for cancer, participants are expected to "budget and prepare for...minor [medical expenses] like trips to the doctor for a child's cold."[4] As Tony Meggs notes, "This is a sharing ministry, and you have a responsibility not to be an undue burden to the other members."[5] Can you imagine a federal bureaucrat ever saying that to a welfare beneficiary?

Just as sharing ministries promote personal responsibility instead of government dependence, so too do ministry members view each other with a compassion that government can never replicate. One Indiana pastor who feared he "was going to lose everything" when his daughter was diagnosed with a brain tumor was stunned by the outpouring of both financial and emotional support: "It was just Christian people helping Christians."[6] Many participants pray for those whose bills they receive and pay, providing comfort and strength to families in times of crisis. Take, for instance, this public testimony from a family in Idaho:

> We are amazed at the care and generosity of God's people! We received over 200 cards and gifts from those who felt led by the Holy Spirit to help bear our financial burden! I now share with others as much as possible about this incredible ministry. We often found ourselves in tears as we read the meaningful notes of agape love and encouragement.[7]

Imagine anyone saying that about a big insurance company! And while ministries are comparable to traditional health insurance in terms of the range of expenses they cover, the cost of participating in most ministries is lower than that of commercial insurance. For instance, in 2011 most ministry participants were required to pay a "share" of $200 to $400 per month, with the highest monthly share totaling $760 for a large family. By comparison, that same year, the average cost of employer-provided health insurance totaled $15,073 per year, or over $1,250 per month (though employees may not be fully aware of the cost, since they see only the portion that comes directly out of their paycheck). So health care sharing is not only more nurturing than traditional health insurance, in many cases it's also more affordable.

The growing popularity of health care sharing testifies to its success—and also contributes to it. Over 160,000 individuals now participate in health care sharing ministries nationwide.[8] The two largest ministries—Christian Care Ministry and Samaritan Ministries—have over 50,000 members each. That is how they are able to cover catastrophic events such as cancer, a major heart attack, or severe injuries from a car crash, while at the same time keeping the cost so low.

And this concept of group self-insurance need not be limited to faith ministries. Other organizations could establish similar mutual aid societies—Rotary, say, or the Elks (after all, the latter's official name is the Benevolent and Protective Order of Elks, a reminder of its history as a mutual aid society as well as a social club; such societies were common in our country before government welfare started taking over in the twentieth century).

Health care sharing stands in stark contrast to most forms of health insurance, and certainly to Obamacare, the essence of Big, which provides tremendous giveaways to big health care interests. In order to ram the unpopular bill through Congress, the Obama administration cut backroom deals with lobbyists for hospitals, the American Medical Association, and others. In fact, the head of PhRMA (the Big association for the pharmaceutical industry) publicly bragged about the windfall Obamacare would bring to his industry, saying he had a "rock-solid deal" with the administration.[9] PhRMA's side of the bargain involved running hundreds of millions of dollars' worth of ads supporting Obamacare, to make sure Congress would enact the special interests' "rock-solid deal." It's the typical Washington "You scratch my back and I'll scratch yours" approach that has Americans sick and tired of big government.

But big pharma wasn't the only special interest supporting Obamacare. Many insurers lobbied for the law, which grants them a captive audience, by commanding us to buy their products whether we like it or not. What's more, Obamacare will raise taxes in order to pay for more than $1 trillion in subsidies for insurance.[10]

Obamacare is perhaps the worst example to date of big

government getting into bed with big business. The law actually helps the larger insurance companies, hospitals, and hospital-based physician groups to get larger still and more powerful, and the Democrats who passed the bill believe that more bureaucrats, regulation, and government bureaucracy will "control" this behemoth. But there's only one real way to control it. That's to dismantle Obamacare, along with all the power structures and connections with special interests that come with it, and give power back to the people and the civic institutions that form the backbone of our society.

Back to Basics: Doctors and Patients

When it comes to health care, nothing is more important than the relationship between doctor and patient. Unfortunately, Obamacare finds numerous ways to meddle in that relationship. Even before Obamacare, Congress and Washington bureaucrats were imposing more and more requirements on doctors participating in government programs like Medicare. Physicians have to report more information, comply with more regulations, and do things Washington's way to get paid for treating patients. It's Washington's version of the Golden Rule—he who has the gold makes the rules. And it means that federal bureaucrats are encouraging a pay-for-conformance culture, where doctors spend more of their time filling out paperwork and checking boxes to get paid, rather than spending that time with their patients.

Obamacare takes government regulation of doctors and accelerates it to warp speed. The law will reduce Medicare payments by 2 percent for doctors who do "not satisfactorily submit data" to government bureaucrats,[11] and by an additional 1 percent for doctors who do not meet bureaucrat-defined standards of "quality" and cost.[12] Doctors also face penalties of up to 3 percent of Medicare payments if they do not follow the latest bureaucratic mandates when it comes to keeping electronic medical records. Overall, politicians and bureaucrats have repeatedly shown their willingness to punish doctors who do not dance to their tune.

Given all this intrusion, it's little wonder that many physicians are abandoning medicine entirely rather than spend all their time following Washington's orders. A survey by Deloitte found that a majority of physicians (57 percent) think the practice of medicine is in jeopardy.[13] More than six in ten (62 percent) say it is likely that they or their colleagues will retire in the next one to three years because of frustration with the health care system.

However, a growing number of physicians have found a solution: direct-care practices. Some call direct-care practices "concierge medicine," but I call it letting doctors be doctors. The physicians in these practices focus on providing personalized, quality care to a smaller group of patients, rather than spending their time filling out insurance paperwork or complying with Washington's latest mandates. Many of them charge patients a set fee per month or per year, which entitles the patients to see their doctor as often as they need.

These direct-care medical practices operate on a common-sense basis: providing a full range of services to patients at a reasonable price. Under the insurance-based system, doctors get paid for performing more procedures. But insurance covers only certain types of services, like lab tests or X-rays. Most insurance companies won't pay doctors to make a quick phone call to check on a patient, or to send an e-mail to the worried parent of a sick child. Direct-care medicine allows doctors to do what's best for their patients, rather than focus on what bureaucratic hoops they need to jump through to get paid.

Concierge medicine also allows doctors to spend more time with their patients. More than 70 percent of these physicians spend half an hour to an hour with their patients during each visit, getting to know their behavior and medical history in a way that will enable the physician to provide higher-quality care.[14] These doctors are also more accessible, with many answering e-mails and phone calls from patients directly. One Texas physician goes so far as to ask his patients to call and wake him up if they need him at two o'clock in the morning.[15] That's the result of a better doctor-patient relationship—and personalized attention by the doctor increases the patient's trust.

Critics claim that only the rich can afford the fees direct-care physicians charge. Looking at the facts shows that's nonsense. A recent survey indicated that the average income of a typical patient is between $50,000 and $200,000 per year—income levels far below the so-called 1 percent.[16] Many families can pay $200 to $400 per month for a family physician to provide them care such as flu shots, routine checkups, and annual physicals; purchase catastrophic insurance to cover unexpected expenses such as treatment for a heart attack, cancer, or injuries sustained in a car crash; and still spend less than the $1,250 per month that the average employer-provided insurance plan costs.[17]

And concierge medicine fees have remained "incredibly stable," according to the American Academy of Private Physicians. As journalist Elizabeth O'Brien reports, the largest concierge network has held fees "essentially flat since 2007"[18]—this while insurance premiums have risen by an average of about $3,000 per family since Barack Obama was elected.[19] While critics claim that only the wealthy can afford to pay a doctor an annual retainer, the numbers indicate that this "concierge medicine" can actually make health care *more* affordable for middle-class families.

Critics also claim that the personalized-care physicians provide their patients in direct-care practices will create health care shortages for others. "Concierge seems so unjust because it's making more care available to people who are willing to pay more," one doctor told a *PBS NewsHour* interviewer.[20] Because some people will receive more care, the thinking goes, others will receive less, and patients who can't afford to pay a monthly retainer won't be able to find a doctor.

More nonsense. If every doctor could spend more time with his patients and less time filling out insurance forms and meeting Washington bureaucrats' latest whims, do you think 62 percent of doctors would say they expect many of their colleagues to retire soon? Of course not. In fact, Gary Dorshimer, a physician at the University of Pennsylvania, said that concierge medicine "helped extend my career." Before he converted his practice to a concierge model, his level of mental burnout had him contemplating retirement.[21]

You know that when critics say "our health system has an equity problem to begin with," as that doctor did on PBS, what they mean is that government hasn't done enough to "fix" all the problems that government intervention has helped to create. These critics think boards and bureaucrats in Washington can set up a system to micromanage areas where there is a shortage of physicians, and "encourage" doctors to practice there. Obamacare includes provisions designed to do just that.

But substituting regulation for free markets and innovation is the old way of thinking, and here's hoping it soon becomes obsolete. The real solution to America's demoralized physician population does not lie in more mandates and red tape. It lies in allowing doctors to be doctors.

America's physicians are incredibly talented individuals who can come up with new treatments and methods that benefit us all—if only big government would get out of the way. Unfortunately, Washington bureaucrats, coupled with Washington lobbyists and special interests, often work to stifle innovation. That's what is happening to another physician-led innovation—the specialty hospital.

Specialty Hospitals: "Focused Factories"

Specialty hospitals stem from doctors' belief that they can innovate better for patients than hospital administrators and bureaucrats can. Harvard professor Regina Herzlinger calls these hospitals "focused factories," as many of them specialize in one element of medicine—orthopedic surgery, for instance, or cardiac procedures—rather than trying to be all things to all people.[22] Just as Adam Smith viewed the division of labor as key to economic growth when he was writing *The Wealth of Nations* more than two centuries ago, so specialty hospitals' concentrated focus allows them to raise the level of quality and lower costs.

Just as important, specialty hospitals take their direction from physicians, not bureaucratic administrators. Most specialty hospitals are physician-owned, and while some see that feature as a defect, in reality it has proven their greatest asset. As owners, the physicians have a real stake in the hospital's success; they are not just hired help working a nine-to-five job. Thus they have an incentive to find ways to enhance quality, from developing care protocols to redesigning operating rooms to make them more efficient.

One of Dr. Herzlinger's Harvard Business School case studies examined doctors in a cardiac specialty hospital that developed new processes for recognizing and treating irregular heartbeat following surgical procedures, reducing complications by two-thirds.[23] Because of their ownership stake, these physicians felt empowered to propose new solutions to improve the quality of patient care.

By contrast, physicians in traditional hospitals often complain about inefficient practices instituted by hospital administrators. For instance, one orthopedic surgeon who practiced in a large general hospital noted that "it drives [my colleagues] crazy to have a staff that's not familiar with a tray of multi-size screws and nuts and bolts"—hardware familiar to orthopedists, but not necessarily to operating room staff, who spend much of their time working on other sorts of surgeries.[24]

An Arkansas cardiologist recounted an incident in which "I did [an] angioplasty at 11:30 p.m. one night on a patient who had been waiting all day," because administrators had shut down operating rooms to save money.[25] Specialty hospitals, by allowing greater specialization and greater physician input into processes and procedures, help make the notoriously inefficient field of health care more productive—and better for patients.

Specialty hospitals prove that innovation—not Washington mandates or regulations—drives improvement in health care. Specialty hospitals have proved to deliver superior quality and have received significant quality improvement bonuses under Obamacare. Of the 161 specialty hospitals nationwide participating in the quality programs, 122—more than three-quarters—received bonuses and only thirty-nine received penalties.[26] On the other hand, 74 percent of traditional hospitals received penalties.[27] Ironically, surgeons and other doctors can best meet the quality standards mandated by Obamacare by being freed from the stifling bureaucracy that comes with Obamacare.

Specialty hospitals' success stems from physician ownership and from their concentration on a few limited disciplines. As one Indiana orthopedist put it, "The single-minded obsession with quality has been the hallmark of our success. . . . It's the difference between renting a home and owning a home: the pride of physicians in owning the hospital."[28] The chief of nursing at the same Indiana facility emphasized the importance of specialization in driving quality improvement: "You don't get too many athletes who play more than one sport. It's the same way with hospitals. If you're allowed to specialize in something you can do one thing great. If you want to specialize in four or five things, you can probably do them okay."[29]

When it comes to health care, I don't want just "okay"—I want the best for my family and me. And by empowering physicians and focusing their efforts on just a few types of procedures, specialty hospitals have been able to provide the best care to patients.

But as you might have expected, the big traditional hospitals don't welcome the innovation that specialty hospitals can provide. Instead, most hospitals worry about other institutions poaching on "their" turf—and they rely on government to protect themselves from competition. Over the past fifty years, some thirty-six states have enacted so-called certificate-of-need laws, which require an organization seeking to build a new medical facility to obtain a certificate from a state board affirming that the facility is "needed" in that particular area.[30] Think about that for a moment: A group of physicians want to build a hospital, and they have to go to a state board and beg, "Mother, may I?" before constructing this facility that will improve patients' health and well-being! Why can't doctors and patients get the benefits of a free market like everyone else?

Unfortunately, it gets worse. In their backroom deal with the Obama administration, big hospitals agreed to support Obamacare in exchange for new restrictions on physician-owned hospitals actually written into the law.[31] Under Obamacare, new physician-owned hospitals cannot receive payments from Medicare, and most existing physician-owned hospitals cannot expand if they want to continue receiving Medicare payments.[32] The hospital industry tightened its grip on power even further with this deal, and patients have been left with fewer care options (yet another reason to repeal this legislation).

Some physician-owned hospitals have found one way to circumvent Obamacare's restrictions. Because the law prohibits most facilities that accept Medicare patients from expanding, some of them have decided to stop taking Medicare patients altogether. The founder of one Texas hospital said he and his colleagues didn't want to end their relationship with Medicare, "but we felt like the law gave us no choice."[33]

The fact is, with 10,000 baby boomers joining Medicare every day for the next two decades, the program will need to attract and retain more doctors and hospitals than ever before.[34] But thanks to the unholy alliance of the Bigs, many seniors will have fewer treatment options.

Some would argue that if specialty hospitals refuse to treat Medicare patients, the federal government should impose new regulations requiring them to accept Medicare. But that's exactly the wrong approach. It's Washington regulations that are forcing specialty hospitals to stop seeing Medicare patients—how can more government regulations fix a problem created by government in the first place?

The problem is that, in the health care field as in so many others, big special interests have used big government to preserve their dominant position. Big insurance supported the individual mandate in Obamacare to require all Americans to buy their products. Big pharmaceuticals bragged about their "rock-solid deal" with the administration, which will increase the number of seniors buying more expensive brand-name drugs. And big hospitals are trying to shut out their upstart competitors by placing restrictions on physician-owned facilities.

None of these tactics have worked—or will work—to control health care costs or to provide better care. The answer instead lies in solutions like health care sharing ministries, concierge medicine, and specialty hospitals. The initiatives outlined in this chapter are guideposts: They are exceptional, they point the way for other individuals and communities, and we need to see more of them.

Each of them puts patients and their doctors—not bureaucrats—in charge of health care decision making. Doctors feel empowered to provide better care, and patients feel empowered to take control of their health. Putting patients first: what a novel concept!

We need to move to a patient-centered, market-based health care system, with emphasis on a free market in health insurance, portability of policies, and health care decisions made by patients with their doctors—not big government.

9

Education and the Power of Choice

We cannot expect a federal-government-controlled school system to provide the intellectual ammunition to combat the dangerous growth of government that threatens our liberties.

—Dr. Ron Paul

When Aristotle was asked how much educated men were superior to the uneducated, he replied, "As much as the living are to the dead."

I wouldn't go as far as Aristotle, but I'm convinced that education is not just *a* key; it is *the* key to realizing the American dream. That's why rescuing our children's education from the Bigs should be at the top of every American's to-do list.

America's fractured public education system has placed us in serious danger of splitting apart into two nations: an educated, self-reliant First World America capable of taking full advantage of the opportunities that technology and globalization are generating on an almost daily basis; and an uneducated, dependent Third

World America that is falling further and further behind, is alienated from First World America, and regards the American dream as a hoax.

The overall state of K–12 education in America is lackluster at best. American students rank in the middle of the pack on international assessments of science and math comprehension; according to education researcher Jay P. Greene, just 6 percent of the 14,000 school districts in the United States have math achievement scores in the top third of international math assessments.[1] And the achievement gap between white and minority students is striking.

The 2013 National Assessment of Educational Progress found a 26-point achievement gap between white and black fourth graders in math, and a 19-point gap between white and Hispanic fourth graders. To put this in perspective, 10 points on the NAEP scale is equivalent to a year's worth of progress. That means black and Hispanic children are roughly two years behind in math by the time they reach fourth grade. The gaps have persisted since 1990, despite significant spending increases and additional federal intervention.

The state of reading achievement, which is so fundamental to future academic success, is even more alarming. For American children overall since the 1970s, reading achievement has remained virtually unchanged. And as with math, minority students lag behind white students. NAEP shows that nationally, while 34 percent of white fourth-grade children are proficient in reading, just 17 percent of Hispanic students and 15 percent of black students are similarly proficient.[2] The lack of academic achievement is especially jarring in some of the nation's largest cities. In Cleveland, just 8 percent of all fourth graders are proficient in reading; in Detroit, just 7 percent can read at grade level.[3]

It should go without saying that these educational disparities are fundamentally wrong and unfair. *All* of our children deserve an education that enables them to make the most of their talents—and it's precisely because we love them that we cannot tolerate an educational system that produces such shockingly unequal results.

Why are American schoolchildren doing so poorly? The Left's answer is that we're simply not spending enough on education. This seems to be what President Obama believes.

In his 2013 State of the Union address, for example, he proposed new federal funding to help states "make high-quality preschool available to every child in America."[4] His call for a significant expansion of federal preschool programs came despite the fact that only a month earlier, a long-awaited study by the Department of Health and Human Services concluded that the federal Head Start program, which costs nearly $8 billion annually, had little or no impact on participants' cognitive or social/emotional development or on their health. On a few measures—such as teacher-assessed math ability and social engagement—access to Head Start actually had *harmful* effects on children. For the four-year-old cohort, teachers reported "strong evidence of an unfavorable impact on the incidence of children's emotional symptoms."[5]

But the failures of massive federal programs like Head Start are of no consequence to friends of big government. It's an article of their political faith that whatever the problem, government isn't spending enough. That's their story, and they're sticking to it.

Of course, everything depends on how you define "enough." I suppose it's possible to argue that $2 trillion in federal spending on education since 1965,[6] a near tripling of federal per-pupil expenditures (on an inflation-adjusted basis), and the existence of more than a hundred federal education programs are simply not "enough."

But then, what *is* enough? $3 trillion? $4 trillion? $10 trillion? And even if we could afford to spend such astronomical sums, could we be confident that all that money would move the needle forward on student achievement? History tells us it's unlikely.

Another explanation for the disastrous state of education in America today is the cultural wreckage caused by the pathologies we looked at in chapter 6: family breakdown, welfare dependency, and crime. For the year 2009, for example, only 16.7 percent of African American children between fifteen and seventeen years of age had grown up in an intact family, with married parents; for Hispanics, the figure was 40.5 percent.[7]

The research strongly indicates that children born outside of stable, married-parent homes are at greater risk of dropping out of school, being involved in delinquent behavior, and having a child outside of marriage themselves. Unless we succeed in repairing our overall culture we can't expect our schools to have much of an impact on student achievement.

I think this emphasis on culture is right on point. Although I've spent a portion of my life in the political arena, I'm convinced that the really decisive figures in history are the prophets and moral leaders, not the politicians, and the really decisive events are the religious revivals, such as America's Great Awakenings, that seemingly come out of nowhere, help people regain their moral bearings, and reawaken a love of God, a love of country, and a love of our fellow man.

Historians tell us that between the early eighteenth century and the late nineteenth century, we had four Great Awakenings— which helped to give birth to such remarkable events as the American Revolution, the abolition movement, and the women's rights movement. In my opinion, nothing would improve our education system more than a fifth Great Awakening that would remoralize our culture and strengthen the fraying bonds between husbands and wives, parents and children, and teachers and students.

But children in underperforming schools can't wait around for the next Great Awakening. America is unraveling before our eyes, and we need to do something about it *now*. Fortunately, there is a path forward for American education: school choice, the brainchild of one of the twentieth century's greatest economists, Milton Friedman.

Heroes of School Choice

A child of immigrants, Friedman was born in Brooklyn in 1912 and became an economist and statistician who taught at the University of Chicago for more than thirty years. He was awarded the Nobel Prize for Economics in 1976 and the Presidential Medal of Freedom in 1988. Friedman wasn't just super-smart; he was also one of freedom's greatest champions. I'm proud to say that he and his wife, Rose, were recipients of The Heritage Foundation's highest honor—the Clare Boothe Luce Award.

As President George W. Bush said in a White House ceremony honoring Friedman on his ninetieth birthday, "He has used a brilliant mind to advance a moral vision: the vision of a society where men and women are free, free to choose, but where government is not as free to override their decisions."[8]

One of Friedman's great passions was improving American education by giving parents the ability to choose their children's schools. As he saw it, education was a commodity produced by our schools, and parents were consumers who paid for this commodity through taxes. In a free-market economy, consumers are free to choose from whom they wish to purchase their commodities. This forces businesses to *compete* for the consumer's money, and the only way they can do so successfully is by constantly improving their products.

In the case of education, however, in most jurisdictions consumers are deprived of choice. Parents *must* send their children to the assigned public school unless they are able to afford private school tuition in addition to paying their taxes to support the public school.

Thus the school's teachers and administrators are in the enviable position of monopolists. They don't have to constantly improve their product, because their customers can't take their business anywhere else. Or rather, they can't go anywhere else if they happen to be of low- or middle-income. If they're affluent, it's a different story. The wealthy can afford to send their children to a private school of their choice, and that's what many of them do.

This is how a great country like the United States begins to unravel. Its fortunate youngsters attend private schools where competition is the rule, and where teachers and administrators know that they have to provide their students with a first-rate education or the parents will simply take them to another school.

Less fortunate youngsters, however, are compelled to attend assigned government schools, where monopoly is the rule, and where teachers and administrators know that even if they fail to educate their students there are no consequences.

We need an education system that lets *all* parents choose what they conclude is the best education they can afford for their children—and "affordable" should include choosing which school gets their tax dollars dedicated to education.

As Milton and Rose Friedman put it in their 1979 best seller, *Free to Choose*:

The tragedy, and irony, is that a system dedicated to enabling all children to acquire a common language and the values of U.S. citizenship, to giving all children equal educational opportunity, should in practice exacerbate the stratification of society and provide highly unequal educational opportunity.[9]

To help solve this problem, the Friedmans came up with a policy idea that was as brilliant as it was bold. Let's say it costs $12,000 to educate a seventh grader in the local public school. Give that seventh grader's parents a choice, the Friedmans argued. If they're satisfied with the local school, they can continue to send their child there. But if they're not satisfied, they'll get a $12,000 scholarship, or "voucher," which they can use to fund their child's education at some other school, either public or private.

This voucher system, the Friedmans argued, will accomplish three things: It will take a child out of a bad school and empower his parents to choose a school that meets his particular learning needs. It will serve as a *catalyst*, forcing bad public schools to stop behaving like monopolies and start instituting much-needed reforms—performance pay for teachers, the elimination of "social promotion" of students who are not performing at grade level—that will improve educational outcomes for all their students. And by giving poorer parents the power of choice that affluent parents already enjoy, it will promote greater equality of opportunity in the educational system.

Milton and Rose Friedman were so passionate about the need to improve our education system that they started the Friedman Foundation for Educational Choice. Their foundation works with parents and communities around the nation, providing research to education advocates and promoting policies that protect school choice. They are two of the heroes of the school choice movement. But there is another heroine who also deserves recognition—Virginia Walden Ford.

Virginia Walden Ford's involvement with school choice began in a very dramatic way when she was a young girl growing up in Little Rock, Arkansas, in the 1960s. Little Rock had been home to the Little Rock Nine—the first black students to integrate Central High School in 1957. She and her twin sister were among about 130 students who were handpicked to desegregate the city's high schools on a larger scale in the mid-1960s.

"By the time I attended that school a few years after [the Little Rock Nine] graduated," she later recalled, "I was called 'nigger' nearly every day there, and not just by the students. The number of black kids in our school felt like a drop in the bucket, but we stuck it out. I actually begged my daddy to let me go back to my old school, but he insisted I stay because the resources and opportunities there so far outshone what we could get in an all-black school—and because he knew that we were paving the way for others to come. Those days definitely firmed my backbone."[10]

Virginia Walden Ford's adult involvement with school choice grew out of personal experience of a very different kind. She was raising three children as a single parent in Washington, D.C. Her two older children completed high school successfully, but her third child was experiencing serious difficulties:

When my son started having problems in and out of school, I knew I did not want him to continue attending a D.C. public school that had (and still has) many problems of its own. I became more disturbed each year by the public school system and its "lowered expectations" for academic achievement. By the time my son, William, entered his freshman year of high school in 1996 he was performing poorly and getting into trouble...in class and out. I joined the thousands of poor mothers without the resources to move to better neighborhoods or put our children in private schools—hopeless and helpless.[11]

Fortunately, Virginia Walden Ford had a neighbor who saw potential in William. One day, this Good Samaritan approached her and offered to pay William's tuition at a local parochial school. That act of kindness proved decisive: "The chance to go to a private school turned his life around. Before, he was struggling to fit in, like a lot of urban kids without fathers do. It isn't necessarily to their benefit to act smart. You have to change their environment. For the first time, my son felt people cared if he learned, and he felt safe."

William's story had a happy ending: He graduated from high school in 2000, served in the U.S. Marine Corps, and is doing well today. But Virginia Walden Ford believes that without her neighbor's help, William's life might have turned out quite differently.

She decided to help turn the lives of other children around the way William's had been. She helped organize D.C. Parents for School Choice and began to lobby for scholarships for low-income children to attend the school of their parents' choice.

Her efforts were crowned by success on January 22, 2004, when President Bush signed the D.C. School Choice Incentive Act into law. It gave hundreds of children from low-income families a way out of the city's failing schools by providing scholarships that could be used at private, parochial, or charter schools.

Because the District of Columbia is our nation's capital, Virginia Walden Ford's successful struggle for school choice was highly visible and energized activists everywhere. She has gone on to fight for school choice in other parts of the country, and she has been impressed by the impact school choice has on low-income parents, as well as on their children:

> We have seen that, when children are placed in environments of their parents' choice, they succeed and their parents become active and involved. It changes their lives so much when their children are doing well in educational environments. It is because of expanded educational opportunities for the families who have had no choice that we see happy endings—not only for the children, but also for their families and their communities.[12]

In the D.C. School Choice Incentive Act, which established the D.C. Opportunity Scholarship Program, Congress also mandated annual evaluations of the program's performance. The most recent study found that students who used vouchers to attend a private school had a 91 percent rate of high school graduation. Graduation rates in D.C. public schools hover around 60 percent. Moreover, the $8,500 for an Opportunity Scholarship is less than half the $18,000 per year that it takes to educate a student in a D.C. public school.[13]

I was happy to read recently about Tsion Abera, whose family came from Ethiopia through London to Washington, D.C., when she was eight. Tsion wasn't all that happy in public school here, but even though both her parents worked steadily—her father driving a cab, her mother working in a shop—they wouldn't have been able to afford a change of school. Fortunately, an Opportunity

Scholarship gave Tsion the opportunity to attend parochial schools in the area with excellent results. As I write, Tsion is eighteen and has been accepted at an Ivy League school, Dartmouth College. She wants to study neuroscience.[14]

In a rational world, government officials, comparing the high success rates and low costs of school choice programs like the Opportunity Scholarship Program with the high costs and multiple failures of federal programs like Head Start would try to expand the former and cut back on the latter. But in the real world, things have worked out rather differently.

As I mentioned earlier, although Barack Obama came into office promising to broaden educational opportunity for all children (on June 26, 2008, for example, he said, "We cannot be satisfied until every child in America—I mean every child—has the same chance for a good education that we want for our own children"),[15] he has consistently attempted to *defund* the D.C. Opportunity Scholarship Program. Teachers' unions, one of the president's core constituencies, haven't appreciated the competition.

It's difficult not to agree with Virginia Walden Ford: "When segregationist politicians blocked schoolhouse entrances, they wanted to keep minority children out to deny them a quality education. Today, as anti-voucher politicians block schoolhouse exits, they want to keep minority children in—again denying them a quality education, condemning them to a life of lost opportunities and unfulfilled dreams."[16]

The "Threat" of School Choice

If you're wondering how such a bizarre situation ever came to pass, I suggest you try looking at the school choice movement through the eyes of a teachers' union official. To such an official, school choice is a grave threat because it's all about competition—and competition brings unwelcome change to those who benefit from the status quo. It might, for example, force schools to adopt reforms that the unions have been resisting for years—like basing teachers' salaries on performance rather than seniority, allowing for alternative teacher certification, and ending "social promotion."

School choice forces public school teachers and administrators to be accountable to parents and taxpayers, as opposed to operating like monopolists. And in all the history of the world, no monopolist has ever surrendered his power without a fight.

Of course, you can't expect big labor officials to come right out and say that in opposing school choice, they're defending the interests of their *real* clients, their union members, rather than the interests of parents and students. Instead, they argue that allowing students to opt out of the public school system hurts those left behind.

But recent research tells a very different story. It turns out that virtually all the data we have on school choice demonstrate that not only did *all* the students who participated in school choice show marked educational improvements, but even those students who stayed behind benefited from it.

Simply put, the competition unleashed by school choice forced poorly performing schools to improve their performance as well. A 2013 meta-analysis of the empirical evaluations of school choice programs by education researcher Greg Forster found that choice improves academic outcomes, has a positive impact on public schools, and saves taxpayers money. The analysis, published through the Friedman Foundation, found that:

Twelve empirical studies have examined academic outcomes for school choice participants using random assign-
ment, the "gold standard" of social science. Of these, 11
find that choice improves student outcomes—six that all
students benefit and five that some benefit and some are
not affected. One study finds no visible impact. No empirical study has found a negative impact.

Twenty-three empirical studies (including all methods) have examined school choice's impact on academic
outcomes in public schools. Of these, 22 find that choice
improves public schools and one finds no visible impact.
No empirical study has found that choice harms public
schools.

Six empirical studies have examined school choice's
fiscal impact on taxpayers. All six find that school choice
saves money for taxpayers. No empirical study has found
a negative fiscal impact.[17]

But if the "students left behind" argument doesn't work,
there's another argument that works all too well. It's spelled M-O-
N-E-Y, and the National Education Association (NEA), along
with the American Federation of Teachers (AFT), have lots of it.[18]
According to Stanford political science professor Terry Moe:

By comparison to other interest groups, and certainly to
those with a direct stake in public education—parents,
taxpayers, even administrators—the teachers unions are
unusually well equipped to wield power. The NEA and
the AFT enlist more than 4 million members between

them, and they blanket the entire country—including virtually every political district where public officials are running for office....

Both can count on a zealous cadre of political activists to ring doorbells, man phone banks, and do all the things that candidates love, need, and fear. Both have massive lobbying organizations for bringing their views to bear on policymakers. Both have public relations machines that can conduct media campaigns on a wide range of educational issues, and are designed with the intention of shaping public opinion and influencing elections.... In addition to all this, the teachers unions are fabulously wealthy.... If some 4.5 million members are paying about $600 per person per year in dues, the total comes to $2.7 billion annually.[19]

The unions vigorously oppose school choice, and since the NEA and AFT are a major force in the Democratic Party, this explains President Obama's opposition as well. But the unions do not enjoy that much influence in Republican circles, and in March 2011 the Republican-controlled House, under Speaker John Boehner, voted to reauthorize and expand D.C.'s school choice program—after repeated attempts by those on the Left to zero-out funding for the program. Eventually, the House and the Senate reached a compromise, and funding for the D.C. Opportunity Scholarship Program was restored. But despite having signed a five-year reauthorization for the program in 2011, President Obama in his 2014 budget has once again tried to eliminate funding for this successful school choice option. The struggle continues.

Of course, not all liberals oppose school choice. Former

senator Joe Lieberman worked with Boehner on that 2011 legislation, and James Carville, the irrepressible Democratic political operative, told *Reason* magazine that he was "very excited about" school choice. "I think we ought to give our children the best we possibly can, and I think we're moving in that direction," he said.[20]

Carville is right. Slowly but surely, America is embracing school choice. More than 245,000 students in seventeen states and the District of Columbia have access to private school choice options.

Other school choice options include charter schools (publicly funded schools that agree to meet state performance standards but are otherwise free from bureaucratic rules and regulations), online learning, and education savings accounts (ESAs). In the latter, a portion of the funds that would have been spent on a child in the public school system goes to an ESA, from which parents can then pay for private school tuition and a variety of other education-related expenses. ESAs allow parents to keep unused funds from year to year and even roll funds into a college savings account.

This proliferation of educational choice has provided customized learning options for children across the country. In 1999, shortly after Jeb Bush became governor, Florida undertook a series of education reforms aimed at providing schooling options tailored to individual learning needs. Florida's school choice landscape means parents are able to customize their children's education with a variety of options, including online learning, public school, homeschooling, private schools, and charter schools.

Sixth grader R. J. Woods attends the International Community School (ICS) in Orlando. Two days a week, ICS students take a full slate of academic courses taught by certified teachers; another two days, ICS students receive instruction at home from their parents using lesson plans developed by ICS teachers. And on Fridays, ICS students take a wide range of electives at the school and attend a nearby gym in the afternoon.

R.J.'s mom, Freddi, is an enthusiastic advocate of her son's à la carte schooling. "When R.J. was approaching school age," she says, "my husband and I were intrigued by home schooling. But I never would have felt comfortable doing everything at home." Now, thanks to the "unique partnership" between ICS parents and teachers, she believes R.J. enjoys "the best of both worlds."[21]

Two Million Free and Counting

In addition to hybrid schooling, there has been significant growth in homeschooling over the past decade. Homeschooling, of course, is one of the oldest forms of school choice. Indeed, before the advent of compulsory education in the nineteenth century, it was the rule rather than the exception. All the presidents whose faces adorn Mount Rushmore were homeschooled, as well as inventors and scientists from Benjamin Franklin to Thomas Edison.

Today, about two million children are homeschooled in the United States, and they've got quite an edge on their forefathers. Dozens of carefully tailored curricula, easy access to almost every book ever published, and a wide array of online courses and tutoring have opened up a world of knowledge for the taking, without the child's ever needing to suffer through roll call.

Each family's reason for opting out of public schooling is different. Some want to make sure that their children receive a strong religious education. Others are afraid that their local public schools won't provide a good education at all. Still others see it as the best way to teach and care for a child with special needs or a developmental disability.

By its nature, homeschooling is generally an individual effort by a mother or father, and it doesn't involve a massive national structure. That's the point of it. However, it is fair to speak of a homeschooling "movement," but it is not a partisan political movement. These moms and dads run the gamut from conservative evangelicals to liberal atheists. What they all have in common is the desire to be intimately involved in the academic and moral formation of their kids.

There are many reasons why you'd think the government and professional educators would support this movement. For starters, homeschooling saves tax dollars. Each child enrolled in public school costs the taxpayer a little over $10,000 a year on average,[22] which is saved when parents take teaching upon themselves—and yet parents teaching their children at home still pay taxes, which fund the public school system.

Homeschooling serves as a constant reminder to teachers in both public and private schools to be at the top of their game: Mom and Dad don't need to settle for a lackluster education for their children if homeschooling is a viable option.

But, for the reasons I've been discussing in this book, the groups that make up big education in the United States are vociferously opposed to homeschooling. The National Education Association is particularly aggressive here. In 2013 the NEA again passed a resolution, as it has annually for decades, stating that "home schooling programs based on parental choice cannot provide the student with a comprehensive education experience." [23]

Note that language carefully. The claim, apart from being

baseless, shows where the NEA's real problem with homeschooling lies: It is based on parental choice. This terrifies the Bigs, both because it presents them with a class of people entirely outside of their control, and because homeschooled students following structured curricula consistently outperform their public school counterparts.[24] By its very existence, the homeschooling movement is a standing rebuke to the educational empire presided over by the NEA and its allies. Homeschoolers also tend to pass along traditional American values to their children—values that are not very popular with the NEA crowd.

Today, all fifty states allow homeschooling, with differing degrees of oversight or regulation, but it wasn't always this easy to teach your own kids. In the early 1980s, some states had virtually banned the practice. Even in the states where homeschooling was legal, many bureaucrats, teachers, and social workers still had a penchant for civil action against families that attempted it—even, in extreme cases, finding excuses to seize children from their homes on the basis of unfounded allegations of neglect.

As a lawyer and homeschooling father of a large family, Michael Farris was all too familiar with this sort of persecution. He wanted to reaffirm the constitutional protection of home educating and ensure that parents could teach their children in peace. In 1983, along with fellow homeschooling dad and attorney Michael Smith, Farris started the Home School Legal Defense Association.

Run out of Farris's and Smith's homes, the HSLDA was a true labor of love from the start. The fee for membership was—and still is—just $100 a year, which entitles a family to legal representation by volunteer lawyers in case of need. This dedication to affordability meant it was years before the HSLDA could afford any salaried employees.

Nonetheless, its unceasing challenges to unconstitutional laws and regulations bore fruit in state and federal courts. Within a decade, the United States was a far safer place to educate one's children. Many states passed explicit protections for home educators, and countless families escaped heinous harassment because Farris and company covered their backs.

Farris went on to found Patrick Henry College in Virginia, a Christian liberal arts school. Many homeschooled students who benefited from Farris's legal efforts have gone on to study there. The HSLDA continues to fight for parental rights in and out of court, and from its humble beginnings has expanded its activism to Canada and Europe.

Farris fully appreciates the ability of grassroots organizations, from the local homeschooling club to national associations like his, to restore educational freedom: "We all know that God used and blessed state organizations, especially through their annual conventions, to build, inform, motivate, and turn out the team to win battles in state after state. Local support groups that pass along critical information about legal and political threats are also absolutely essential to our future defense, as they were in the past. This is not a time to be fat and happy. It is the time to get fit and ready for battle."

But you don't need to be a lawyer or the president of a college to revolutionize education. Sometimes all it takes is the energy and dedication to share your experience, asking nothing in return.

Laura Berquist didn't have an advanced degree in education, but she knew exactly what she wanted her six children to learn. Modern schooling had produced generations of students who could recite facts but couldn't put them in any critical context, and thus were easily led by faddish ideas rather than focusing on the quest for truth. Mrs. Berquist wanted to raise critical thinkers, children whose education would prepare them to reason independently at an early age.

She was greatly influenced by the acclaimed writer Dorothy L. Sayers's essay "The Lost Tools of Learning," which advocated a return to primary education based on the medieval Scholastics' Trivium—the traditional studies of grammar, logic, and rhetoric. In the process of collecting various materials to fill out this model—classic poems, speeches, essays, and so on—Mrs. Berquist discovered she had enough to fill a book. Like-minded friends who were homeschooling their own children came to her for recommendations, and she received invitations to speak at various homeschooling conventions.

There was a clear demand for a radical shift away from the textbook culture that is part of what so many home educators wanted to avoid in the first place. The well-educated student, in her mind, "needs to judge the conformity of the facts he learns to the reality outside. That is what truth is, conformity of the intellect with reality. Such a person will be an independent learner and thinker, and we live in a time when we have to be able to resist collective thinking. We want to order our lives to the truth, specifically the eternal Truth, not to what is popular."[25]

Thus *Designing Your Own Classical Curriculum* was born.[26] Including important historical, philosophical, and literary samples, Mrs. Berquist carefully composed this guide on the basis of her own homeschooling experience and offered recommendations for how families can pick and choose the readings and methods that fit their needs. Even so, there was significant clamor for more practical advice and guidelines; parents wanted the nuts and bolts of how to turn the kitchen table into an effective classroom.

To fill this need, Mrs. Berquist founded her own long-distance learning program, Mother of Divine Grace School. It combines the formal grading and tutoring of professional instruction with the stay-at-home, personalized experience of traditional homeschooling.

Today, the MODG program is used by thousands of families across the nation, guided by two hundred teachers and consultants. Laura Berquist never intended to start an entire business, but she now employs assistants and tutors to keep up with demand. From her home base in Southern California, she travels the country every year, telling homeschooling groups about her courses and helping them to design their own.

One of the newest entrants in the homeschooling field is my friend and former colleague Dr. Ron Paul, who launched his own curriculum last year. As he said in his farewell address to Congress, we should "expect the rapidly expanding home-schooling movement to play a significant role in the revolutionary reforms needed to build a free society with constitutional protections. We cannot expect a federal-government-controlled school system to provide the intellectual ammunition to combat the dangerous growth of government that threatens our liberties."[27]

I think Dr. Paul is on to something. I know that homeschooling is tough work, and it might not be the best choice for every family. Still, it remains an important avenue of escape for parents who are fed up with the incompetence and political correctness of our public education system and—to borrow from Mrs. Berquist—want to "foster in our children a love of the beautiful and true and a corresponding distaste for what is ugly and false."[28]

Even those of us who aren't directly engaged in homeschooling, or in any other aspect of the broader school choice movement, have a vested interest in defending the parental rights and familial freedoms that school choice represents.

It shows that the Bigs aren't all-powerful, that alternatives to top-down, one-size-fits-all federal programs still exist, and that America's little platoons are alive and well.

It shows how thinkers like Milton and Rose Friedman, activists like Virginia Walden Ford, and moms and dads like Laura Berquist, Mike Farris, and Michael Smith can take on the Bigs and win.

It shows that despite the crime, the drugs, and the challenges facing single parents, inner-city children *can* succeed, once they escape from the stranglehold of the Bigs.

Most important, perhaps, the school choice movement shows that huge reserves of concern, compassion, and, yes, love exist throughout our great nation. Once we succeed in drawing on these reserves, we can raise a generation that knows it has been loved by America's little platoons, and that will in its turn come to love the Good Samaritans—and the nation that sustains and nurtures them.

As Supreme Court Justice McReynolds wrote in *Pierce v. Society of Sisters*, the landmark 1925 decision banning compulsory public education, we must work to protect "the liberty of parents and guardians to direct the upbringing and education of children under their control," recognizing that "those who nurture [a child] and direct his destiny have the right, coupled with the duty, to recognize and prepare him for additional obligations."[29]

Loving Work

Why did the chicken cross the road? To escape federal regulators, of course.

I 'm a great believer in learning from other people's mistakes, and one of the greatest mistakes of the twentieth century, in my view, was the Soviet Union.

The basic idea behind the Soviet Union's formation was that the Communist Party would create a New Man, who would usher in a golden age of universal peace and prosperity. But in order to create a New Man, you first have to get rid of the Old Man. And since the people already living in the Russian Empire when the Communists took over had been formed and nurtured in their society's little platoons, they too had to be gotten rid of—or at least tightly controlled.

That's why, from 1917 to 1991, the Soviet authorities waged a ruthless war against families, communities, and churches. These institutions were seen as transmitters of the old "bourgeois" values: love of God, love of country, and love of one's fellow man. In their place, the Communists promoted revolutionary, Marxist-Leninist values: love of the Communist Party, love of the Soviet state, and hatred of "capitalist exploiters." And heading up the list of capitalist exploiters were bankers. After all, what good could these heartless "bloodsuckers" possibly do?

Of course, the Soviets had it exactly wrong. The little platoons are to societies what skeletons are to human bodies. Destroy them and everything else collapses. And in 1991, everything in the Soviet Union *did* collapse, much to the surprise of most of our Sovietologists, who couldn't understand how such a mighty "superpower" could dissolve so quickly—like the Wicked Witch of the West in *The Wizard of Oz*.

Well, as I said, I'm a great believer in learning from other people's mistakes—and one reason I love the little platoons is that the Soviet Union hated them. I have an especially warm spot in my heart for community bankers, for the simple reason that they help create the jobs on which our economy depends.

If you find that hard to believe, let me tell you the story of A. P. Giannini.

The Banker Who Changed America

Amadeo Pietro Giannini was born in San Jose, California, in 1870, the son of Italian immigrants. When he was thirteen years old, he dropped out of school and began working as a produce dealer for his stepfather. He was extremely successful, and retired at the age of thirty-four.

He became a banker quite by accident. His father-in-law was a director of the San Francisco–based Columbus Savings and Loan Society, and when he passed away, A.P. took his place. He soon discovered that Columbus Savings and Loan, like all other banks at the time, was run for the benefit of the wealthy and well connected, and was uninterested in making loans to the area's struggling immigrant community. A.P. decided to remedy that, and in so doing he became what his biographers called "the greatest innovator in modern banking."

"The only other to approach his stature," continue the biographers, "was J. P. Morgan, the elder. It is easier to contrast than to compare the services to society of these dissimilar men. Morgan was the banker for men of great wealth and for combinations of greater wealth. The locomotive fireman who worked on the railroad systems Morgan unified and the puddlers in the Morgan-financed steel mills never entered the great banker's consciousness, or his Wall Street banking house. Can you imagine J. P. Morgan carrying on a conversation with a track laborer? Giannini could talk to anybody."[1]

Not surprisingly, Giannini's sympathy for the "little fellow" encountered fierce resistance from his fellow directors, and in 1904 Giannini founded a bank of his own in a converted San Francisco saloon—the Bank of Italy. It catered to the inhabitants of North Beach, San Francisco's Italian colony:

> The majority of the Bank of Italy's early patrons were immigrants who had never been inside a bank before. They had hidden their surplus cash under the mattress. When they borrowed they had usually borrowed from loan sharks at merciless rates. Giannini taught them the advantage of interest-bearing savings accounts. He would loan $25 at bank rates, often with no better security than the calluses on the borrower's hands. Very few San

Francisco banks would loan as little as $100, in the belief that such small transactions were more trouble than they were worth.[2]

The Bank of Italy grew quickly, and most of its depositors were small tradesmen who had never had bank accounts before. But they had faith in Giannini, and Giannini had faith in them.

Then, on April 18, 1906, the great San Francisco earthquake struck; between the earthquake itself and the resulting fires, about three thousand people were killed and around 80 percent of the city was destroyed. The building housing the Bank of Italy was one of those destroyed—but not before Giannini succeeded in getting the bank's cash out of it. He moved the money to his home in San Mateo, eighteen miles away, in a horse-drawn wagon, covering it with garbage to guard against possible theft.

As a result, while every other San Francisco bank was shut down for at least a month, the Bank of Italy reopened nine days after the earthquake. It did so in a "branch" on San Francisco's waterfront. The branch consisted of a plank laid across two barrels and a bag of money Giannini brought back from San Mateo.

But it wasn't only A.P.'s quickness in getting the Bank of Italy's cash out of the damaged building that enabled him to help San Francisco recover from disaster; it was also his closeness to the community. As his biographers explain, "Unlike the big bankers, who were hampered by the loss of records, A.P. did not need them. He knew every one of his distressed clients and, almost to the penny, their balances before disaster struck. Moreover, he knew how much they could stand in the way of loans. He made decisions quickly. It was unnecessary to turn to municipal assessment rolls, if any survived, for Giannini carried in his head the appraised values of all North Beach properties and of some other sections as well."[3]

While the Bank of Italy had grown impressively before the earthquake, its growth after the disaster was phenomenal. It doubled its business virtually overnight, and A.P., impressed by the loyalty of his depositors, decided to become a banker for life.

Giannini reminds me a lot of Jimmy Stewart's character, George Bailey, in the inspiring film *It's a Wonderful Life*. A.P. went on to make many more contributions to his community, his country—and the world. In 1928 he changed his bank's name from the Bank of Italy to the Bank of America. During the Great Depression, the Bank of America bought the bonds that financed the construction of the Golden Gate Bridge. In World War II, it bankrolled many of the enterprises that spearheaded the war effort. And after the war, it helped rebuild war-torn Italy.

But Giannini's major contribution, I believe, is that he transformed America's banking industry. Before A.P., as we've seen, banks catered mainly to the wealthy; after A.P., banks opened their doors to small businesses. And since small businesses create the great majority of America's jobs, it's fair to say that an Italian immigrant's son who became a banker by accident laid the basis for much of our nation's economic growth and prosperity.

The Farmer Who Lowered Your Grocery Bills

Another hero, even less well known than A.P., is Carl A. "Skip" Pescosolido Jr. If you love oranges the way I do, you owe Skip a major debt of gratitude. Let me explain why.

In 1937, the federal government organized orange producers into cartels—known as "marketing orders"—that regulated the number of oranges farmers could sell. Farmers were assigned a weekly quota telling them what proportion of their orange crop they could bring to market. Any extra oranges could not be sold, and if they spoiled and had to be discarded—well, that was just too bad.

Cartels are generally illegal in America, since they interfere with the operation of the free market. But an exception was made for marketing orders. The theory was that by limiting the supply of oranges offered for sale, the federal government would prop up orange prices and protect small farmers.

Of course, the other side of the coin is that this system forced American consumers to pay more for oranges at their local grocery stores. And it led to enormous waste, with millions of oranges being left to rot every year because the cartel had blocked their sale. But—so you might think—at least it protected America's small orange growers, whose livelihoods were secured against the vagaries of supply and demand.

So you might think, that is, if you hadn't been reading this book. In fact, as we've seen in so many other fields, marketing orders served the interests of the Bigs, not the little guys. Sunkist, the largest California orange grower, used the cartel to maintain its market dominance. In a free market, smaller producers would be able to compete with Sunkist and grab a larger share of the market for themselves, but in a government-run cartel, Sunkist simply relied on the coercive power of the federal government to prevent small orange producers from expanding their business. The marketing-order system was a perfect way for Sunkist to advance its own interests and suppress competitors while pretending to stand up for the small producers.

And then, in 1971, Skip Pescosolido came along.

Like Giannini, Pescosolido got into his profession by accident.

A Harvard-educated economist, he planned to join his uncle in a bulk oil distribution operation. But while viewing potential properties, he visited the San Joaquin Valley town of Exeter and saw a better business opportunity in citrus farming.

"I had never been in the San Joaquin Valley before, and I was quite taken by the place," he later recalled.[4] Pescosolido liquidated his other holdings, moved his family to Exeter, acquired four thousand acres planted with orange, plum, and cherry trees, and became an independent producer. And soon enough, he also became an outspoken opponent of the orange cartel.

His position was very simple. He described the marketing-order system as one that allows "a committee of my competitors to sit around in a smoke-filled room and tell me how many oranges I can sell each week." Pescosolido thought this arrangement was grossly unfair, and of course he was right.

But he did more than criticize. He filed over a dozen civil suits against Sunkist, and, being a trained economist, he was able to demolish the flimsy arguments advanced by Sunkist's lawyers. His research provided the basis for federal suits that were also filed against the giant producer. Nonetheless, Pescosolido didn't think he would ever succeed in changing the system. "There's a political battle going on when it should be an economic battle," he declared. "When it comes to politics, I'm very weak. I'm a minority."

But despite being badly outgunned politically, Pescosolido fought on, and ultimately prevailed. By 1991, the marketing-order system was gone, not only for oranges, but for other fruits and vegetables as well. Today, not only are small farmers free to expand their businesses and create more jobs, but your grocery bill is a lot lower than it would otherwise be, thanks in large part to the courage and determination of Skip Pescosolido.

Big Government versus Community Banks

But while entrepreneurs like Giannini and Pescosolido changed America for the better, today bankers in the A. P. Giannini mold are in serious trouble. One such banker is James Hamby. He's not a global banker, not a Wall Street financier, not a derivatives trader—just an old-fashioned community banker. The bank he runs, Vision Bank, has served Ada, Oklahoma, longer than Oklahoma has been a state, starting up in Indian Territory over a century ago. Like thousands of other small banks, Vision Bank is an integral part of its community, lending to "businesses, farmers, ranchers, oil and gas companies, Indian tribes, doctors, and hospitals, and anything else that walks in the door."[5]

But Vision Bank, along with the community it serves, is threatened by a wave of new regulations coming from Washington. In particular, the Dodd-Frank "financial reform" law, some of whose distortions of the financial industry I discussed in chapter 4, is hitting community banks like Vision hard. Over the past three years, it has had to spend an extra $1.4 million on regulatory compliance. And Hamby calculates that every dollar of compliance costs means as much as $10 less available for creditworthy borrowers.

The scope of Dodd-Frank is hard to comprehend. Running twenty-three hundred pages in length, the statute calls for 398 individual rulemaking proceedings by eleven separate regulatory agencies, many of which have nothing to do with the financial crisis that spurred the law's passage. Even the regulators are overwhelmed: As of June 2013, barely a hundred of the required rules have been finalized, adding uncertainty to the cost of the legislation. Small banks are hit particularly hard by the new rules, as

they lack the specialized staff to deal with the multitude of requirements. I'm happy to say I voted against the legislation when I was
in the Senate.

Some of the most problematic rules for small banks come from
the Consumer Financial Protection Bureau, a new agency created
by Dodd-Frank. Independent of the president and—thanks to
automatic funding from the Federal Reserve—free of congressional budget constraints, the CFPB enjoys broad powers to restrict
anything it sees as "abusive" behavior by financial firms, in areas
ranging from overdraft fees and the interest charged on payday
loans to student loans and mortgage financing.

For instance, in early 2013 the CFPB adopted a new rule defining "qualified residential mortgages." Ostensibly meant to protect consumers from mortgages they can't afford, the rule limits
options for responsible Americans who know what their prospects
and obligations are.

Other provisions of Dodd-Frank have also had counterproductive results. A provision known as the "Durbin rule" (after
Democratic senator Richard Durbin of Illinois) requires the Federal Reserve Board to impose price controls on debit cards, limiting how much banks can charge retailers for their use. This was
billed as a way to save merchants some money. But banks needing
to make up the lost revenue have responded by raising fees elsewhere. One frequent target has been free checking accounts—
which have become an endangered species since the Durbin rule
was implemented.[6]

Dodd-Frank has jeopardized rather than stabilized the financial industry. I believe that Congress should repeal it and instead
put in place a real alternative to "too big to fail" based upon the

principles of markets, private property, and the rule of law. The centerpiece of such a system should be the time-tested institution of bankruptcy, rather than regulatory whim.

The goal of policymakers should not be to *favor* small bankers like James Hamby, but to free them from unnecessary regulation. Just as A. P. Giannini's success turned his tiny Bank of Italy into one of the largest financial institutions in the world, so James Hamby's Vision Bank should have the right to serve its customers, compete, and grow without either interference or favoritism from Washington. But that becomes harder and harder as big government grows increasingly involved in every aspect of our economy.

Barriers to Job Creation

Today, members of Congress and federal bureaucrats have come to believe that *they* are responsible for our nation's prosperity. They like to portray themselves as compassionate defenders of the "little guy"—and perhaps that's how they see themselves. In reality, however, their interventions invariably end up raising new barriers to job creation. Let me give a few examples.

Taxation

The power to tax is the power to destroy. That statement is as true today as it was in 1819 when Chief Justice John Marshall wrote it in his landmark *McCulloch v. Maryland* decision.

Take, for example, the new tax on medical devices imposed by the Obamacare legislation passed by Congress in 2010. The tax applies to all manner of medical devices—everything from X-ray and MRI machines, to artificial knees and hips, to syringes, stethoscopes, and tongue depressors—and it is levied on the manufacturers of the devices. If markets won't let manufacturers pass along the burden of the tax as part of the price of the device, the manufacturers must absorb the cost, cutting innovation or workforce costs.

Before the tax went into effect, the Stryker Corporation of Kalamazoo, Michigan, announced it would lay off about a thousand employees—about 5 percent of its workforce—because of the tax. Many of those job losses occurred in the company's research and development department, stifling the company's ability to create new products or improve existing ones. And Stryker was not the only device manufacturer that laid off workers in response to the tax.[7]

The federal estate tax, a.k.a. the death tax, is also a destroyer of jobs and opportunity. The family that runs Reliable Contracting, a construction business in Maryland, faced the death tax when one of the founders, Frank Baldwin, passed away, followed by his wife. While the family was dealing with these painful losses, the IRS assessed a death tax on the full value of the company, even though many of its assets were tied up in machinery and supplies and were not available as cash.[8]

"You're trying to capture that American dream," recalled Patricia Baldwin, Frank's granddaughter, "and yet you're [also] trying to figure out how not to lose it." In order to hold on to Reliable Contracting, the family was forced to work out a payment plan with the IRS, in which it had to hand over hundreds of thousands of dollars per year, over an agonizing ten years, out of the firm's profits. As a result, said Patricia, "We didn't have that extra cash flow to invest in the company." Rather than being able to use the money to buy new construction equipment and hire new workers, they had to send it to Uncle Sam.

President Obama has often called for an end to the tax deduction for corporate jets. He thinks that higher taxes on the rich Americans who own those jets will benefit other, less wealthy Americans. He forgets our recent history. In 1990, a 10 percent luxury tax on yachts went into effect. Congress passed the measure assuming that the rich buyers of yachts would accept the burden. But when the price of yachts rose, orders dried up, and the yacht-building industry dried up as well.

As the *New York Times* chronicled at the time, it was blue-collar workers who built the yachts who ended up bearing the pain of the tax by losing their jobs. The situation was so bad that Congress repealed the devastating tax in 1993.[9] Ending the tax deduction for corporate jets would similarly end up hurting the blue-collar workers who build the planes.

For twelve years Congress debated what to do when the Bush tax cuts expired. Liberals wanted the government to have and spend the revenue that allowing the cuts to expire would bring in. Conservatives warned that letting the cuts expire would cost the economy hundreds of thousands of jobs. The accounting firm Ernst & Young ran the numbers and found that just allowing the tax cuts to expire for singles making more than $400,000 per year and married couples making more than $450,000, as President Obama favored, would reduce the number of jobs in the economy by more than 700,000 over ten years.[10] Unfortunately for American workers, Congress did not heed that warning. It passed most of President Obama's tax hike on New Year's Day 2013.

Of course, Congress needs to collect taxes to fund the legitimate functions of the federal government, like national defense, homeland security, and the courts. But too often in recent years it has forgotten that when it raises taxes to pay for new spending and grow the government, it is taking money out of the economy that might have been spent on growing investment and hiring workers.

As the social thinker George Gilder has observed, "Entrepreneurs must be allowed to retain the wealth they create because only they, collectively, can possibly know how to invest it productively among the millions of existing businesses and innumerable visions of new enterprise in the world economy."[11]

Regulation

But it's not just taxes that kill jobs. Oppressive regulations do too—in addition to increasing the cost of living and eroding our freedoms. Unlike federal taxation and spending, however, there is no official accounting of total regulatory costs. (Estimates range from hundreds of billions of dollars to nearly $2 trillion annually.) But the number and costs of *new* regulations can be tracked, and the results are alarming, to put it mildly.

Despite our weak economy, the Obama administration has increased the regulatory burden on Americans, adding twenty-five major regulations that imposed regulatory costs of $23.5 billion in 2012 alone.[12] From Obama's first year in office through 2012, 131 major regulations were issued, with costs approaching $70 billion a year.[13] While the president has acknowledged the need to rein in regulation, the problem is actually growing worse on his watch, with hundreds of costly new regulations in the pipeline.

Keeping track of all these regulations is next to impossible. But my Heritage colleagues publish an ongoing series of reports—"Tales of the Red Tape"—that highlight the impact of selected regulations on American life. Here are a couple of recent "Tales of the Red Tape" that focus on job creation—or rather, job destruction. As you'll see, they describe a world much closer to Lewis Carroll's *Alice in Wonderland* than to the America you and I grew up in.

USDA Lays a Regulatory Egg

The Obama administration fervently opposes state laws requiring voter identification to cast a ballot. But it is insisting that the nation's farmers prove the identity of every chicken transported across state lines. (I am not making this up.)

Under the fowl rule proposed by the U.S. Department of Agriculture (USDA), a flock that has been hatched, fatted, and butchered as a single unit may be transported from state to state with a "group identification." But such groups are as scarce as hen's teeth.

The vast majority of poultry owners are not part of a vertically integrated commercial operation. They routinely co-mingle chicken stock of varying sources and ages. Consequently, under the rule, they will have to attach sealed and numbered leg bands *to every bird* they transport.

The federal coop cops say the regulation is needed to enhance the "traceability" of livestock to control animal disease. But that explanation doesn't add up. The Regulatory Impact Analysis that accompanies the proposed rule lacks any quantification of (supposed) benefits or the very real costs.

Nearly 9 billion chickens went to market last year, moving from hatcheries to farms to slaughter houses.

Most broilers live only five to eight weeks. In that short span, their IDs will have to be changed a number of times—with documentation—to accommodate leg growth. And the USDA wants all such records to be maintained for *five years*—the costs of which ain't chicken feed.

As the Small Business Administration noted, "Small poultry operations have very thin profit margins that cannot absorb the cost increases from the tagging and record keeping requirements of this rule."

The benefits of the poultry rule would be paltry. It's unclear, for example, how forcing thousands of people to maintain billions of documents on dead chickens for years would enhance traceability. As it is, evidence of disease typically results in the destruction of the flock. Only healthy birds are eligible for slaughter and sale.

There is one upside to the USDA action in that it finally solves the nagging question of why the chicken crossed the road.

To escape federal regulators, of course.[14]

EEOC Disables Employers

A high school diploma has long served as the most basic requirement for an entry-level job (notwithstanding declining standards in public schools). But now comes the Equal Employment Opportunity Commission (EEOC) declaring that a sheepskin prerequisite constitutes discrimination.

In the opinion of the EEOC Legal Counsel staff, requiring a high school diploma has a "disparate impact" on individuals with a learning disability. In other words, requiring a high school diploma discriminates against those who don't have one by holding them to a standard they fail to meet.

Proponents of this rather expansive rendering of the Americans with Disabilities Act (ADA) undoubtedly believe they are advocating for the learning disabled. In actuality, it's an insult. Many millions of students with learning disabilities graduate from high school—with or without the multitude of accommodations that public schools are required to provide. And their diplomas affirm the discipline and determination that a business owner dreams of.

Alas, the EEOC's interpretation of the ADA effectively renders their accomplishments as meaningless, while also eroding the incentive to graduate.

Any employer who dares to require a diploma must be prepared to prove that it's a "business necessity" and to establish that the work cannot be accomplished otherwise. But that's not all. According to EEOC staff, the employer must also demonstrate that the job cannot be performed adequately even when the company "accommodates" the applicant lacking educational qualifications.

That's an enormous burden. As noted by Heritage researchers James Sherk and Andrew Grossman, such legal risks discourage businesses from hiring altogether.

What we have, then, is a government policy that discourages educational achievement and inhibits hiring—a real disabling of employers.[15]

Now, it's not just the regulators who are responsible for the mountain of red tape that's smothering America. Under the Constitution, Congress is responsible for the rules governing Americans. It has a duty to ensure that unnecessary and excessively costly regulations are not imposed on our economy. For decades now, though, it has been ignoring that duty. Until it changes its ways, the costs of red tape will continue to skyrocket, and jobs will continue to be destroyed.

Mandated Benefits

Part of our legislators' motivation, as we have seen so many times already in this book, is to serve the special interests that help them get elected. But the nobler motive is the tendency to respond to problems by saying, "There ought to be a law." And so well-intentioned legislators reason, "Wouldn't the world be a better place if everyone got paid sick leave and health benefits? So why not *require* employers to provide them?"

Unfortunately, not even Congress can repeal the law of unintended consequences. Laws often work quite differently from the way their sponsors intended them to. This especially applies to workplace regulations.

The reality is that it is the workers who often pay for these benefits.

When the government mandates a particular benefit, employers comply. But they then make up the cost by cutting their workers' cash pay.[16] Government mandates do not force companies to pay their workers more; they force workers to take more of their pay as benefits and less as cash income.

Sometimes this is a good trade-off. Workers' compensation laws, for example, provide important protections for employees injured on the job. But it *is* a trade-off. Workers often do not get the new benefit for free on top of their old pay.

Currently, some members of Congress have proposed requiring businesses to provide paid sick leave. Four-fifths of full-time employees already get paid sick leave, but that still leaves one-fifth who do not.[17] Will they benefit if Congress passes the Healthy Families Act and forces businesses to provide seven days of paid sick leave per year? Perhaps not. They will get paid sick leave— but will also see their wages drop concomitantly. They will have more time off and seven days' less pay each year.

The cost of some regulations cannot be passed on to employees. In that case, the regulations cost jobs instead. France illustrates this problem well. French businesses with fifty or more employees must comply with very extensive rules: They must set up profit-sharing plans, appoint union representatives, incur greater costs for workplace accidents, and set up a "work council." Complying with these rules is very expensive, and businesses cannot easily take the costs out of their employees' pay.

However, firms with forty-nine or fewer workers avoid these regulations. The result? French employers do not hire their fiftieth employee unless they absolutely must.

As you might expect, France therefore has more small businesses than medium-sized ones, and more medium-sized businesses than large ones. There are more French companies employing twenty-five workers than there are employing thirty, more companies employing thirty workers than there are employing thirty-five, and so on.

But something very strange happens when you hit forty-five employees. All of a sudden the number of firms at each level starts increasing. More French companies have forty-seven workers than forty-five, and even more have forty-nine employees. But at that point the number of businesses falls off a cliff. A total of 416 French manufacturers have forty-nine workers. Only 160 employ fifty workers. French businesses take great pains to avoid hiring that fiftieth worker.[18]

Fortunately, America is not in that bad a situation—yet. Similar studies in the United States do not show employers clumping at certain levels to avoid regulations. But we are headed in that direction—the Obamacare employer mandate/tax applies to all employers with fifty or more full-time workers. It remains to be seen how many employers will avoid hiring—or will either lay workers off or cut their hours back to part-time—to avoid the mandate.

Licensing

Tens of millions of workers lost their jobs in the Great Recession that began in 2008–2009.[19] Workers in construction and manufacturing got hit especially hard—and these industries are unlikely to return to their former size anytime soon. Many laid-off workers now need to find jobs in different fields.

Unfortunately, the government has effectively declared one of every three American jobs off-limits to them. One-third of U.S. jobs require a government license to perform them, a license that takes time and money to obtain.[20] For unemployed workers without a license—or the time and money to get one—these job openings are like the spots on ancient maps marked, "Here be dragons." Try to earn a living here and you may end up in court.

Of course, some occupational licensing makes sense. You wouldn't want just anyone performing brain surgery, or even filling your teeth. But occupational licensing now goes far beyond stopping quacks and snake-oil salesmen.

In every state of the Union you need the government's permission to work as a barber. Two-thirds of states require licenses to work as a makeup artist. In Florida it takes six years of study to legally work as an interior designer.[21] These restrictions have nothing to do with consumer safety. A bad haircut takes maybe three weeks to grow out. Only two other states besides Florida think interior designers need licenses.

Some licenses border on the ridiculous; others cross the line. Maryland, for example, licenses fortune tellers: "A Fortune Telling License is required for persons who practice or carry on the business or art of spiritualism, mind reading, fortune telling, clairvoyance, astrology, horoscope preparation and reading, palmistry, phrenology, crystal gazing, hypnotism (except as administered by a licensed physician or psychologist in connection with the practice of medicine or psychology), psychometry or any similar business or art and to ensure compliance with all applicable City Code regulations."[22] Does Maryland fear that unlicensed fortune tellers might make inaccurate predictions?

For those on the inside, licensing is a sweet deal. They get to freeze out their competitors. That is why most of the pressure for licensing occupations comes from the already-in-business practitioners themselves, not concerned consumers.[23]

Unnecessary licensing puts unemployed workers in a horrible position. They cannot even apply for one-third of available jobs. That forces them to look either for very low-paying jobs, or for jobs that may be difficult for them to land—or to excel in. A laid-off autoworker in Michigan might make a good security guard, but unless he completes three years of specialized education he cannot apply. An unemployed carpenter in Nevada might want to start installing security systems, but he must first pay the government $1,000 in licensing fees.[24] Thus licensing walls off large sections of the economy to unemployed workers while in many cases giving no real protection to consumers.

Licensing serves the interests of insiders, at the expense of outsiders. But entrepreneurs succeed by serving insiders, outsiders, and everyone in between. That's why CrossFit, a fitness company founded by Greg Glassman in 2000, has been such a hit. Its exercise program is practiced by about seven thousand affiliated gyms—or "boxes," as Glassman prefers to call them. CrossFit licenses them for a fee and certifies their trainers, but otherwise leaves them alone. They can set up their "boxes" in garages, warehouses, or any other location that suits the needs of their customers. They can charge what they want and train how they want. A passionate libertarian, Glassman leaves it to the free market to provide quality control.[25]

Killing Cupcakes

Unfortunately, governments don't think like entrepreneurs. Instead of welcoming diversity, many state and local governments enact onerous regulations to stop newcomers from competing against established firms. A prime example of this was attempted in the spring of 2013 in our nation's capital.

Washington, D.C., has incredibly expensive real estate—some of the costliest in the country. This makes renting space for a restaurant very pricey. Unless you are already fairly well off, you probably can't afford to do it.

But in 2009 some clever entrepreneurs in the District found a way around this problem: food trucks. The trucks get regular business licenses, follow food service health regulations, and cook delicious meals while parked along the streets in downtown Washington. They offer quick service, reasonable prices, and amazing variety. They serve everything from Korean BBQ tacos to Ethiopian stews to Cajun catfish. Unlike traditional restaurants, food trucks can move to where their customers work. And setting up a food truck is a way for someone with less money to become a small business owner and work his way up the economic ladder. Who would oppose that?

The Restaurant Association of Metropolitan Washington, that's who. The food trucks are cutting into its members' business. So it lobbied the D.C. government to pass "safety" regulations sharply limiting where the trucks could park. They would have to stay at least five hundred feet away from "specialty vending areas" (read: far away from restaurants) and in areas with at least ten feet of unobstructed sidewalk (read: not many places).

"These regulations will kill the food truck industry as we know it," said Kristi Whitefield, the co-owner of Curbside Cupcakes. "It will be smaller. It will be dispersed out to Lord knows where."[26] The regulations would wipe out hundreds of food truck jobs, while protecting brick-and-mortar restaurants from competition. This is government cronyism at its worst, the bureaucracy protecting the interests of the well connected.

In this case, the story has a happy ending. Washingtonians

revolted at the prospect of losing their beloved food trucks. After public outcry, including thousands of letters, blog posts, and tweets, the D.C. City Council rescinded the new regulations.[27] This was a rare victory. The food trucks survived because they were highly visible—people working in the city enjoyed their services every day. But special interests pressing legislators for job-killing favors in lower-profile industries often get their way.

It took a court order in Louisiana, for example, to permit Benedictine monks to make coffins. The monks wanted to support themselves by selling (relatively) inexpensive cypress coffins. But in Louisiana only registered funeral directors were allowed to sell coffins. They charged a lot more than the monks intended to—and they wanted their cozy monopoly protected. This law had remained on the books for decades. Each coffin is used only once, so the legislature faced little public pressure to allow coffin competition.

When the monks finally filed suit, however, the court ruled in their favor. But monopolists like to keep their monopoly power, so they filed a petition with the U.S. Supreme Court, asking the Court to overturn the lower court decision and prohibit the woodworking monks from making caskets.[28]

These are just a few examples of how big government destroys American jobs. This is obviously bad for the American economy—but it's even worse for the American soul. It makes us less brave, less optimistic, and less proud of our wonderful country. It divides Americans into two antagonistic classes: a ruling class that enacts and administers an endless stream of job-killing rules and regulations, and a subject class that must somehow find ways to cope with the adverse consequences of the ruling class's decrees.

Conservatives recognize this problem, and many of us are doing everything we can to limit the size and scope of government. But I believe we would make our case more effectively if we explained that the coercive power of the state doesn't just destroy jobs; it also destroys the love that Americans should feel for their country. That love is gradually being drained away by a ruling class that uses the power of government to make it harder and harder for ordinary people to live the American dream.

Loving the Poor

As earlier generations of Americans knew, individuals in
need are not statistics but human beings with physical,
relational, mental, emotional and spiritual needs.

In his farewell remarks to his cabinet ministers in 1955, Prime
Minister Winston Churchill urged his colleagues always to bear
in mind that man is not just a physical being, he is also spiritual. "The destiny of man," Sir Winston said, "is not measured by
material computations. When great forces are on the move in the
world, we learn we're spirits, not animals."

As usual, Sir Winston was right. Men and women aren't interchangeable cogs in some vast social machine. They're spiritual as
well as physical beings, created in God's image. Great political
leaders can awaken their people's spirits and inspire them to great-
ness. Effective antipoverty fighters achieve great results because
they know that more than material assistance, the neediest among
us require a firm set of spiritual values on which they can build new
lives.

Think of some of the wonderful people in Bob Woodson's network whom we met in chapter 1—Freddie and Ninfa Garcia, Bob

Coté, Shirley Holloway. They all understand that men and women who are down and out need more than regular meals and a place to sleep—"bunks for drunks," in Coté's memorable phrase. They need someone who will connect with them as individuals, who will offer them unconditional love but in turn will expect them to develop a sense of responsibility and discipline.

How an Earlier America Fought Poverty

Historically, America's method of helping those in need took a similarly personal approach. As Marvin Olasky describes in his book *The Tragedy of American Compassion* (which, I'm pleased to say, he began researching while at Heritage in the 1980s as a Bradley scholar), in the earliest days of our country, Americans believed that help should come from those closest to the person in need: family, community, and church. The "family, church, and neighborhood" comprised the "three-legged stool" on which every poor person could sit.[1] Olasky adds that relationships between those proffering assistance and those receiving it were key: "[I]t was important for the better-off to know the poor individually, and to understand their distinct characters."[2]

As the population increased and cities grew, more organized forms of charity began to spring up. Numerous charitable enterprises, such as orphanages and societies to provide assistance to widowed women with children, were founded.

For example, Olasky reports, the Society for the Relief of Poor Widows with Small Children, which started in 1797 in New York, "was cautious in distributing aid. Volunteers checked the means, character, and circumstances of each applicant to make sure that relatives were unable to help and alcoholism was not contributing to the general misery."[3] Giving away charity too freely was seen "as destructive both morally and materially,"[4] as an annual report from the Society for the Prevention of Pauperism in the City of New York noted in the early 1800s. Olasky adds that "the report also firmly distinguished between 'the unavoidable necessities of the poor' and those that resulted from wrongdoing."

"Enforcing work among the able-bodied," says Olasky, "was not seen as oppressive."[5] For example, the Female Charitable Society, established in New York in 1816, "distributed raw wool to the 'industrious poor' among women so they could spin and weave the material into finished products."[6] The objective was to "treat all as human beings, as members of the community with responsibilities."[7]

Today, such privately run organizations to help the poor are still very much with us. For example there are organizations like Harvest of Hope in Somerset, New Jersey, which I mentioned briefly in chapter 1. Harvest of Hope is a faith-based organization that recruits and trains prospective foster and adoptive parents. As Harvest of Hope's website puts it, the organization operates "to develop a network of partnerships with faith-based, as well as other community-based organizations in identifying homes for children." Founded in the late 1990s by the Reverend Dr. DeForest Soaries Jr., Harvest of Hope has recruited 285 families to become foster homes, and placed 490 children in temporary foster care.[8]

Bud's Warehouse in Denver is another example. A "home improvement thrift store," it was created by Belay Enterprises, a not-for-profit group of business leaders, community servants, and pastors, in order to engage individuals who face significant barriers to employment in work and work training.[9] They also provide help to individuals recovering from substance abuse, mental illness, or homelessness. Bud's keystone program is a yearlong curriculum that not only includes employment, but also education for job skills, healthy living, personal finance, and a host of other life lessons to transition participants back to independent living.

In 2013, Bud's "enter employment" rate was 75 percent for program participants.[10] Executive director Jim Reiner explains that he sees opportunities for hope in the terrible brokenness of poverty. "[T]here is a unique role that specially-gifted Christian entrepreneurs can play in addressing these problems" he writes.[11]

Reiner tells the story of Viana, a twenty-seven-year-old woman who spent eight months at Bud's recovering from alcohol addiction and the misdemeanors and employment gaps that accompanied it.[12] "What Bud's has done is it's given me a job history, it's given me a lot of responsibility," Viana says. "It's a huge blessing."

And in the words of Jason, another recent graduate:

> Before I came to Bud's I was drinking, using drugs a lot. Getting in trouble with the law. And I decided I needed to change my life around. I was just coming out of jail, and I needed a sober place to live. . . . [Bud's] helped me out with work ethic, showing up to work every day. People here helped me out really good, with just life in general.[. . .] It was a positive experience. I'd recommend it to anybody just trying to change their life around. Hard work pays off.

Big Government's War on Poverty

In 1964, when President Lyndon B. Johnson launched his famous "War on Poverty," he emphatically stated that his newly crafted welfare system "strikes at the causes, not just the consequences of poverty."[13] He also noted that the "aim is not only to relieve the symptom of poverty, but to cure it and, above all, to prevent it."[14] He said, "[W]e want to offer the forgotten fifth of our people opportunity and not doles."[15] His array of programs would accomplish this by giving Americans "the opportunity to develop skills, continue education, and find useful work."[16]

While Johnson's statements speak to self-sufficiency, the ideology undergirding federal antipoverty programs is in reality very different. As Olasky explains, that ideology essentially ignored personal responsibility and behavior and recast the causes of poverty as a function of society. And if poverty was a function of society, the new mentality reasoned, society could eliminate it. How? By redistributing resources. Olasky cites a Johnson administration official as saying, "The way to eliminate poverty is to give the poor people enough money so that they won't be poor anymore."[17] Thus over the last five decades the federal government's approach has been one of pouring billions and billions of taxpayer dollars into programs that purport to be fighting poverty. The dollar amount never seems to be high enough, however, with advocates of welfare programs continuously clamoring for more, with little accomplishment to show for it.

Today's Big-Government Welfare System

Their clamoring has been quite successful, I regret to report. Total welfare spending (federal, state, and local) has seen a sixteenfold increase (adjusting for inflation) since the 1960s, and today amounts to nearly $1 trillion annually. Yes, I said *one trillion dollars*. The federal government has spent more on the War on Poverty than it has on all our military wars combined.[18] Today the United States' welfare system consists of a complex web of roughly eighty means-tested programs providing cash, food, housing, medical care, and social services to poor and low-income individuals. These include:

twelve food-assistance programs,
twelve programs funding social services,
twelve educational assistance programs,
eleven housing assistance programs,
ten cash assistance programs,
nine vocational training programs,
seven medical assistance programs,
three energy and utility assistance programs, and
three childcare and child development programs.

As of 2008, despite Johnson's grand statements back in 1964, only four of these programs included any type of work requirement for able-bodied adult recipients (or even a requirement to train for work or look for a job). By 2012, because of controversial changes made by the Obama administration, only two of these programs included a work requirement.

Liberal supporters of big government welfare buy into the false assumption that compassion for the poor means providing public assistance with nothing expected of the individual in return. This idea is very far from that of the early American providers of charity cited by Olasky, and of Bob Woodson and the people in his network, who understand that indiscriminate giving can be useless and even harmful.

Where has this new approach left us? The respected political scientist Charles Murray says in his landmark work *Losing Ground* that it has indeed left the poor worse off in many regards. "The changes we made were not just policy errors, not just inexpedient, but unjust," he says.[19] "We tried to remove the barriers to escape from poverty, and inadvertently built a trap."[20]

How does this trap work? Once again, to quote Murray, the welfare system makes it "profitable for the poor to behave in the short term in ways that [are] destructive in the long term" and then "mask[s] these long-term losses" by "subsidiz[ing] irretrievable mistakes."[21] We saw one such case in Rodrick Yarborough's account, in chapter 6, of how the girls in his neighborhood decided to have out-of-wedlock babies so as to get on government assistance. Bob Woodson, in his testimony at a Senate Budget Committee hearing, provides another example of a young woman who had fallen into this trap:

> When my daughter was earning her degree in pastoral counseling, she was an intern in a high-school class for low-income kids with behavioral problems. One girl she met with was under a lot of stress. She was 15 and had a two-year-old baby. She and her boyfriend were living with her grandmother because her father was out of the picture and her mom was on drugs. But one day she came into my daughter's office and was very excited. She had figured out a plan. She would try to get pregnant again, and then would qualify for more money and more food stamps, and she and her boyfriend would move into Section 8 housing. The girl even knew how much of the rent she would have to pay. That was her dream. She had her whole life figured out within the government programs.[22]

This fifteen-year-old girl's story is one tragic example of the casualties of the welfare state. As Woodson noted at the hearing,

"It's not surprising that, regardless of intention, a system that rewards failure and punishes success has generated ever-increasing dependency." Welfare becomes an endless cycle. A 2002 study revealed that women whose families received welfare during their childhood are approximately three times as likely to be welfare recipients as adults.[23]

And then there are the Lumbees. Never heard of them? Well, neither had I, until I read Steve Forbes's *Freedom Manifesto*. The Lumbees are a North Carolina Indian tribe that is *not* recognized as a tribe by the federal government. As a result, the Lumbees aren't eligible for the assistance big government provides to other Native American tribes.

In case you're still undecided about whether government handouts help or hurt their recipients, the experience of the Lumbees should help you make up your mind. Whereas too many recognized Indian tribes stagnate on reservations and rely on casinos to generate income, the Lumbees own their own homes and many have become successful entrepreneurs. Prominent Lumbee businessmen include Jim Thomas, who used to own the Sacramento Kings, and Jack Lowery, who helped start the Cracker Barrel restaurant chain.

"We don't have any casinos," says Ben Chavis, another Lumbee businessman. "We have 12 banks....I can take you to one neighborhood where my people are from and show you nicer homes than the whole Sioux reservation."[24]

It's the old story: You subsidize poverty—either on reservations or in housing projects—and you get more poverty. You give people the opportunity to succeed, and you get...more Lumbees.

It is little wonder, then, that the welfare rolls have ballooned and poverty rates have not declined since Johnson promised to "cure" poverty.

In 1966, two years after the beginning of Johnson's antipoverty program, the rate of U.S. poverty stood at 14.7 percent.[25] In 2011, after nearly $20 trillion of welfare spending and the creation of eighty new welfare programs, the poverty rate stood at roughly the same level: 15 percent. It has fluctuated over the years, dipping after welfare reform in 1996, and rising with the economic downturn beginning in 2007. Yet the poverty rate has stayed the same since the mid-1960s.

It's important to understand how the poverty rate is calculated. The majority of welfare assistance that individuals receive is not included in the calculation as part of their income, meaning that many of the people counted as below the poverty line actually have a good deal more money than that would suggest. On the other hand, it can provide a decent measure of self-sufficiency, because it estimates the number of individuals not able to provide for themselves without assistance. So what the poverty rate tells us is that there has basically been no improvement in self-sufficiency since the War on Poverty began.[26] In fact, some researchers point out, the rise of welfare is connected with an erosion in self-sufficiency.[27]

This isn't to say that government welfare programs have done nothing to help raise the living standards of lower-income Americans over the last several decades. Not even the federal government can spend $20 trillion and have no impact! According to 2009 federal census data, as outlined by my Heritage colleague Robert Rector:

Eighty percent of poor households have air conditioning (only 36 percent of all Americans had air conditioning in 1970); 92 percent of poor households have a microwave; nearly three-fourths have a car or truck, and 31 percent have two or more cars or trucks; nearly two-thirds have cable or satellite TV; two-thirds have one or more DVD players; half have a personal computer; and more than half of poor families with children have a video-game system. The majority of the poor also have comfortable housing in good repair. In 2009, 96 percent of poor parents reported that their children had never gone hungry at any time during the year because they couldn't afford to pay for food, and 82 percent of poor adults reported never having gone hungry at any time during the year because they couldn't afford food.[28]

Of course, America's poor are not living in the lap of luxury. Many American families face very real challenges and struggle to make ends meet. But severe material poverty is mercifully uncommon (although supporters of big government fail to admit this, as it would undercut their argument for even more government welfare spending).

Unfortunately, big government seems to believe that the success of our welfare programs should be measured not by how many people get off welfare and start supporting themselves, but instead by how many are receiving welfare. There are even instances of welfare agencies recruiting people to join the rolls.

For example, the U.S. Department of Agriculture has run advertisements announcing, "Food Stamps Make America Stronger."[29] States have even been encouraged to create special "outreach plans" to make sure that individuals receive the benefits they "deserve." A *Washington Post* article highlighted some of these activities:[30] SNAP-themed bingo games in Rhode Island primarily for the elderly (SNAP, or the Supplemental Nutrition Assistance

Program, is the new name for food stamps); fliers in Alabama that read, "Be a patriot. Bring your food stamp money home"; and food-stamp parties in the Midwest at which new recipients can sign up for food stamps in groups. Florida even has its own food-stamp "recruiter," who is supposed to reach a monthly quota of new enrollments. She comes equipped with a training manual that provides guidance on what to say when seniors are reluctant to sign up for the program, including phrases such as, "You worked hard and the taxes you paid helped create SNAP."[31]

Welfare Reform

There was, however, a notable breakthrough in the 1990s. The welfare reform of 1996, significantly shaped by Heritage research, aimed to recast the conversation about government welfare and change policy in ways that would encourage self-sufficiency.

The 1996 welfare reform was arguably one of the most significant social policy changes in the last two decades. It fundamentally restructured the largest cash assistance program, transforming Aid to Families with Dependent Children into what is now known as Temporary Assistance for Needy Families (TANF). Work requirements were the centerpiece of the reform, and time limits were another element. Also, whereas prior to 1996 states would receive more federal dollars as their welfare rolls increased, the new law made it so that states would receive a fixed amount of federal funding. Thus instead of having incentives to increase welfare rolls, states would now be rewarded for helping able-bodied welfare recipients find jobs.

Although the reform law was signed by a Democratic president, Bill Clinton, liberal opposition was adamant. Some charged that this "awful policy" would do "serious injury to American children" and would result in "more malnutrition and more crime, increased infant mortality, and increased drug and alcohol abuse" as well as "increased family violence and abuse against children and women." Others said the reform was like "beating up children," a "horror," "a cleverly concocted scam," and an "outrage."[32] Peter Edelman, an assistant secretary for planning and evaluation at the Department of Health and Human Services, resigned in protest at the law's passage and claimed it would fail to promote work because "there simply are not enough jobs now."[33]

In fact, just the opposite occurred. As my colleague Robert Rector has explained, prior to the reform "the number of Americans on welfare had never significantly decreased. By 1995, nearly one in seven children was on AFDC. The typical AFDC beneficiary was on welfare for an estimated average of 13 years."[34] Within five years of the reform's implementation, welfare rolls had declined by half, the employment rates among low-income Americans had increased, and child poverty rates had plummeted.

Liberals claimed that welfare reform would push an additional 2.6 million persons into poverty.[35] Instead, by 2003 there were 3.5 million fewer people living in poverty than in 1995. Nearly three million fewer children lived in poverty, with poverty rates among African American children reaching all-time lows. Hunger rates among children also dropped by half.

The employment rate of never-married mothers grew by 50 percent, and employment among single mothers with less than a high school education increased by two-thirds.[36] As Rector and Jennifer Marshall point out, "Both decreases in dependency and increases in employment were largest among those most inclined to long-term dependence, that is, among younger, never-married mothers with little education."[37]

Bob Woodson told the Senate committee how welfare reform was key in helping his own niece break out of the cycle of government dependence:

> I had a niece who was in her 30s and had been on welfare for years. She was living with her child in one of the most dangerous public-housing projects in Philadelphia. The apartment complex was so dangerous that my nephew who was a police officer warned me about going there and said he wouldn't even go in there with his gun.
>
> I spent thousands of dollars trying to help her relocate. I found an apartment for her in Arlington...and found a job for her. But when I went to pick her up, she was in a bathrobe with a beer in her hand in the middle of the afternoon. She couldn't bring herself to make the move and leave the situation she had. My efforts to help her help herself couldn't compete with the welfare system. In the system, she knew she had a place to live, no matter how dangerous, and she had food and day-care benefits.[38]

But then the 1996 reform law passed. Says Woodson, "It wasn't until welfare reform became a reality that [my niece] changed. Welfare reform did what all of my efforts to persuade her could not do. It compelled her to go out and get a job. She had been on welfare for years and the only thing that interrupted that cycle was welfare reform."[39]

Bishop Holloway agrees with the earlier generations cited by

Olasky about the right way to help the poor. As she puts it, "It is wrong for the government to just take care of people. It's an impoverished mind not to let people take care of themselves. I believe in assistance, but I also believe it can be enabling and it can cause the weakening of a generation.... If they are on welfare, nothing is asked of them. They can have as many babies as they want to. Life has no value and they have relationships that are meaningless.... And that is the real problem with the welfare system.... It's easy to get on welfare, but it's hard to get off."[40]

That's one of the beauties of the 1996 reform: It decreased the "moral hazard" that a welfare system can create. Instead of competing for "clients," TANF case workers encouraged individuals to take advantage of the resources around them provided by civil society.

Barbara Elliott gives an example of this in her book *Street Saints: Renewing America's Cities*. She notes, "When the first flurry of activity followed the Welfare Reform Act in 1996, there were many efforts [by faith-based programs] to help single mothers with the job search." However, these women needed more than just help with job skills. "[I]t became clear," Elliott explains, "that women making the transition had a whole complex of issues that needed to be addressed before they could become stable in the workplace."[41]

Civil society, with its ability to reach individuals as individuals, went to work. "Holistic care groups sprang up in churches all over the country to make mentors available to provide assistance in each of these areas, to impart life skills as well as offering Bible study and personal encouragement to solidify character and motivation.... Neither job-search coaching, résumé assistance, childcare, transportation, nor Bible study alone would have guaranteed success. But the combination had a profound effect."

For example, Elliott writes, Good Samaritan Ministries in Michigan "trained small teams from local churches to assist low-income families with budgeting, goal setting, developing self-esteem, and managing day-to-day problems. The organization collaborated with Ottawa County and was the first in the country to successfully transition 'every able-bodied welfare recipient into a job.' "[42]

In addition to its clearinghouse, which acts as an information hub and referral service for eighty area churches and provides assistance for almost four thousand cases a year, the ministry now runs a Housing Assessment and Resource Team dedicated to finding affordable housing for the needy and homeless, as well as the Faith in Youth Partnership, which conducts volunteer mentoring and education programs for at-risk children.

However, while welfare reform saw much success, the reform touched only one program of the more than eighty federal programs providing assistance to poor and low-income Americans. On top of this, the friends of big government have been looking for ways to undo the 1996 reforms since day one. Unfortunately, under President Obama, they have been quite successful. Government welfare has resumed its growth, as has the number of Americans dependent on it.

If America plans to help the poor help themselves, this trend must change. As my former colleague Senator Jeff Sessions of Alabama told the Senate Budget Committee in early 2013, "No longer can we measure compassion by how much we spend on poverty but how many people we help to lift out of poverty.... It is time to return to the moral principles of the 1996 welfare reform. That reform was guided by the principle that, over time, unmonitored welfare programs were damaging not merely to the Treasury but to the recipient."[43]

Moving Forward

How do we make sure that America's most vulnerable are cared for, while at the same time ensuring that we are fostering, not discouraging, self-sufficiency?

First, we need to admit that the current welfare system has failed the poor. For decades, its approach has been the opposite of what President Johnson stated in 1964: Instead of curing the disease of poverty, it has poured ever more dollars onto the symptoms. In doing so, it has propped up living standards, yet it has also encouraged destructive behaviors. As Rector and Marshall put it:

> Material poverty has been replaced by a far deeper "behavioral poverty"—a vicious cycle of unwed childbearing, social dysfunction, and welfare dependency in poor communities. Even as the welfare state has improved the material comfort of low-income Americans by transferring enormous financial resources to them, it has exacerbated these behavioral problems. The result has been the disintegration of the work ethic, family structure, and social fabric of large segments of the American population, which has in turn created a new dependency class.[44]

Work, as we have seen time and again in this book, is a crucial component to human thriving. In Bob Coté's pithy phrase, "Work works." Tragically, participation in the workforce has declined among working-class American men over the last five decades. This is particularly troubling, as this decline has taken place not only during the Great Recession and the subsequent slow recovery, but also during good economic times.[45]

Work is a crucial component of human life. There is more to work than simply a paycheck. It connects individuals to their communities and gives them opportunities to contribute and gain self-respect. Additionally, research shows that employment is connected to higher levels of health and well-being.[46]

Americans understand the importance of work. A 2013 Rasmussen survey found that over 80 percent of Americans agree that work is the best way out of poverty.[47] Another poll by Rasmussen shows that about the same percentage agree that individuals receiving welfare should be required to work (only 7 percent said they disagreed with this statement, and the rest were unsure).[48]

Besides the failure to work, one of the greatest drivers of poverty today is the epidemic of broken relationships. As we saw in chapter 6, over the last five decades the most important little platoon, the family, has experienced significant fracturing.

Today, over 40 percent of children are born outside marriage. This is tragic because children in single-parent homes are nearly six times as likely to be poor as their peers born into married-parent homes. To look at it from the other direction, 70 percent of poor families with children are headed by a single parent. Research shows that over half of single mothers who remain unwed are poor. On the other hand, if these women marry the fathers of their children, only 17 percent remain in poverty, a decrease of roughly two-thirds.[49]

Policies that incorporate the principles of work and self-respect help people rise out of poverty. Most important, such policies help individuals get back on their feet rather than getting caught in the trap of government dependency.

Toward a Just Society

As earlier generations of Americans knew, individuals in need are not statistics, but human beings with physical, relational, mental, emotional, and spiritual needs. They need the helping hands of those who care to encourage them toward positive independent behavior.

And those helping hands that can restore the whole person are going to be found only in the little platoons, not in impersonal big welfare programs. By their very nature, government programs cannot focus on the unique needs of the individual person. But families, churches, and charitable organizations can and do. Whether it's Bob Woodson helping his niece, or Pastor Soaries's Harvest of Hope facilitating adoptions, or Bud's Warehouse teaching through employment, these are the people helping individuals in need.

For fifty years the ever-growing welfare state has not only failed to address the causes of poverty, but has created a trap for many. Overall, it has almost certainly done more harm than good, because it has ignored Churchill's insight about our spiritual nature.

We need to take a good look at ourselves. Are we truly a just society—a society in which we all seek to do justice, love mercy, and walk humbly with our God—or have we contracted out love, justice, and mercy by calling for ever more spending and programs from big government, while we go about our daily lives oblivious to the needs of our neighbors?

The safety net exists to catch those who fall and need assistance with the emergency material needs. But for too many, the safety net has become a snare. One reason is that we have misdiagnosed poverty in America. It's not merely about material need. It's about fatherlessness and the breakdown of human dignity and community. Politicians can't solve problems like that.

Freedom: America's Inexhaustible Energy Source

When people like George Mitchell figure out a safe and inexpensive way to take something that had been thought useless and put it to a thousand different uses, we all benefit.

I am old enough to remember the address to the nation that President Jimmy Carter delivered on April 18, 1977. "Tonight," President Carter declared, "I want to have an unpleasant talk with you about a problem unprecedented in our history. With the exception of preventing war, this is the greatest challenge our country will face during our lifetimes. . . . The oil and natural gas we rely on for 75 percent of our energy are running out."[1]

Well, it turned out that President Carter, along with most experts at the time, had it all wrong. Today we know that our country has enough oil and gas to last us, our children, and our children's great-great-grandchildren. We're an energy-rich country and we're developing those resources at a blistering clip today, thanks in large part to the pioneering efforts of George Mitchell. Let me tell you his story.

In 1901 Savvas Paraskevopoulos stepped off the ship *Kalamata* and passed through Ellis Island as the first in his Greek family to come to America. He was able to get a job on the railroad, where they needed able-bodied men, and he worked for the railroad for three or four years. It was the Irish paymaster on the crew who changed Savvas's name to Mike Mitchell because he couldn't manage Savvas Paraskevopoulos. Savvas couldn't read or write when he came here, but his foreman, who was also Greek, started teaching him.

Eventually he moved to Houston with a cousin who had come here separately, and they set up a shoe-shining shop together. Soon Savvas married a Greek girl who had emigrated to Florida, and they had four children. Though Savvas and Katina stressed to their children the importance of hard work and education, they could not imagine that their third son, George, would become one of America's wealthiest men.

After paying his own way through Texas A&M and serving in the Army Corps of Engineers during World War II, George, along with his brother Johnny, began a start-up oil drilling company with several friends. George and Johnny eventually took the company over and renamed it Mitchell Energy and Development Corporation.

They started small and worked hard and cheaply—instead of buying the gas and oil logs that identified potential reserves, George borrowed them overnight for a smaller fee and studied late into the night. They leased some land and started drilling. "This little company had a rig, one little rig," George remembers.[2] By the 1980s Mitchell Energy was a Fortune 500 company and one of Texas's best in the business.

Around this time, George, like others in the industry, realized that opportunities to drill natural gas were slowly shrinking. George also knew there was some natural gas in the Barnett Shale, where his company had been drilling, but no one knew how to free the gas trapped in pockets amid the dense, tight rock, or whether there was even enough of it there to make the venture worthwhile.

Determined and willing to take a risk, George ignored the people around him who said he was a fool. He organized a research team to figure out if there was a way of doing what others had dismissed as impossible. There was no guarantee of success—in fact, the team faced many dead ends and discouragements along the way. "I had a lot of engineers and geologists say, 'You're wasting your money, Mitchell.' We knew enough to go on and keep doing it, because we were making progress."[3]

They had begun with a technique known as hydraulic fracturing, which had been first developed for oil drilling in the 1940s. Back then, mud was pumped into the oil wells to release the deposits. George's team experimented with different liquids and different methods of pumping them in. After many tries, millions of dollars, and eighteen years of effort, they finally came up with a method of fracturing the shale to extract the gas.[4]

George's story marks the start of one of the biggest breakthroughs in America's energy sector. The technological developments in hydraulic fracturing, better known as fracking, that George and his team discovered have opened up a whole new energy chapter in America's history.

Of course, any energy venture has environmental risks, and given the high profiles of some antifracking activists, most Americans have probably heard more about the risks than the benefits.

I'll have more to say about that later on, but for the moment, suffice it to say that state governments, with local and community involvement, have been successfully regulating the use of fracking since it began in the late 1940s. Private and nonprofit organizations have been formed to ensure that fracking continues to make the most of America's energy wealth while protecting communities. These governments and individuals have accepted the responsibilities and privileges of controlling their own resources, bringing America great profit.

America's Energy Boom

Because vast stores of natural gas locked up in shale can now be tapped cheaply, America has enough natural gas to meet our needs for the next 175 years. Yes, I said 175 years, almost two centuries. And even that number keeps changing as scientists and industry people keep finding more reserves.[5]

Despite constant cries of oil scarcity, America actually has nearly 1.5 trillion barrels of oil that can be extracted with today's technologies. U.S. exports of crude oil and petroleum products have tripled since 2002, to over 1 billion barrels in 2011,[6] and the International Energy Agency expects North America to be a net oil exporter by 2035.

The development of our oil and gas resources is projected to add 549,000 jobs to the economy by 2020.[7] And exporting natural gas stands to increase GDP by as much as $47 billion by 2020 if exports are permitted by the federal government.[8]

This means jobs for all sorts of people, from those who have nothing more than a high school diploma to those who went through years of education and training. North Dakota is a good example of the promise and prosperity the energy boom is bringing to America.

As Ward Koeser, the mayor of Williston, North Dakota, put it, "[The pioneers] came west to find a place to start over. We're finding again today, the people who come here.... They're not complaining. They're just grateful to have a good-paying job, benefits, and a company that appreciates them."[9]

Because of fracking, advancements in drilling techniques, improved access to information, and an efficient state regulatory regime, in just five years shale oil production has increased more than fivefold in North Dakota, which has passed Alaska to become the country's second largest oil-producing state after Texas. That means more work for geologists, engineers, rig workers, truck drivers, and pipe welders. But it also means increased demand for restaurateurs, mechanics, salespeople, construction workers, and even florists—a result of husbands working away from home for two to three weeks at a time. It is no surprise that North Dakota has the lowest unemployment rate in the country, and the state government has enjoyed multi-billion-dollar surpluses for the past several years.

Even for low-skilled workers there are well-paying jobs. Fast-food restaurants located near the shale gas and oil fields are paying $15 an hour. And if you thought signing bonuses were just for investment bankers and NFL quarterbacks, think again. The McDonald's in Dickinson, North Dakota, was offering $300 signing bonuses.[10]

The shale-oil and shale-gas revolution is having profound impacts on our lives. It is creating good jobs in this otherwise sluggish economy and has lowered the cost of natural gas, and the increased oil supplies will help lower gasoline prices. Families have to devote less of their budgets to energy costs and have more freedom to save money or to spend it elsewhere—taking the kids on vacation, say, or going out to eat. Businesses are more competitive and are able to take risks and invest in new and better ways to do business—and consumers are once again the beneficiaries as businesses are able to lower their prices.

Take Pennsylvania, which is rich in natural gas. It went from generating 2 percent of its electricity from natural gas in 2001 to generating 18 percent from natural gas in the first quarter of 2011.[11] "I never would have expected that as a region we'd have a second chance to be a real leader in American manufacturing. Suddenly we're back in the game," said Bill Flanagan of the regional business group the Allegheny Conference on Community Development.

For Penna Flame Industries, a family-run metallurgy company in western Pennsylvania, the new abundance means their gas bill dropped from $10,000 a month in 2008 to as little as $3,000 a month in 2012. The money saved has allowed them to be more competitive by dropping fuel surcharges and investing in new staff and robotic technology.[12] Some people think of robots as stealing jobs from people, but general manager Gary Lopus, speaking of a newly hired robotics technician, pointed out, "That guy wouldn't have a job if it wasn't for the robots.... When you're not spending as much in other areas, you can spend more on things like this."[13]

Again, we've all heard that fracking threatens farms and water supplies, but in fact the extra income from leasing mineral rights and collecting royalties has enabled some hard-pressed farmers, like Vern and Jan Herfindahl from outside of Tioga, North Dakota, to hold on to their way of life. Hard economic times had forced the Herfindahls into bankruptcy, and they would have lost their family farm if not for the money they now receive for leasing the mineral rights underneath their land.

"We thought we had lost everything," recalled Jan. "And by the grace of God we were able to take control again and now we have a little bit of oil money. We're still paying on the house; we had it paid at one time. We're paying on land again, and so it just feels good to know that we do have some kind of income that we can rely on. It's a gift and we're so grateful for it."[14]

Even people in states that do not have rich energy resources benefit from the energy boom. Besides lowering energy costs for households, inexpensive electricity and cheap natural gas make America an attractive place to do business both inside and outside of the energy sector. Natural gas is also used for transportation and as a basic building block for fertilizers, chemicals, and pharmaceuticals. Cheap natural gas has people talking about a "manufacturing renaissance" in America as major companies around the world plan to make investments and build new factories here.[15] We're already beginning to witness it.

Enter the Bigs

As I said earlier, state governments, with local and community involvement, have been successfully regulating the use of fracking since it began in the late 1940s. Fortunately for us, many of the shale-oil and shale-gas reserves are on private or state-owned lands and do not have to go through the onerous regulatory process that extracting energy on federal lands does.

Part of the wisdom of allowing states to continue to regulate fracking as they have done for decades is the ability of state and local governments to respond quickly to changes in technology and to the specific needs of their communities. "Where [other states] started to see some of these problems, we thought, 'Well, let's not wait and have the problem in Ohio. Let's address it,'" Scott Nally, director of the Ohio Environmental Protection Agency, said of regulating fracking within the state.[16] This kind of quick reaction is not possible from Washington.

In November 2011, then EPA administrator Lisa Jackson said, "States are stepping up and doing a good job. It doesn't have to be EPA that regulates the 10,000 wells that might go in."[17] In Ohio there have been over 71,000 oil and gas wells fracked since the 1950s with no instances of contaminated groundwater. The same is true in Pennsylvania, where over 97,000 oil and gas wells have been fracked. The Interstate Oil and Gas Compact Commission has compiled statistics for fracking in each of the states, and it has found no case in which the process of fracking has caused any groundwater pollution.[18] And when there have been concerns, local and state governments are more accountable to their constituents than if the concerns were brought to the federal government in Washington.

And yet both the U.S. Environmental Protection Agency and the U.S. Department of the Interior are proposing federal regulation of fracking. Their proposed one-size-fits-all regulations would stifle one of the most productive sectors of the American economy with rules that would interfere with what states have done successfully for years. It just doesn't make any sense to slow the progress and add costs in time and money to businesses and local governments.

However, the media find antifracking activists like Mark Ruffalo and Yoko Ono more interesting than the people in small communities who are benefiting from the energy revolution fracking has started. It is hard, very hard, for small communities to stand up against the hulking federal government. And fracking is not the only area in which big government is at risk of shutting down America's energy revolution.

Never So Much Promise or Frustration

Why does big government have a seemingly irresistible urge to step into a promising situation and mess it up?

Politicians, I think, are forever on the lookout for a crisis they can "solve"—thereby ensuring both their reelection and their place in history. In Jimmy Carter's day, it was the energy crisis. Now that that crisis no longer exists, politicians have discovered a new crisis to occupy them: global warming.

The theory behind global warming is that carbon dioxide emissions are raising the earth's temperature, melting the polar ice caps, and threatening to create an ecological catastrophe. Unless we act promptly to curtail the carbon dioxide in our atmosphere, the argument goes, the earth is doomed.

Part of the problem with the debate over climate change is how sensationalized it has become. Yes, the earth is warming, although that warming has slowed over the past decade and a half, something the climate models failed to predict. And the fact that the earth has warmed doesn't mean we're headed toward *catastrophic* warming. The reality is, the science behind global warming is controversial, and many prominent experts think it's unsound and have competing theories as to why the earth is warming and how fast that warming is occurring.

But supporters of big government have been quick to jump on the global warming bandwagon, since it justifies their efforts to gain control of ever larger sections of the American economy.

Thus, arguing that the use of coal is a major contributor to global warming, the Obama administration has surrounded the entire coal industry with interminable permit applications and costly, time-consuming operating rules and safety regulations. These regulations essentially make it too expensive to build new coal-fired power plants or operate existing ones.

For instance, in January 2013, Georgia Power announced that it would close fifteen of its forty-three[19] electric power plants by 2016, ten of which use coal as their fuel (the others use oil). This will affect 480 employees.[20] "These decisions were made after extensive analysis and are necessary in order for us to maintain our commitment to provide the most reliable and affordable electricity to our customers," said Paul Bowers, the president and CEO of Georgia Power. The company specifically cited low natural gas prices and the costs of complying with new federal environmental regulations as reasons for the closings.[21] Once again, federal bureaucrats have put utilities and businesses in a no-win position where they must choose between regulatory compliance and their communities.

What *is* the cost of these federal regulations to the affected communities? Georgia Power's coal-fired Plant Branch has been operating in Putnam County for over sixty years. "They've been great corporate citizens," Putnam County manager Paul Van Haute said of Georgia Power. District 4 county commissioner Billy Webster said of Plant Branch's scheduled closing, "This, to me, is the time when we have to seriously—and I mean seriously—look to eliminating all but essential government services in the county. Otherwise, we may be looking at tax increases the like of which we have not seen before."[22]

The sad thing is, the people of Georgia will never see the climate "benefits" the federal regulations are supposed to achieve. While the Obama administration wants to end the use of coal in the United States, twelve hundred coal-powered electricity plants are being planned in fifty-nine foreign countries to supply homes, businesses, and communities with over 1.4 million megawatts of electricity.[23] Meanwhile, if America stopped emitting any carbon dioxide today, the predicted global effect would be a decrease of 0.17 degrees Celsius (0.31 degrees Fahrenheit) by the year 2100.[24] In other words, ending the use of coal would impose a heavy burden on American individuals and businesses, but with no noticeable impact on the earth's temperature.

Lower energy prices, based on healthy competition in generating energy, help Americans live healthier and more productive lives, but federal policies that artificially increase energy prices negate this effect. Especially hard hit are America's rural communities and the poor, since they spend a larger share of their income on energy. According to a study by America's Power, low-income families spend 24 percent of their budgets on energy bills, compared to the median family, which spends 9 percent. For individuals with after-tax incomes of $10,000 or less, this share jumps to 78 percent.[25]

In the end, these global warming policies aren't something we do for our children, but something we do *to* them.

The Problem with Subsidies

While big government has tried hard to cut the use of coal as part of its global warming policy, it has tried equally hard to subsidize "green" (wind and solar) technology. Politicians like to pretend that such subsidies promote fairness by "leveling the playing field." In fact, energy subsidies promote unfairness. When some companies get extra help from the government to win the competition for Americans' business, other companies must compete at a disadvantage. The game is no longer fair.

Government at any level should have no stake in the success or failure of particular industries or companies. Nor should the federal government play market investor either. And that goes for all types of energy, whether it's green or conventional. That privilege rightly belongs to the American people—that is, individuals, families, schools, religious institutions, hospitals, businesses—who risk their own money and don't draw from a collective pool of taxpayer dollars.

There are two kinds of companies that receive corporate welfare from the government: profitable companies that don't need it, and unprofitable companies that don't deserve it.

If Americans believed that big government's favorite green technologies were worth investing in, then the companies would not need the federal government to subsidize them.

The real irony of energy subsidies, however, is that in the long run they hurt the very industries they were meant to help. Rather than standing on their own feet, learning from their mistakes, and earning the business of their fellow Americans, lobbyists for subsidized industries usually circle back to Washington to ask for "just one more" favor. It reminds me of a little book I used to read to my kids, *If You Give a Mouse a Cookie*.

The CEO of one of America's largest wind energy producers has called out his own industry and the federal government on the perverse effects of subsidies. Patrick Jenevein, president and CEO of Tang Energy, writes:

> My own company began by delivering clean energy (in the form of natural gas) to rural China, where families still used animal dung for cooking fuel. We entered the wind business in the late 1990s, when a wind-turbine company asked us to provide electricity from its site when the wind wasn't blowing. Years later, we oversaw a similar project but in reverse: In 2008, without a government subsidy, we built a wind farm in Lubbock, Texas, to supplement at lower costs the delivery of electricity to a cottonseed-oil company....
>
> Without subsidies, the wind industry would be forced to take a hard fresh look at its product. Fewer wind farms would be built, eliminating the market-distorting glut. And if there is truly a need for wind energy, entrepreneurs who improve the business's fundamentals will find a way to compete.[26]

But perhaps the most insidious cost of subsidies falls on entrepreneurs who do not produce one of the politically preferred energy types, or whose ideas may be too risky to qualify for a government handout. Because subsidies channel public and private investment to selected technologies, the long-term success of innovation in America is stunted.

Don't get me wrong; none of this is to say that efficient, low-emission technology isn't the way of the future: As the energy sector progresses with demand, we can only expect to see greener and cheaper cars, power plants, and appliances everywhere. And if they're worth it, they'll sell themselves.

Who knows what great energy innovation awaits us around the corner but isn't on the government's radar screen? And yet the person working on the next breakthrough must compete against less promising technologies subsidized by big-government bureaucrats who pretend to know how to read tea leaves when it comes to the future of the energy sector.

Back to Basics

We need to get back to basics—and that means recognizing that America's greatest resource is the ingenuity and determination of entrepreneurs like George Mitchell. Unlike the bureaucrats and politicians in Washington—who risk nothing, build nothing, create nothing—it's pioneers like George who move America forward. When people like George figure out a safe and inexpensive way to take something that had been thought useless and put it to a thousand different uses, we all benefit. For George and others like him to move America forward, it took the same persistence despite failure, and the same courage to *use* failure, that characterized the pioneers who built America in the first place.

George Mitchell's success is also our success. We use energy every day—it's what lets you bake that cake for your son's birthday, what gets you to work every day so you can provide for your family, what turns on your camera to capture your daughter's wedding, and what keeps the lights on at your local grocery store. This isn't something to apologize for, as many of today's politicians would have Americans think. This is something to celebrate, enjoy, and be thankful for.

America's energy scene still looks like a land of great opportunity. And in many ways it is—we are only just beginning to discover what this rich land has and the ways we can find, repackage, and use it safely. It's sad that we have to overcome our own government to realize this great potential. In many cases, all this requires is for Washington to fade out of the picture, creating room for individual Americans in their little platoons to carry America's energy sector into the future.

Loving the Planet (and People Too!)

Freedom unleashes the forces most needed to make our environment cleaner, healthier, and safer.

I have always considered myself an environmentalist. I think conservatism and environmentalism are a natural fit, since one of the things we conservatives seek to *conserve* is this magnificent land of ours. But I'm not an environmental absolutist—I don't think concern for the land invariably trumps concern for the folks living on it. I favor the balanced approach Ronald Reagan laid out in 1973: "We do not have to choose between the environment and jobs. We can set a commonsense course between those who would cover the whole country with concrete in the name of progress, and those who think you should not build a house unless it looks like a bird's nest or a rabbit hole."[1]

Unfortunately, Ronald Reagan's commonsense approach has become the exception rather than the rule. Today, what we see time and time again is big government—in this case, the Environmental Protection Agency and the Departments of the Interior and of Agriculture—riding roughshod over the rights of Americans in the name of the environment.

David versus Goliath

Generally speaking, we don't hear about the victims of the EPA unless, like David in the Bible, they stand up to the bureaucratic Goliath and fight back. Two such "Davids" are Mike and Chantell Sackett, who stood up to a Goliath-sized EPA when they believed they were being wronged.

Mike and Chantell set out to build a house on a half-acre plot they had purchased in 2005 in Priest Lake, Idaho. After all the necessary county permits were completed and work had begun, the EPA found the Sacketts guilty of disturbing wetlands, in violation of the Clean Water Act. Even though their dry plot was separated from Priest Lake by a road and a neighbor's house, they were ordered to stop construction, remove the gravel they had already laid, and return the land to its original state or face daily fines of $75,000. Yes, I said *$75,000 per day*. Removing the gravel alone would cost more than the $23,000 the Sacketts had paid for their land.

Mike and Chantell were given no written explanation of how their dry property qualified as wetlands under federal jurisdiction. They couldn't even get a hearing. After seven months of asking, they were told that to get a hearing they needed to file for a wetlands permit, a process that would cost hundreds of thousands of dollars and take years to complete. (I know "years" sounds crazy, even for a federal agency, but as you'll see from some of the other stories in this chapter, it really can take that long.) With the help of the Pacific Legal Foundation, the Sacketts fought for their hearing all the way up to the Supreme Court, which found in March 2012 that they did indeed deserve a hearing to review the EPA's determination.

Looking back over the ordeal, Mike said, "As this nightmare went on, we rubbed our eyes and started to wonder if we were living in some totalitarian country. Now, the Supreme Court has come to our rescue, and reminded the EPA—and everyone—that this is still America, and Americans still have rights under the Constitution."[2]

So David won this round. But the Sacketts still have to challenge the EPA's wetlands determination in the federal district court in Idaho. And there are many more Davids out there who do not have the means to fight or someone to help them.

The EPA versus Small Business

It's not only individuals' rights that are being bulldozed by the EPA. Small businesses are also being attacked.

Oilfield CNC Machining in Broussard, Louisiana, is the definition of a small business. Thomas Clements and his wife, Melissa, own and work for CNC, a metal machining shop that supports the oil industry. Besides themselves, they had only four employees.

Following the BP oil spill in April 2010, seven experts from the National Academy of Engineering said that a blanket moratorium on drilling was not the solution. A special commission that President Obama convened to study the spill basically agreed. But the Obama administration ignored their recommendations, as well as the direction of federal courts. It unilaterally banned deep-water drilling, and it put permits for shallow-water drilling in an indefinite holding pattern while it assessed the risks of drilling and prepared to add more layers of regulation. Doing so did nothing to reduce risk—the problem wasn't that the regulations for offshore drilling were inadequate; it was that they hadn't been enforced. And it treated all drilling companies as if they were as responsible for the spill as BP. But that shouldn't surprise us: When something goes wrong, big government's reaction is to add more red tape rather than enforce the rules on the books and actually work to identify the problem.

Meanwhile, when drilling activity stopped, the Clementses had to lay off all four of their workers. As Thomas Clements told some folks from Heritage and the Institute for Energy Research, "I calculate the [economic] risk that, you know, I might mess up something, I might make mistakes and stuff like that. But you don't calculate the federal government, the president, and the administration coming into your business and shutting it down."[3]

Four laid-off workers may sound like small potatoes, but tell that to those who lost their jobs from a senseless regulatory roadblock. And the numbers add up quickly. As a result of the moratorium and an extremely slow permitting process for getting new oil and gas projects off the ground, the Obama administration was responsible for the loss of more than 90,000 jobs in 2011 alone.[4]

Adding insult to injury, on a trip to Brazil in 2011, President Obama declared that the United States wanted to help develop Brazil's offshore oil fields and import Brazilian oil. "That was the most devastating thing I heard him say," Clements recalled. "We felt like it declared war on America's energy workers."

Environmental regulations have been one of the biggest roadblocks to job creation. Some regulations are necessary for setting the bounds of good management of our natural resources. But Congress wrote the laws intended to protect our land, our air, our waters, and human health so broadly and vaguely that the federal agencies tasked with carrying them out have had carte blanche to impose expansive regulations that do less to protect the environment and our health and more to tie the hands of entrepreneurial Americans.

For example, there is the National Environmental Policy Act of 1969, which requires environmental assessment of every project in which the federal government is somehow involved. Unlike some recent monstrosities like Obamacare and the Senate version of so-called comprehensive immigration reform, it is a mere thirty-two hundred words long—but it has a 475-page compliance manual.[5] It kicks in whenever there is government financing, permitting, regulation, or technical assistance involved in a project that *might* significantly affect the environment. The average time it takes to get through the assessment process is more than four years (though there are cases like the Revett Minerals mine in Montana, which took seventeen years).[6] The act leaves a project facing rounds of public-comment periods, lawsuits, and bureaucratic redundancy and squabbling.

The process is so burdensome that the Obama administration actually cut the red tape for projects receiving federal grants under the stimulus bill. "It's about putting our citizens back to work," then energy secretary Steven Chu said when exempting stimulus projects from NEPA assessment.[7] If only the federal government were equally concerned about jobs that didn't receive federal tax dollars!

One person who didn't get the red tape cut for him was Steve Lathrop, an independent homebuilder in Granite City, Illinois. In 1990, Steve bought an abandoned dump at the end of his road. His neighborhood had been suffering severe flood damage for decades, and his plan was to clean up the dump and turn it into a lake to collect the runoff from rainstorms. Steve secured the financing and formed partnerships to build a lakeside housing community. "I was sure I had stumbled across my American dream," he said.[8] But his dream got in the way of bureaucratic self-interest.

Under the Clean Water Act of 1972, the EPA, along with the Army Corps of Engineers, has been able to regulate almost every body of water in America. Their reach extends to "streams (including intermittent streams), mudflats, sandflats, wetlands, sloughs, prairie potholes, wet meadows, playa lakes, or natural ponds."[9] According to the Corps, "wetlands" also included Steve's dump, because some cattails, a form of wetland vegetation, had been seen growing between the concrete slabs and other refuse.

The Corps had been tasked—in 1965, twenty-five years before Steve bought the dump—with solving Granite City's flooding problem. Eight studies and millions of tax dollars later, it had come up with plans costing yet more millions. Steve's initiative to solve the problem, create construction jobs, and build a housing community got in the way of those government plans.

The Corps ordered Steve to stop the project immediately, on penalty of $25,000-a-day fines. It also ordered him to restore the dump to its previous state or face almost two years in jail. Yes, that's right: While Steve wanted to hire people to build houses, the Corps wanted to put him to work restoring an unsanitary dump.

"The red tape and regulatory intransigence have shut down my effort to build affordable homes," says Steve. "It has me, my wife Ruth, and our two daughters teetering on the brink of financial ruin. And with government officials seemingly blocking my every avenue, I wonder in this post-9/11 world what it means to be an American."[10]

Two decades and over $300,000 in permit fees and other expenses later, Steve is facing bankruptcy.[11] As I write, the government has not taken any substantive action on his case.

Mountains of regulations mean years and dollars spent complying with government requirements rather than growing a company, creating jobs, and producing goods and services people want. Larger businesses can often weather this regulatory storm with full-time staffs of lawyers and compliance managers. But many small businesses cannot.

Environmental Protection or a Big-Government Agenda?

Protecting human health and keeping our environment clean and safe has become a handy tool for government overreach into our lives. How is it that the EPA stopped working for the safety of Americans and started hounding them like criminals?

I think the problem goes back to the basic environmental laws passed by Congress starting in the late 1960s. Not satisfied with what states and individuals were already doing as stewards, Congress passed laws that imposed centralized solutions from Washington. NEPA, the Clean Air Act (1970), the Clean Water Act (1972), and the Endangered Species Act (1973) were the first pillars of federal environmental policy, but many more laws have followed since.

Because the laws were so broad and vague in their wording, federal agencies and courts have been able to greatly expand the definitions of what the federal government can regulate. The result has been more federal power at the expense of freedom. To be sure, the conservation of our environment, the wise management of our natural resources, and the protection of human health are all important goals. But there are much better ways to achieve them than by one-size-fits-all regulations.

Empowered by these laws, bureaucrats at the EPA and other agencies treat local people and local expertise with disdain, not respect. They operate under the assumption that renewable natural resources are so fragile and finite that environmental protection and economic activity can't be pursued at the same time.

The current state of things cannot become the new normal if we are to protect our freedoms as well as our environment, both of which are part of the very fabric of our nation's heritage. Recalling Mike Sackett's words, we might ask: How do we turn this country back into the America we love?

The American Conservation Ethic

Based on the work of my colleagues at The Heritage Foundation, I'd like to put forward eight commonsense principles that can get environmental regulation back on track. We call it the American Conservation Ethic. Rather than the top-down, one-size-fits-all bureaucratic approach, these principles are grounded in experience of what actually works. It's exciting to see that when these principles are applied—as they often are by individuals, communities, and states—real environmental benefits result.

1. The first and most important principle is that *people* are our most valuable resource. All environmental policy should start from this assumption, both in the letter of the law and in its implementation. Why affirm such an obvious principle? Because so often human well-being—health, safety, the ability to live productive

and full lives—is ignored for the sake of a threatened subspecies of deer or a filthy dump designated as "wetland."

The people of King Cove, Alaska, are an unfortunate example of why we must uphold this important principle. King Cove is located in the Aleutian Islands and is accessible only by plane or boat. The only practical way residents can get to a hospital in a medical emergency is to fly from Cold Bay Airport, but Cold Bay is twenty miles away. Thus it would be logical to build a road between King Cove and Cold Bay. But as I write, the Department of the Interior has prohibited this because the two hundred acres of federal land needed to complete eleven of those twenty miles of road are part of a federal wildlife refuge—as if wildlife cannot coexist with a road!

I believe that one of the things that make human beings special is that we have the ability to protect wildlife *and* pursue our other interests at the same time. But some just don't see it that way. Too much of our environmental regulation assumes that the environment can be protected only at the expense of every other human activity and aspiration. I could not disagree more with John Muir, founder of the Sierra Club, who said, "Man is always and everywhere a blight on the landscape."[12] In my view, an environmental policy is good for the environment only if it is also good for people.

As Ronald Reagan put it, "People are ecology too, and most of us are looking for answers that will preserve nature to the greatest extent possible consistent with the need to have places where we can work and live."[13]

2. The second principle of the American Conservation Ethic is that renewable natural resources are resilient and dynamic, and respond positively to wise management. President Teddy

Roosevelt, responsible for setting aside many of today's national forests, explained his purpose: "to protect ourselves and our children against the wasteful development of our natural resources, whether that waste is caused by the actual destruction of such resources *or by making them impossible of development hereafter*" (my emphasis).[14]

President Roosevelt appreciated a fact that the Bigs (whether big government or big green environmental extremists who make every issue *their* issue in big lawsuits) fail to make: that locking up our natural resources is just as damaging as squandering them.

3. Private property and free markets provide the best chance for environmental improvements. Property rights and proximity to a problem (or an opportunity) encourage wise stewardship. Too often, federal rules do not do so because they are one-size-fits-all, top-down stipulations of how environmental protection must be done. Nature, technology, and human ingenuity are more dynamic and diverse than this approach recognizes.

Regrettably, government often impedes nongovernment solutions to environmental and resource problems. Private ownership, on the other hand, gives people incentives to be good stewards of land and natural resources, just as it does with a home or a car.

For example, one of the biggest successes in restoring an endangered species has been through the efforts of Texas ranchers. The African scimitar-horned oryx, a species of antelope, is extinct in its natural habitat. But by charging for limited and guided hunts of the antelope, these ranchers have been able not only to maintain populations but to help them grow. Some six thousand to ten thousand oryxes now thrive in Texas.

The ranchers were able to accomplish this because the U.S. Fish and Wildlife Service allowed an exemption from the Endangered Species Act for them and others engaged in similar programs. But in 2012 big green—in the form of Friends of Animals and the University of Denver's College of Law—successfully sued the FWS, denouncing the ranchers' version of conservation as vile profiteering. As a result, the FWS now requires any rancher or conservation group seeking an exemption from the Endangered Species Act to acquire a federal permit and go through a public-comment period. This means more time and money spent complying with government rules, leaving less available for saving endangered animals.

Environmental laws should allow the people closest to a resource or a source of pollution—the ones who stand to gain or lose the most from it—to exercise the responsibilities *and* privileges due to private property rights.

4. Efforts to reduce, control, and remediate pollution should achieve *real* effects. For example, the Clean Air Act has been successful in reducing the major air pollutants—although they were already in decline before the act was even enacted, because of technological advances. The federal government, however, has since become so stringent as to attempt to regulate pollution to an unnoticeable vanishing point—at enormous cost. Today, any connection between the EPA's expensive air regulations and improved health is becoming ever more difficult to see or prove.[15]

5. In contrast to the government's penchant for spending more and accomplishing less, the fifth principle of the American Conservation Ethic acknowledges the power of the free market to do the very opposite: to get more from less. Economist Warren Brookes put it this way: "The learning curve is green."[16] Over time we learn how to come up with innovative ways to manage wasteful by-products. And we learn to do things more efficiently. Efficiency is not only in the interests of business, it's also green.

Whole libraries can now be accessed on electronic devices the size of a single book, and nationwide phone books can be accessed at the click of a button. But one of the best examples of increased efficiency can be found in America's agriculture sector. America's farmers feed and clothe a population that has more than doubled since 1949, and our agricultural exports have increased more than twentyfold in that period. At the same time, total acreage under cultivation has decreased from 387 million acres to 330 million acres, a difference roughly the size of Idaho.

The saying in Jonathan Swift's *Gulliver's Travels* holds true today: "whoever could make two Ears of Corn, or two Blades of Grass to grow upon a Spot of Ground where only one grew before, would deserve better of Mankind, and do more essential Service to his Country than the whole Race of Politicians put together."

6. Management of natural resources should be conducted on a site- and situation-specific basis. Though there may be times when the federal government should have a role in setting an environmental standard, generally, environmental solutions should rely on the decisions of communities and states and reflect their needs, values, and priorities. This kind of weighing of all the factors simply cannot be done by a distant government that does not have on-the-ground knowledge of the problem and the possible solutions.

In the previous chapter, I wrote a lot about the promise of shale oil and natural gas thanks to developments in fracking and other drilling techniques. But success hasn't been without controversy. For a time, the small town of Dimock, Pennsylvania, was the epicenter of that controversy.

Several families complained that a nearby fracking operation had ruined their water. The drilling company immediately supplied the families with bottled water and started to conduct testing.

Meanwhile, however, the complaints had attracted the attention of antifracking activists, documentary filmmakers, and state and federal politicians. The Pennsylvania state government reacted by putting a moratorium on natural gas production in Dimock.

Inaccurate journalism painted Dimock as a wasteland instead of the quiet farming community that coexisted with the drilling company. Yes, there were growing pains. Having a lot of trucks roll through your neighborhood isn't pleasant. But on the whole, most people in Dimock said they were glad for the improvements natural gas had brought to their community—fuller restaurants, jobs for young people, royalties from leasing land and mineral rights—and were tired of the negativity from outsiders. But when the state government voted to spend $11.8 million on a twelve-mile pipeline to deliver water to residents, that was too much.

Appalled by the expensive and unneeded pipeline project no one had consulted them about, the residents of Dimock banded together to form a group called "Enough Already." In a petition signed even by some who feared their water was contaminated, Dimockers demanded that the pipeline project be stopped. And a good thing: Private and government studies have since repeatedly shown that the fears of contaminated water were mistaken. Pride in their community inspired the people of Dimock to stop the over-reaction and save Pennsylvania taxpayers nearly $12 million.[17]

7. Science should be employed as *one* tool to guide public policy. But other factors—like human well-being, ethics, and good judgment—must also be taken into account when Congress is writing new laws and the regulatory agencies are enforcing them. But when it comes to something like energy efficiency, this isn't the way the federal government operates. Laws passed by both parties in Congress and the Department of Energy regulations stemming

from them ignore the fact that people don't all use energy the same way. They have to make choices based on their budgets, regardless of the fact that science and technology can always come up with a more efficient car or home appliance to meet ever-tightening efficiency regulations. When the government mandates efficiency, it's taking decisions away from families and business owners and making us *worse* off, not better.

The fact is that Americans *do* care about saving energy—just ask 3M,[18] Chicago's Shedd Aquarium,[19] or any other company. Businesses naturally want to cut operating costs in order to make their products more competitively priced, and families want to get the most out of their energy dollars. But Americans have the right to set their own priorities in deciding how much to spend now and how much to save for future goals, like a child's education, a new home, or hiring a new employee. This is a freedom Congress must respect. It is a freedom the Founders called "the pursuit of happiness," and it mustn't be overridden through the dogmatic invocation of "science."

8. The eighth and last principle in some ways underlies all the rest: Successful environmental policies flow from liberty. The most polluted places on earth are also the most politically oppressive. The abuses of the Soviet Union created the human and environmental disaster of Chernobyl, not to mention the Aral Sea, once one of the world's largest lakes and now reduced to one-tenth its historic size in order to feed a massive irrigation project. The oppressive government of Zimbabwe has turned Africa's breadbasket into a wasteland. Primitive and irresponsible management of waste from the mining of rare earth metals has cost the lives and health of too many in Mongolia.

More than two centuries ago, Americans chose a system of governance that empowers individuals and their little platoons rather than entrusting all decisions to a select few. Free people, not centralized policies and mandates, come up with superior solutions to environmental problems.

I can't put it better than my Heritage colleagues did when they formulated the American Conservation Ethic: "Freedom unleashes the forces most needed to make our environment cleaner, healthier, and safer. It fosters scientific inquiry, technological innovation, entrepreneurship, rapid information exchange, accuracy, and flexibility."[20] We must protect the right of states and individuals to exercise the responsibilities *and* privileges of environmental stewardship.

Moving Forward

The word "unique" comes from the Latin *unus*, meaning "one." It should look familiar: *e pluribus unum*—"out of many, one"—is stamped on every quarter. This is how Americans solve environmental problems—not with top-down regulations or one-size-fits-all rules, but as individuals working in freedom to find solutions.

Conservatives are committed to the defense of our environment because it makes our nation, in William F. Buckley Jr.'s words, "safer, lovelier, and more precious." We oppose big-government environmentalism because it makes America less safe, less beautiful, and less lovable.

Free people and free markets are the engines of prudent environmental stewardship. We must reorient our environmental policies so that our laws uphold private property rights and free markets, and empower the little platoons that define America as much as its beautiful lands and sparkling waters. I know we Americans are up to the task.

14

And the Greatest of These...

Loving America is the result of God's love for us and our love for one another.

None of us is completely lovable, which means true love says more about the lover than the loved. If those who know you the best genuinely love you, it means you have been blessed to live among people who are able to forgive, forget, and love unconditionally.

What does this have to do with falling in love with America?

Love begins with individuals—you and me. The Bible says that we are able to love others because God first loved us. That was the purpose of Jesus's life on earth: to forgive us and convince us that God loves us as individuals, as we are. Once we realize God has forgiven us, we can forgive those who have wronged us. We can love those who are not always lovable, including ourselves.

But what does this have to do with America? Well, it is hard to love a country full of often unlovable people if we haven't first grasped the love and forgiveness of God. I'm not suggesting

Americans are less lovable than other people. I'm just suggesting that if we know God loves us despite our faults and flaws, we are much more likely to love others despite their shortcomings.

This is what makes the little platoons in our lives work—our families, our friends, and all those who live and work around us. Forgiveness and love are also what make our nation work—the millions of diverse people who feel loved by God and by those closest to them. This is the inspiration for us to love our country regardless of all the things that can divide us. Loving America is the result of God's love for us and our love for one another.

Boundaries, Ownership, and Affection

Loving America is also the result of a basic respect for the rights and dignity of the individual. People do not feel or express love as groups. Love can be given or received only by individuals. While love cannot be legislated, public policies that protect the property and the rights of individuals can create an environment for peaceful cooperation and mutual respect.

One of the first words children learn is "mine." Human nature leads us to acquire and possess things, and to make our own decisions about what's ours. This drives us to work and compete, which can have both positive and negative impacts on our relationships. I remember our children drawing imaginary lines on the floor in their playroom to claim an area of the room as their own. They would then warn their siblings not to cross the line. Those invisible lines caused a lot of conflict.

Many philosophers and politicians over the years have agreed with Karl Marx's proposition that if there were no individual boundaries or personal ownership, everyone would live in peace.

Centrally controlled communal living, they insist, will create equality and promote harmony among the people. But history tells us that just the opposite is true. Where boundaries are non-existent, poorly defined, or unprotected, people—and countries—will either take what doesn't belong to them or lose the incentive to work. Real boundaries that are respected by all parties reduce conflict and create peace and incentives to work.

Growing up in a large family with a single mom, I had very little that was actually mine. I shared a room with my older brother, and many of my clothes were his hand-me-downs. If I wanted my favorite seat at the dinner table, I had to get there before my competitors. And if I wanted a prime spot in front of the television, I sometimes had to fight for it. None of us four children had much that was really ours, so everything was up for grabs. And grab we did. It was every man for himself.

Things began to change when I was twelve years old. I had saved enough money from my paper route to buy a new set of Slingerland drums, and you'd better believe those drums were *mine*. I bought them with my own money—money I had worked for. They were my prized possession. No one touched those drums without my permission, and the area of the basement where they were enshrined was off-limits to everyone.

My brothers and sister respected my boundaries, and there was peace throughout the land. I controlled a little piece of my world, and that made it easier to accept those things I couldn't control. I loved my drums and my family.

I earned some extra money in middle and high school playing my drums in a rock-and-roll band. That fun work, along with the routine of bagging groceries and delivering restaurant equipment, earned me enough money to buy my own car when I was in the eleventh grade—a brand-new 1968 Super Sport Camaro with a 350-cubic-inch high-performance engine, a four-speed Muncie transmission, and an eight-track tape player. It's hard to overstate how cool I was (at least in my own mind).

I practically washed the paint off that car because it was mine. I owned it, and it gave me the freedom to go wherever I wanted to go. The road outside belonged to everyone, but inside the boundaries of those doors and windows was my space. It was the only place in the world where I was in charge. I loved my Camaro.

Boundaries became really important to me when my wife, Debbie, and I bought our first house. It was a new contemporary home, nineteen hundred square feet, with two rock fireplaces, big plate-glass windows, and natural wooden shake siding. Sitting on a third-of-an-acre lot in a suburban middle-class neighborhood, this was our dream house. It cost $49,900, and we prayed we could handle the payments.

There were actually three levels of boundaries relevant to our new home. The neighborhood had a boundary. Those who lived inside the neighborhood and paid our homeowners' association dues had the privilege of using the community pool and tennis court, and we all shared the responsibilities of taking care of the plants in the common areas and serving on various committees. Privileges and responsibilities came with living in the neighborhood.

Then there were the boundaries around our yard. Debbie and I had a lot of freedom within those boundaries; we could make all the decisions about plants and landscaping on our property, and we could do anything we wanted (within the laws of decency and noise ordinances) in our own yard.

But to live in the neighborhood we had to agree to a few rules:

no boats or campers in the driveway or yard, and no exterior reno-
vations or external structures without the approval of the archi-
tectural committee. We were willing to submit (sign a contract)
to these restrictions on our freedom in return for the privilege of
living in the neighborhood.

The final frontier—the area that was completely controlled
by Debbie and me—was within the boundaries of our home. The
doors and walls protected the space that was exclusively ours. We
could do what we wanted, decorate the way we wanted, eat what
we wanted—this was our area of unrestricted freedom.

It was illegal for anyone to enter our space uninvited, and the
primary purpose of our local government was to protect our private property.

The government and the public recognized the boundaries of
our home and lot, which meant that anyone who violated our space
would be arrested by the police and punished by the justice system. I didn't have to fight for what was mine because my neighbors
respected my boundaries and the government was committed to
defending my rights. And of course, we respected our neighbors'
private property too. That made me feel good about my neighbors,
us, and my government.

Boundaries do not necessarily divide people; they can help
define and protect what is inside them. This allows people to have
relationships without losing control of their space. Good fences
make good neighbors, because tangible boundaries help avoid
arguments, prevent unwanted intrusions from children and pets,
and allow people to do their own thing without infringing on the
rights of others.

Harold was my neighbor who lived directly behind our house.
Every July 3 he dug a pit in his backyard, filled it with wood and

charcoal, and stayed up all night roasting a whole pig for his Fourth of July party. The big, smoking pit was always very close to my back fence. It was not something I would have done in my yard, but I was happy for him to do it on his own property. And the fence prevented any argument about whether he was in my yard or his.

Harold and I had only spoken casually over the fence during the first few years we were neighbors. But one July 3, I had stayed up all night with Debbie at the hospital as she delivered our second child, Ginger. When I arrived home tired and groggy about 6 a.m. on the Fourth, I saw Harold sitting in his lawn chair beside the smoking fire pit. I walked to the back fence to tell him the good news about Ginger's birth, and he invited me to join him for a cold beer (at 6 a.m.!). I opened the gate, and we sat in his lawn chairs, talked for an hour, picked at some pig, and enjoyed a couple of beers. I loved that neighborhood.

Contracts: Boundaries That Define Relationships

Boundaries can be property lines, or they can be contractual agreements that establish ownership and roles between parties. Marriage is, among other things, a contract that establishes a boundary around a husband and wife, with commitments to support and care for each other for the rest of their lives. My neighborhood has a contractual agreement between all homeowners and the neighborhood association. It tells us what the association will do for us and what we're expected to do for the neighborhood.

Businesses use hordes of lawyers to write contracts and agreements to define the terms of all kinds of relationships. Churches, clubs, and associations have contracts or membership agreements that define the role of the organization and the role of its members.

Contracts define the terms of agreements between parties to help avoid conflicts and to provide remedies for disagreements if they should occur.

When two parties voluntarily and willingly enter into a contractual agreement, the terms are legally binding. One of the most important roles of government is to enforce contractual agreements and provide a system for settling contract disputes peacefully. America's prosperity is often (and rightly) attributed to our insistence on protecting property rights and our enforcement of contract law. Well-established boundaries have proved to be the key to our free enterprise system, our wealth of opportunities, and our incredible economic growth.

Laws and the Constitution: America's Boundaries of Freedom

The goal of America's Founders was to have only enough federal laws to protect the rights and property of citizens, promote commerce, ensure justice, maintain civil order, and defend America. With only limited government intrusion into civil society, the people through voluntary relationships and associations—such as marriage, church, neighborhoods, associations, and job—could decide for themselves how to order their lives.

Politics is the process people use to decide how they will live together. If you think about it, you realize that most politics does not involve government. Debbie and I had to decide for ourselves how to raise our children and how to manage our home. Members of our church wrote bylaws to formalize what was expected from everyone. Businesses have employee manuals so all workers can follow the same set of rules and work together harmoniously.

Politics works best when it is a voluntary process that is managed by the people who will actually be living by the decisions.

When elected officials or government bureaucrats make decisions, membership is not optional and compliance is not voluntary. Once the government makes a law, it is authorized to use force if necessary to make sure the law is followed. Laws force everyone to follow the same rules, even if some of the rules make no sense in a country with hundreds of millions of people in a wide variety of circumstances. Every business can have a different employee manual, and every church can have its own set of beliefs, but excessive government laws and regulations create discord and dysfunction by keeping people from making their own decisions about how they want to live together.

The one-size-fits-all aspect of laws is why lawmaking should be very limited at the federal level. Federal laws apply to the whole country. Not only do they supplant individual decision making and choices, but they also supersede the decisions of state and local lawmakers, who better understand the problems and opportunities within their communities. No matter how many special rules and exceptions federal law has, it can't possibly be tailored to the unique needs and circumstances of every community in the country, so the federal government should be wary of one-size-fits-all and Washington-knows-best solutions.

Our Founding Fathers understood the inherent problem with centralized decision making, and that is why the original thirteen states signed a contract with each other to put boundaries around the federal government when they created it in 1787. This contract is called the Constitution of the United States of America. It gives the federal government the authority to form an army and a navy to defend the states, to print a common currency, to encourage interstate commerce, to establish postal routes, to ensure justice—and very little else. All other authority was left to the states and the people.

One of the most disheartening aspects of being in Congress was watching presidents, congressmen, senators, and judges take an oath to defend the Constitution, and then ignore what it says. And unfortunately, few Americans today seem to understand what it says or why it's important. Few seem willing to accept the boundaries and limits placed on the federal government by the Constitution. The boundary lines between the federal and state governments and between government and the people have become blurred and uncertain.

Federal politicians and bureaucrats are now pushing policies that supersede individual decision making in almost every area of our lives. This has caused discord among the American people. In the absence of clear and well-defined boundaries, the American people have become politically polarized and have come to believe that political participation means electing federal officials who will force their views on others rather than insisting that the federal government allow people to make their own decisions.

Over the last century, and especially over the last fifty years, the federal government has grown well beyond its original boundaries. States have been persuaded by money from Washington, D.C., to accept more federal programs, but every federal program has come with more rules, regulations, and red tape and with more spending at the state level. Too many state governments are now bloated and broke. Even large businesses and organizations have shifted their focus from competing and serving to lobbying for federal money and special privileges. This has led to fewer choices, higher taxes, diminished opportunities, and less freedom for the states and the people.

Today the federal government makes many of the decisions about our education, health care, transportation, energy, banking and finance, the environment, workplace rules, law enforcement, charity, and morality. This means that American citizens have fewer and fewer choices because the decisions that affect our lives are being made by people we don't know in Washington, D.C.

Freedom is determined by who makes the decisions. When people are free to choose for themselves within the boundaries of law and order, they tend to work harder and lead happier lives. And they tend to be more accepting and loving of others who choose differently. Freedom is diminished when others make decisions that control us and those we love.

The federal government has become an overbearing behemoth—wasteful and increasingly indifferent to the wishes of the people. Politics has become a mean and negative competition to determine who will make the decisions about how we will live.

Politics is increasingly polarized because, instead of protecting freedom and individual rights, the federal government is now a winner-take-all trophy for politicians and interest groups who want to control our lives. When liberals win the White House and Congress, they consider it a mandate to control health care, education, transportation, and energy decisions from Washington and to unionize government programs to reward union bosses for helping them win. If conservatives win... well, I'm hoping we would see a return to real federalism—although as we saw in chapter 3, it is a herculean task to dismantle any part of this behemoth.

When individuals or governments violate our boundaries, invade our space, take what is ours, and limit our choices, we resent it. If it happens repeatedly, our resentment grows. If the government approves my neighbor moving the boundaries and taking part of my land, I will resent both my neighbor and the government. Any government that redistributes property instead of protecting it will create resentment and division among the people.

After I was on ABC's *This Week* with George Stephanopoulos, ABC had a car take me to the airport. A few minutes after I got into the car, the driver turned around and said, "When are you conservatives going to get your act together and learn how to communicate with people?" I was surprised he even knew who I was, but he proceeded to give me a few examples of how we needed to communicate. The big immigration debate of 2013 was at a fever pitch, so he began with that issue.

He said, "Here's what you need to tell the naturalized American citizens who came here lawfully." I suspected he was speaking about himself. "Imagine you came home from work and found another family living in your home, wearing your clothes, and eating out of your refrigerator. You call the police, but they tell you since these people are already there, you have to let them stay. And you have to let them keep eating your food and wearing your clothes! That little story would help Americans understand how amnesty really works."

The driver was using the very personal boundaries of our homes to underscore the importance of our national boundaries. America's failure to defend and control our borders has created division, resentment, and disrespect for the rule of law. After decades of ignoring our national boundaries, the government is now violating personal boundaries by taking a larger part of everyone's income to pay for millions of uninvited guests.

The political motivations for amnesty are the same as the motivations for welfare and many other government programs—charity and votes. Many public officials and citizens now view the government as an instrument of compassion. This justifies, at least in their minds, taking individuals' property and ignoring the boundaries that were established to restrict government action.

If expanded federal action were actually helping people, strengthening our country, and building a brighter future for all Americans, then perhaps such disregard of constitutional limits might be understandable (though not excusable). But federal welfare programs have spent trillions of dollars to reduce poverty, and instead have created more poverty. Federal education programs have spent hundreds of billions while diminishing the quality of public schools.

The federal government has taken billions from state gas taxes and actually reduced the quality of America's highway infrastructure. The federal government took control of the nation's home mortgage business and created the disastrous housing bubble that burst in 2007. The federal government created Social Security and Medicare to give retirement security to seniors, but diverted this money to other uses, leaving these programs unfunded and unsustainable. There are numerous other examples, but you get my point.

A Plan to Unite America

The solutions to America's fiscal, economic, and cultural problems are the same solutions that will cause Americans to rediscover their affection for each other and for their country. These are liberty-minded solutions that will come from the ground up—beginning with all of us as individuals. We all need to ask less from the federal government, work harder, and expect more from ourselves.

As President John Kennedy, a liberal Democrat, said, "Ask

not what your country can do for you—ask what you can do for your country." Senator Barry Goldwater, a conservative Republican, challenged voters to elect public officials "who understand that their first duty...is to divest themselves of the power they have been given." We must all ask ourselves how we can serve others and work in our little platoons to make our families stronger, our communities more compassionate, our states more business-friendly, and our country more free.

None of this can be accomplished from the top down. Central planning is a utopian notion that has failed wherever it has been tried and is failing us again today. Small usually works better than big, so let's work to keep things small whenever we can. Big government breeds big business, big organizations, and big problems. Big can be beneficial, but only if Big has boundaries, is not propped up by government, and is supported by many little platoons that make their own decisions.

America was built on big ideas, big dreams, big principles, and big hearts, but our strength has always come from individuals in their little platoons, building from the ground up.

America's fifty states are essential political building blocks for uniting and rebuilding our country. They must reclaim their constitutional authority to govern themselves on most issues, and work together to push the federal government back inside its boundaries. This will not only reduce federal spending and improve public services, but it will also help unite America by allowing states, localities, and individuals to make more of their own decisions. This is what *federalism* means.

Where there is no clear constitutional mandate or general welfare requirement that cannot be efficiently implemented by the states, separately or collectively, the federal government should not act.

In other words, Congress needs to mind its own business, and let the states mind theirs.

Americans must insist that Washington return dollars and decisions to the states and to the people. States should have more flexibility to revamp their public school systems, and parents should have more choices about the education of their children. Doctors and patients should have more freedom to make their own decisions about health care and health plans. States should also have more choices about transportation infrastructure, energy development, and law enforcement issues.

States should take the lead in protecting unborn children. States should not wait for Washington to implement commonsense protections for unborn children. Even when confronted with the gruesome truth of late-term abortions in cases such as the infamous trial of Dr. Kermit Gosnell, who was ultimately convicted of murder, there are only a few on the political Left in Washington who will even admit that anyone has the authority to say whether an unborn child is a human being...at any stage of development. States such as Arkansas and North Dakota are leading the way with basic protections for human life that the majority of their citizens support.

States should also take the lead in recognizing marriage correctly, as the union of one man and one woman. And the courts should respect the authority of states to make this decision. I personally find it abhorrent that government at any level would presume to have the authority to redefine the millennia-old institution of marriage. No one in Washington, judge or politician, has the constitutional or moral authority to redefine marriage for the entire nation. The people and their elected representatives in the states—hopefully with guidance from their religious leaders—have constitutional authority to make marriage policy.

Unfortunately, through a narrow 5–4 decision in 2013 the Supreme Court allowed California's Proposition 8, which defined marriage as between a man and a woman, to be struck down on technical grounds. By the same margin the court invalidated a similar provision in the Defense of Marriage Act, a federal law. However, the court has not fabricated a new constitutional right to same-sex marriage. Some thirty-six states continue to support the truth about marriage—that it is the union of one man and one woman to provide children with a mom and a dad. States should continue doing so.

States don't have to wait for federal welfare reform to make sure welfare recipients are pointed toward work or getting the skills they need to find work. They're also in a better position than the federal government to know how to direct those dependent on public assistance to the transformative relational resources of voluntary organizations, as we saw through the inspiring stories of Bob Woodson's network of stellar individuals and organizations in chapter 1. We need to rescue the millions of Americans who have been trapped in dependency, robbed of their dignity, and deprived of hope.

Liberals will still argue that allowing over half of Americans to "share the wealth" of others will foster a more united country, but the opposite is true. As personal responsibility is replaced with collectivist entitlement programs, community spirit is replaced with an attitude of entitlement—a sense that the country owes you more than you have earned. Author Mark Steyn captures this attitude of entitlement in his inimitable style:

> Nothing makes a citizen more selfish than socially equitable communitarianism: Once a fellow's enjoying the fruits

of government, health care and all the rest, he couldn't give a hoot about the broader societal interest; he's got his, and if it's going to bankrupt the state a generation hence, well, as long as they can keep the checks coming till he's dead, it's fine by him. "Social democracy" is, it turns out, explicitly anti-social.[1]

Rebuilding America doesn't require the removal of social safety nets, but it will require a redesign of programs now forcing people into dependency and trapping them there. Instead of continuing to have federal programs that discourage personal responsibility and hard work, we should transfer authority for most social programs to communities and states. Federal programs like Social Security and Medicare, which have been paid for out of workers' paychecks, should be protected for today's seniors. But new options should be created that allow younger workers to be independent of government control when they retire.

Those who call themselves liberals and progressives often talk about how the federal government needs to help different groups: the poor, minorities, women, children, veterans, the disabled, students, immigrants, seniors. But by dividing America into groups, they build resentment and mistrust by suggesting that some groups are getting more than their fair share. They promise to take from the groups that have more to help those that have less. For generations, their promises have proved to be empty. Their top-down policies have only grown the Bigs and hurt the little platoons that can really help those in need.

Instead of promoting the positive aspects of diversity, the Left uses our differences to divide us. This creates tension between groups instead of emphasizing and building the commonality that holds us together. As the prominent British Conservative leader Liam Fox told me, "Diversity without commonality leads to fragmentation." Collectivism and central planning force businesses to lobby for favors rather than freedom, lead to suspicion among the people that the decision makers favor one group over another, and turn politics into a game of winner-take-all. However, a country blessed with strong little platoons and enduring institutions will be united by the commonality they find close to home.

Now, of course, pushing decision making out of Washington and restoring the authority of states to address important issues will not solve all our problems or eliminate political controversy. But if one state adopts an unpopular or ineffective policy, the people living in the other forty-nine are not forced to accept it. They can seek a better way. When fifty states are competing to create the best quality of life and business environment, all Americans will benefit—and we'll all feel better about being Americans.

15

Falling in Love Again

In America, "We the people" are supposed to tell the government what to do, instead of the government telling us.

—Ronald Reagan

The ideas and principles set forth in this book are often referred to as "conservative" ideas. They are more than that: They are *American* ideas—limited constitutional government, free enterprise, individual freedom, and traditional values—that have guided America from the founding of the Republic.

I call myself a conservative because I love people and I love my country. For me, conservatism has always offered a balance of liberty and order, of faith and reason. In his bestselling manifesto, *The Conscience of a Conservative*, Senator Barry Goldwater wrote that conservatism "puts material things in their proper place—[it] has a structured view of the human being and of human society, in which economics plays only a subsidiary role."[1]

While acknowledging that man is an economic creature, Goldwater insists that he is also "a spiritual creature with spiritual needs and spiritual desires." And furthermore, these spiritual needs and desires "reflect the superior side of man's nature and thus take precedence over his economic wants." Liberals, in contrast, regard the satisfaction of economic wants as the dominant mission of society.

That Marxist view of man and government I totally reject, and I believe you do too.

I also reject the view that the founding ideals of our country are out of date, and that instead of remaining what Abraham Lincoln called "the last, best hope of earth" we Americans must resign ourselves to becoming subjects of yet another European-style social democracy. I regard this approach as a betrayal of everything our country stands for—and again, I believe you do too.

So what is to be done in this present crisis? I believe there are three major categories of issues on which a large majority of Americans are in agreement, issues that should unite rather than divide.

1. Competitive Federalism: More Choices, More Freedom

As we have discussed throughout this book, moving dollars and authority from Washington to the states and to the people should be a top priority for all freedom-loving Americans. This can be done through a thoughtful, transitional approach that does not disrupt public services. The process can begin by giving states more flexibility in areas such as education, health care, transportation, and energy. Instead of having Washington control programs and the purse strings, we should allow the states to develop their own approaches, with the federal government getting itself out of programs that belong at the state level.

2. Fiscal Responsibility: Responsible Government, Free People

The degree to which Congress and a succession of presidents have mismanaged America's finances cannot be overstated. Washington politicians for decades have mortgaged our future to buy votes and accolades from special-interest groups. We now have a national debt that is larger than our annual production of goods and services and, even worse, has robbed money from programs such as Social Security and Medicare, leaving future generations with trillions of dollars of unfunded liabilities.

A platform to unite America would insist that Washington must balance the federal budget, create a simple, pro-growth tax code, reform Social Security and Medicare to save them for the future, reform welfare programs to rescue Americans from dependency, reduce federal taxes, and move programs to the states. Congress should also assert its constitutional power to manage our currency and establish a rules-based monetary system to rein in the out-of-control Federal Reserve.

3. Strong Defense and a Focused Foreign Policy: Strong America, Free America

Everything we love about America depends for its continuance on a strong defense and secure borders. Every nation and person in the world must know that if they violate our boundaries or harm our citizens, they will pay a heavy price. When our enemies question our ability to protect ourselves or our commitment to respond to any attack, they will attack.

America's military and defense systems are in desperate need of modernization. Budget cuts and politicization over the past decade have weakened our capabilities and enticed our enemies. America must have a strong and technologically advanced defense.

As the cab driver I quoted in chapter 14 said so memorably, America cannot be secure and prosperous if we do not control our borders. Our immigration policy should not be designed to reward those who are here illegally; it should be designed to improve the lives and increase the incomes of citizens and of immigrants who are here legally.

Our borders are currently porous invitations to drug smugglers, sex traffickers, terrorists, and illegal workers. Thousands of people have died near our southern border because of Washington's lack of resolve to protect the boundaries that define our sovereignty.[2] America's foreign policy is now a hodgepodge of confusing policies and mixed signals. We have spent billions on foreign aid attempting to buy friends in nations that hate America and our way of life. We are entangled with the utopian and corrupt ventures of the United Nations. This nonsense has got to stop. America's foreign policy must be refocused on strategies that protect and benefit our citizens and our allies. When America is strong, moral, and prosperous, we will shape the rest of the world by our example—not by meddling.

Loving America

Since joining The Heritage Foundation in January 2013, I have traveled all across the country and met with thousands of people who are anxious to join us in building a stronger and more prosperous America. I have met with many governors and state legislators who are ready to throw off the yoke of the federal government—even turn down federal money—to develop more effective and less costly public policies.

It has been exhilarating to see states compete with each other. Texas has created a great business climate (jobs, jobs, jobs!), it has no income tax, and it has reduced lawsuit abuse and streamlined regulations. But it is lagging behind Florida and other states when it comes to more choices and competition in education. Texas governor Rick Perry, who has helped create one of the most prosperous states in the nation, doesn't like being behind Florida governor Rick Scott in education. Governor Perry is now working with the Texas Public Policy Foundation and other education groups to make Texas schools the best in the country. Other states are joining the competition.

Many governors have recognized that states with no income tax, like Florida and Texas, have a huge advantage when it comes to recruiting businesses. Mike Pence in Indiana, Pat McCrory in North Carolina, and Bobby Jindal in Louisiana are among the governors who are pushing their legislators to eliminate or reduce their income taxes. It's friendly competition, but believe me, it is serious business.

One of the biggest competitions between states is for freedom in the workplace. The economic growth of many states has been suffocated by the barnacles of antiquated forced unionization. As we saw in chapter 4, this is a relic of a federal law that forces workers to join unions and pay dues unless their state passes a law that gives them the freedom not to join. Almost half of the states have liberated their workers from this federal overreach, while other states, with political systems influenced by government unions, have been languishing with declining economies and increasing unemployment. Governors Mitch Daniels and Rick Snyder led their courageous legislatures to free their states' workers from union control. The courage and determination of these governors and legislators have demonstrated that states can wrestle free themselves from suffocating federal control.

The most inspiring example of this sort of courage and determination has come from the states that are fighting against the federal takeover of health care. Twenty-six states joined together to file suit against Obamacare, and while they did not win the complete victory they hoped for in the Supreme Court in 2012, they won the freedom not to accept a federal expansion of Medicaid that would have cost them billions of dollars. Most of these states have now turned down the federal money that would come with yet more red tape and mandates.

Watching states standing together to restore the constitutional boundaries of freedom has given me hope that we can restore America's founding principles. The friendly competition between governors has on many occasions made me smile. Working side by side with volunteer organizations and citizens who are already busy rebuilding America from the ground up has given me confidence that our best days still lie ahead.

How good those days will be depends upon one thing: we the people. Our future rests with us and—you guessed it—the little platoons. I simply do not see any other way out of our present crisis. We certainly can't look to the federal government.

I believe deeply in the little platoons, which are so American. They are made up of decent, honest citizens like you, who work hard, pay your bills, worship God, love your spouse and kids and want the best for them, and are deeply worried about where America seems to be headed. Well, I'm worried too, but I will not give in to despair. We have been here before, and we have come through every crisis stronger and better prepared for the future than before.

At the beginning of our Republic, we took on and defeated the mighty British Empire, which had the most powerful army in the world. A few years later, when our young nation seemed to be on the verge of splitting up into thirteen independent states, we ratified the Constitution and laid the firm foundation for a government of the people, by the people, and for the people.

In the 1860s, we fought a terrible, bloody civil war that preserved the Union and affirmed that, in the words of the Declaration, all men are created equal. By the end of the nineteenth century America had become the most prosperous and envied nation in the world.

In the twentieth century, we fought two world wars, overcame the Great Depression, survived the cultural counterrevolution of the 1960s, applauded the triumph of the civil rights movement, welcomed the equal treatment of women in the workplace, won the Cold War without firing a shot, and began a great public debate about the future of America—whether it would be an entitlement society dominated by the federal government and its myriad regulations and bureaucrats, or a free society of individuals who work together to solve their problems and who call on government as the court of last and not first resort.

That debate is still going on. How it will be resolved depends on us. I know Americans will do everything we can to ensure that the America we have known and loved all our lives prevails. I am confident, because I believe in the American people, just as our greatest leaders, from George Washington to Abraham Lincoln to Ronald Reagan, did. They understood that the people are the very foundation of America.

In his farewell address, President Reagan talked about the American Revolution and what made it possible. "Ours was the first revolution in the history of mankind," he said, "that truly reversed the course of government and with three little words: 'We the people.' In America, 'We the people' are supposed to tell the government what to do, instead of the government telling us." The idea of "we the people," he explained, was the underlying basis for everything he had tried to do as president.[3]

And it is "we the people" who make up the little platoons of society that will decide our tomorrow. It is the people, not the government, who are responsible for the many successes—some large, some small, but all life-changing—that we have highlighted in these pages.

Consider, for example, the town of Union, Iowa. It has only 394 residents, and so you wouldn't think that what goes on there makes much of a difference for the world. But Floyd Hammer and Kathy Hamilton are from Union, and in 2004 they founded Outreach, Inc., a nonprofit organization designed to combat hunger and offer medical care to millions of children in the United States and East Africa. Outreach has provided more than 229 million free meals to families in more than fifteen countries, and Kathy and Floyd were recently honored for their work by President Barack Obama and President George H. W. Bush at a White House ceremony in July 2013.[4] Both presidents recognized that a little platoon can have a very big impact.

And what has been the major motivation of Kathy and Floyd and all the other people we have met in this book? Faith? Yes. Hope? Yes. But most of all it was love, love of family, friends and neighbors, workplace and church, fraternal and social organizations. And it was love of something greater than themselves—a love of America, this once-in-a-millennium nation.

I have fought in the political arena because I have seen how liberal policies have hurt our people and hurt our country. I left politics to serve with the conservatives at The Heritage Foundation, because if we don't convince enough Americans that big government is destroying the things we love, they will continue to believe the promise that big government will solve all our problems. If you're still with me at the end of this book, you now know there is a better way—the freedom way.

And so, my friends and fellow Americans, let's fall in love with each other and this exceptional nation, with this land of the free and home of the brave. Let's fall in love with America, again and again and again.

Notes

Introduction

1. Edmund Burke, *Reflections on the French Revolution* (Cambridge, MA: Harvard Classics, 1909–14), paragraph 75.

Chapter 1: A Love Story

1. Robert L. Woodson Sr., "Is the Black Community a Casualty of the War on Poverty?," Heritage Lecture #245, March 15, 2009.
2. Robert L. Woodson Sr., Stephan Thernstrom, and Fred Siegel, "The Kerner Commission Report," Heritage Lecture #619, June 24, 1998.
3. Woodson's statement at a meeting following the Hudson Institute's book discussion on *Fables of Fortune: What Rich People Have That You Don't Want*, by Richard Watts, August 13, 2012.
4. Robert L. Woodson Sr., *The Triumphs of Joseph: How Today's Community Healers Are Reclaiming Our Streets and Neighborhoods* (New York: Free Press/Simon & Schuster, 1998), 82–94.
5. Freddie and Ninfa Garcia, *Outcry in the Barrio* (San Antonio: Freddie Garcia Ministries, 1988), 46.
6. Robert L. Woodson Sr., introduction of panelist Jubal Garcia at an antipoverty conference cosponsored by The Heritage Foundation and the Center for Neighborhood Enterprise, September 12–13, 2012.
7. Jubal Garcia at the antipoverty conference. A video of a portion of this testimony is available at http://blog.heritage.org/2012/11/01/how to-cure-poverty-in-america-video/.
8. Robert L. Woodson Sr., *Winning with a Losing Hand*, forthcoming.
9. Harvest of Hope, "Believe in Our Children: Open Your Heart and Your Home," http://harvestofhopefamily.com/services.php.
10. Statement by Cortez McDaniel of the Homecomers Academy reentry program for ex-offenders, who participated in a roundtable discussion at the antipoverty conference on September 12–13, 2012.

11. "Work Works" and "Success Stories," www.Step13.org.
12. "Work Works."
13. Telephone interview with Collette Caprara, March 2, 2013.
14. Woodson, Thernstrom, and Siegel, "Kerner Commission Report."
15. Center for Neighborhood Enterprise, "About CNE," http://www.cneonline.org/about-cne/.
16. Woodson, *Triumphs of Joseph*, 10.

Chapter 2: Too Big to Love

1. Gallup, "Americans' Confidence in Congress Falls to Lowest on Record," http://www.gallup.com/poll/163052/americans-confidence-congress-falls-lowest-record.aspx.
2. "In Nothing We Trust," *National Journal*, April 26, 2012, http://www.nationaljournal.com/features/restoration-calls/in-nothing-we-trust-20120419.
3. Hartford Institute for Religion Research, "Fast Facts About American Religion," http://hirr.hartsem.edu/research/fastfacts/fast_facts.html.

Chapter 3: The Mother of Big

1. "Epilogue: Securing the Republic," *The Founders' Constitution*, http://press-pubs.uchicago.edu/founders/documents/v1ch18s11.html.
2. U.S. Census Bureau, *Income, Poverty, and Health Insurance Coverage in the United States: 2011*, http://www.census.gov/prod/2012pubs/p60-243.pdf.
3. Heritage Foundation, "The 2012 Index of Dependence on Government," http://www.heritage.org/research/reports/2012/02/2012-index-of-dependence-on-government#_edn64.
4. Centers for Medicare and Medicaid Services, "Trustees Report & Trust Funds," http://www.cms.gov/Research-Statistics-Data-and-Systems/Statistics-Trends-and-Reports/ReportsTrustFunds/index.html?redirect=/reportstrustfunds/.
5. John C. Goodman and Laurence J. Kotlikoff, "Medicare by the Scary Numbers," *Wall Street Journal*, June 24, 2013, http://online.wsj.com/article/SB10001424127887323393804578555461959256572.html.
6. Jeffrey M. Jones, "Americans See Medicare, Social Security 'Crisis' within 10 Years," Gallup Politics, May 2, 2011, http://www.gallup.com/poll/147380/americans-medicare-social-security-crisis-within-years.aspx.

Chapter 4: The Rule of Big

1. Frederick Douglass, "Self-Made Men," in *Douglass Papers*, vol. 5, 556, 569.
2. P. J. O'Rourke, *Insight Magazine*, January 15–25, 35.

3. As quoted in Tom McCarthy, "JP Morgan Boss Jamie Dimon Faces Shareholders—As It Happened," *Guardian*, May 15, 2012.

4. As quoted in Ben Protess, "Citigroup's Pandit Shows Love for Dodd-Frank," *New York Times*, March 7, 2012.

5. As quoted in Vicki Needham, "Blankfein Supports Financial Reform Bill," *The Hill*, April 27, 2010.

6. Letter from American Wholesale Marketers and National Association of Tobacco Outlets to U.S. House of Representatives, March 13, 2009, http://legacy.library.ucsf.edu/tid/lra21i00/pdf;jsessionid=A0B0C9A10395D014F83CC3B116CEFFE7.tobacco03.

7. Ryan Donmoyer, "H&R Block, Jackson Hewitt Must Register with U.S. IRS," Bloomberg, January 4, 2010.

8. Timothy Carney, "Food Safety Regulation: A Tale of Big Business, Small Business, Big Government and Jobs," *San Francisco Examiner*, July 18, 2011.

9. Timothy Carney, "Mattel Exempted from Toy Safety Law It Helped Write," *Washington Examiner*, March 15, 2012.

10. Amy Ridenour, "Five Myths About the Federal Incandescent Light Bulb Ban," *National Policy Analysis*, December 2011.

11. Claudia Owen, "California Truckers Take EPA to Court over Emissions Rules," FoxNews.com, January 6, 2012.

12. Michael Kinsley, "The Washington Lobbying Dance," *Los Angeles Times*, April 5, 2011.

13. Tom McGinity and Brody Mullins, "Political Spending by Unions Far Exceeds Direct Donations," *Wall Street Journal*, July 10, 2012.

14. James Sherk and Todd Zywicki, "Obama's United Auto Workers Bailout," *Wall Street Journal*, June 13, 2012.

15. Matthew Boyle, "Emails: Geithner, Treasury Drove Cutoff of Non-Union Delphi Workers' Pensions," *Daily Caller*, August 7, 2012.

16. Jason Richwine, "'Overpaid and Underworked' Federal Employees? It's Not Just a 'Perception,'" *The Foundry*, March 1, 2013, http://blog.heritage.org/2013/03/01/overpaid-and-underworked-federal-employees-its-not-just-a-perception/.

17. Franklin D. Roosevelt, "Letter on the Resolution of Federation of Federal Employees Against Strikes in Federal Service," August 16, 1937. Online by Gerhard Peters and John T. Woolley, *The American Presidency Project*, http://www.presidency.ucsb.edu/ws/?pid=15445.

18. "Meany Looks into Labor's Future," *New York Times*, December 4, 1955.

19. Art Hughes, "Bus Strike Ends but Not All Drivers Are Happy," Minnesota Public Radio, April 16, 2004.

20. Bill Frezza, "Governor Walker's Victory Spells Doom for Public Sector Unions," *Forbes*, June 5, 2012.

Chapter 5: Federalism: Our Founders' Priceless Legacy

1. Matthew Spalding, preface to Eugene W. Hickok, *Why States? The Challenge of Federalism* (Washington, DC: Heritage Foundation, 2007), viii.
2. Hickok, *Why States?*, 2.
3. Ibid., 60.
4. Ibid., 76.
5. Ibid., 88.
6. Edwin J. Feulner, "What Is the Role of the People?," Understanding America series, Heritage Foundation, 2012, 10–11.
7. Heritage Foundation, "Solutions for America: Re-embracing Federalism," August 17, 2010, http://www.heritage.org/research/reports/2010/08/re-embracing-federalism.
8. David Leonhardt, "Budget Hawk Eyes Deficit," *New York Times*, January 4, 2011, http://www.nytimes.com/2011/01/05/business/economy/05leonhardt.html?pagewanted=all.
9. "The Right Stuff," *Economist*, August 19, 2010.
10. "Gov. Jindal's Accomplishments," http://www.bobbyjindal.com/index.php?option=com_content&view=article&id=47.
11. WMTV (Madison, WI), "Walker Says Budget Surplus Is 'Good News,'" May 9, 2013, http://www.nbc15.com/election/headlines/Wisconsin-Budget-Gets-500M-Boost-206768371.html.
12. Felicia Sonmez, "Rick Snyder Signs 'Right to Work' Legislation," *Washington Post*, December 11, 2012, http://www.washingtonpost.com/blogs/post-politics/wp/2012/12/11/rick-snyder-signs-right-to-work-legislation/.
13. The Honorable Mary Fallin, Governor, Oklahoma, *State of the State 2012*, http://www.ok.gov/governor/documents/Governor%20Mary%20Faliin%20State%20of%20the%20State%20Address%202012%20UPDATED.pdf.
14. ALEC, "History," http://www.alec.org/about-alec/history/.
15. Lee Edwards, *Leading the Way: The Story of Ed Feulner and The Heritage Foundation* (New York: Crown, 2013), 189.
16. Ibid.
17. "Boots-on-the-Ground for Liberty," SPN News, March–April 2013, 4.
18. Jonah Goldberg, "To Heal Government, Go Local," *Los Angeles Times*, March 20, 2012.
19. Michael S. Greve, "But What Kind of Federalism?," *Insider* (Winter 2013): 5.

20. *Federalist* No. 45.

21. Lindsey Burke, "Reducing the Federal Footprint on Education and Empowering State and Local Leaders," The Heritage Foundation, *Backgrounder* No. 2565, June 2, 2011, at http://www.heritage.org/research/reports/2011/06/reducing-the-federal-footprint-on-education-and-empowering-state-and-local-leaders.

22. Patrick Caldwell, "Outmatched," *American Prospect*, March 7, 2013.

23. Joseph G. Lehman, letter to Mackinac Center supporters, March–April 2013.

24. Caldwell, "Outmatched."

25. "Right to Work in Michigan: A Visual Time Line," Mackinac Center, February 19, 2013, http://www.michigancapitolconfidential.com/18295.

26. "Michigan Becomes 24th Right-to-Work State in the Nation," CAPCON: Michigan Capitol Confidential, December 11, 2012, http://www.michigancapitolconfidential.com/pubs/mcc/article.aspx?id=18056&print=yes.

27. Lindsey Dodge, "The New Civil Society," Mackinac Center, May 2, 2013, http://www.mackinac.org/18600.

28. Joseph Lehman, "In Praise of Those Unpraised," Mackinac Center, May 2, 2013, http://www.mackinac.org/18586.

Chapter 6: Love Begins at Home

1. "Family Structure and Children's Education," Heritage Family Facts Brief #35, http://familyfacts.org/briefs/35/family-structure-and-childrens-education.

2. "Parents' Influence on Adolescents' Sexual Behavior," Heritage Family Facts Brief #42, http://thf_media.s3.amazonaws.com/familyfacts/briefs/FF_Brief_42.pdf.

3. "A Wise Investment: Benefits from Families Spending Time Together," Heritage Family Facts Brief #15, http://familyfacts.org/briefs/15/a-wise-investment-benefits-from-families-spending-time-together.

4. "Parental Involvement and Children's Well-Being," Heritage Family Facts Brief #40, http://thf_media.s3.amazonaws.com/familyfacts/briefs/FF_Brief_40.pdf.

5. Robert Rector, "Marriage: America's Greatest Weapon Against Child Poverty," Heritage Special Report #117, September 5, 2012.

6. Ryan Messmore, "Finding His Calling," *World Magazine*, August 13, 2010, http://www.worldmag.com/2010/08/finding_his_calling.

7. Ibid.

8. "Family Environment and Children's Prospects for Marriage," Heritage Family Facts Brief #39, http://thf_media.s3.amazonaws.com/familyfacts/briefs/FF_Brief_39.pdf.

9. Elisabeth Donahue, Ron Haskins, and Sara McLanahan, "The Decline in Marriage: What to Do," The Future of Children Policy Brief, Princeton–Brookings, Fall 2005, http://www.brookings.edu/es/research/projects/wrb/publications/pb/200509foc.pdf.

10. Elizabeth Marquardt, "The Revolution in Parenthood: The Emerging Global Clash Between Adult Rights and Children's Needs," Institute for American Values, 2006.

11. Hanna Rosin, *The End of Men and the Rise of Women* (New York: Riverhead, 2012).

12. Prof. Douglas W. Allen and Maggie Gallagher, "Does Divorce Law Affect the Divorce Rate? A Review of Empirical Research, 1995–2006," Institute for Marriage and Public Policy, *iMAPP Research Brief* 1, no. 1 (July 2007), http://www.marriagedebate.com/pdf/imapp.nofault.divrate.pdf.

13. Census Bureau, "Survey of Income and Program Participation, 2008." Or the report is: Rose M. Kreider and Renee Ellis, "Number, Timing and Duration of Marriages and Divorces: 2009," U.S. Census Bureau, *Current Population Reports* (May 2011): 70–125, http://www.census.gov/prod/2011pubs/p70-125.pdf.

14. "Divorce Rate Is Declining but Still High," Heritage Family Facts Chart #120, http://familyfacts.org/charts/120/the-divorce-rate-is-declining-but-still-high.

15. Anne C. Fletcher, Laurence Steinberg, and Elizabeth B. Sellers, "Adolescents' Well-Being as a Function of Perceived Interparental Consistency," *Journal of Marriage and the Family* 61 (August 1999): 599–610; Sara McLanahan and Gary Sandefur, *Growing Up with a Single Parent: What Hurts, What Helps* (Cambridge, MA: Harvard University Press, 1994).

16. Susan Gregory Thomas, "The Divorce Generation," *Wall Street Journal*, July 9, 2011.

17. Susan Gregory Thomas, "All Apologies: Thank You for the 'Sorry,'" *Huffington Post*, August 23, 2011, http://www.huffingtonpost.com/susan-gregory-thomas/all-apologies-thank-you-f_b_931718.html.

18. "The Proportion of Married Adults Has Decreased," Heritage Family Facts Chart #150, http://familyfacts.org/charts/150/the-proportion-of-married-adults-has-decreased.

19. "Men and Women are Marrying Later," Heritage Family Facts Chart #102, http://familyfacts.org/charts/102/men-and-women-are-marrying-later.

20. "Unwed Childbearing Has Increased Dramatically, Regardless of Mother's Age," Heritage Family Facts Chart #207, http://www.familyfacts.org/charts/207/unwed-childbearing-has-increased dramatically-regardless-of-mothers-age.

21. "Nearly 12 Percent of Couples Living Together Are Unmarried," Heritage Family Facts Chart #110, http://familyfacts.org/charts/110/nearly-12-percent-of -couples-living-together-are-unmarried.

22. "Cohabitation vs. Marriage: How Love's Choices Shape Life Outcomes," Heritage Family Facts Brief #9, http://www.familyfacts.org/briefs/9/cohabi tation-vs-marriage-how-loves-choices-shape-life-outcomes.

23. "Most Unwed Childbearing Occurs Among Females in Their Twenties," Heritage Family Facts Chart #209, http://familyfacts.org/charts/209/most -unwed-childbearing-occurs-among-females-in-their-twenties.

24. Robert Rector, "Marriage: America's Greatest Weapon Against Child Poverty," Heritage Foundation, September 5, 2012, http://www.heritage.org/ research/reports/2012/09/marriage-americas-greatest-weapon-against -child-poverty.

25. Kay Hymowitz, Jason Carroll, W. Bradford Wilcox, and Kelleen Kaye, "Knot Yet: The Benefits and Costs of Delayed Marriage in America," National Marriage Project at the University of Virginia, National Campaign to Prevent Teen and Unplanned Pregnancy, and RELATE Institute, 2013.

26. Kathryn Edin and Maria Kefalas, *Promises I Can Keep: Why Poor Women Put Motherhood Before Marriage* (Los Angeles: University of California Press, 2007), 6.

27. Ibid., 121.

28. Ibid., 122.

29. Ibid., 117.

30. Ibid., 172.

31. Ibid., 173.

32. Kathryn Edin and Timothy J. Nelson, *Doing the Best I Can: Fatherhood in the Inner City* (Berkeley: University of California Press, 2013), 58.

33. Ibid., 109.

34. Jennifer Roback Morse, "Privatizing Marriage Will Expand the Role of the State," Witherspoon Institute Public Discourse, April 3, 2012, http://www .thepublicdiscourse.com/2012/04/5071/.

35. Rector, "Marriage: America's Greatest Weapon against Child Poverty."

36. Chuck A. Donovan, "A Marshall Plan for Marriage: Rebuilding Our Shattered Homes," Heritage Backgrounder #2567, June 7, 2011, http://www.heritage .org/research/reports/2011/06/a-marshall-plan-for-marriage-rebuilding -our-shattered-homes.

37. Chuck A. Donovan, "Obamacare: Impact on the Family," Heritage WebMemo #2857, April 12, 2010, http://www.heritage.org/research/reports/2010/04 /obamacare-impact-on-the-family.

38. Robert H. Bork, *Slouching towards Gomorrah: Modern Liberalism and American Decline* (New York: Regan Books, 1996), 173.

39. Ryan T. Anderson, "What Three Dissents Signal for Marriage's Future," Heritage Foundation, July 3, 2013, http://www.heritage.org/research/commentary/2013/7/what-three-dissents-signal-for-marriages-future.

40. Ryan T. Anderson, "Marriage: What It Is, Why It Matters, and the Consequences of Redefining It," Heritage Backgrounder #2775, March 11, 2013, http://www.heritage.org/research/reports/2013/03/marriage-what-it-is-why-it-matters-and-the-consequences-of-redefining-it.

41. Thomas Messner, "From Culture Wars to Conscience Wars: Emerging Threats to Conscience," Heritage Backgrounder #2543, April 13, 2011, http://www.heritage.org/research/reports/2011/04/from-culture-wars-to-conscience-wars-emerging-threats-to-conscience.

42. Julie Baumgardner, "What's the Point of Marriage?," *First Things First*, http://firstthings.org/whats-the-point-of-marriage.

43. "First Things First 2011 Report Card," http://firstthings.org/fullpanel/uploads/files/2011-report-card.pdf.

44. Rector, "Marriage: America's Greatest Weapon against Child Poverty."

45. Donovan, "A Marshall Plan for Marriage."

46. Robert Rector and Katherine Bradley, "Confronting the Unsustainable Growth of Welfare Entitlements: Principles of Reform and the Next Steps," Heritage Backgrounder #2427, June 24, 2010, http://www.heritage.org/research/reports/2010/06/confronting-the-unsustainable-growth-of-welfare-entitlements-principles-of-reform-and-the-next-steps.

Chapter 7: Faith: Learning to Love

1. George Washington, "Letter to the Hebrew Congregation of Newport, Rhode Island," http://www.heritage.org/initiatives/first-principles/primary-sources/washington-s-letter-to-the-hebrew-congregation-of-newport-rhode-island.

2. Ronald Reagan, "Farewell Address to the Nation, January 11, 1989," http://www.reaganfoundation.org/tgcdetail.aspx?p=TG0923RRS&h1=0&h2=0&sw=&lm=reagan&args_a=cms&args_b=1&argsb=N&tx=1749.

3. "Press Statement of David Green—September 13, 2013," Becket Fund, http://www.becketfund.org/davidgreenpressstatement/.

4. Sen. Max Baucus, "Obamacare Delay Was the Right Call," RealClearPolitics, July 18, 2013, http://www.realclearpolitics.com/2013/07/18/obamacare_delay_was_the_right_call_311788.html.

5. Manya A. Brachear, "Last Faith Agency Opposed to Civil Union Adoptions out of Foster Care," *Chicago Tribune*, November 16, 2011, http://

articles.chicagotribune.com/2011-11-16/news/ct-met-evangelical-foster-care -gone-20111116_1_ken-withrow-faith-agency-catholic-charities-agencies.

6. Nancy Frazier O'Brien, "Bishop Addresses House Panel on 'Grave Threats to Religious Liberty,'" Catholic News Service, October 26, 2011, http://www .catholicnews.com/data/stories/cns/1104218.htm.

7. Ross Douthat, "Defining Religious Liberty Down," *New York Times*, July 28, 2012, http://www.nytimes.com/2012/07/29/opinion/sunday/douthat-defin ing-religious-liberty-down.html?_r=0.

8. John Adams, "Address to the Military," October 11, 1798.

9. Andrew T. Walker, "Rick Warren: Religious Freedom Ensures Other Freedoms," *The Foundry*, February 26, 2013, http://blog.heritage.org/2013/02/26/ rick-warren-religious-freedom-ensures-other-freedoms/.

10. Dr. Martin Luther King Jr., "A Knock at Midnight," June 11, 1967, Martin Luther King, Jr. Research and Education Institute, http://mlk-kpp01.stanford .edu/index.php/encyclopedia/documentsentry/doc_a_knock_at_midnight/.

11. Prison Fellowship, www.prisonfellowship.org.

12. Alyson R. Quinn, "One Father, One Son, One Gift," *Inside Journal* 20, no. 3 (2011).

13. Electa Draper, "Adoption Initiative Halves Numbers of Kids Needing Families," *Denver Post*, March 5, 2010, http://www.denverpost.com/news/ci _14516591.

14. Transcript of Small Group Study on DVD: "Serving the Whole Person: Churches and Ministries," video: http://seeksocialjustice.com/index.php/ serving-the-whole-person-churches-and-ministries/; transcript: http://www .slideshare.net/seeksocialjustice/seek-social-justice-guide-lesson-3.

15. Alexis de Tocqueville, *Democracy in America* (Chicago: University of Chicago Press, 2000), 275.

16. "For 38th Consecutive Year, A.M. Best Reaffirms Top A++ Rating for Knights of Columbus," Sys-Con Media, July 11, 2013, http://www.sys-con.com/ node/2733428.

17. Arthur Brooks, *Who Really Cares: The Surprising Truth About Compassionate Conservatism* (New York: Basic Books, 2006), 47.

18. Ibid., 39.

19. Ibid., 126.

20. Mary Eberstadt, *How the West Really Lost God* (West Conshohocken, PA: Templeton Press, 2013), 198.

21. Ibid.

22. Ibid.

23. Byron Johnson, *More God, Less Crime: Why Faith Matters and How It Could Matter More* (West Conshohocken, PA: Templeton Press, 2011).

24. Patrick F. Fagan, "Why Religion Matters Even More: The Impact of Religious Practice on Social Stability," Heritage Backgrounder #1992, https://www.google.com/#bav=on.2,or.r_qf.&fp=ac66d152b2e67cf5&q=%E2%80%9C Why+Religion+Matters+Even+More:+The+Impact+of+Religious+Practi ce+on+Social+Stability%2C%E2%80%9D+.

25. W. Bradford Wilcox, "Religion, Convention, and Paternal Involvement," *Journal of Marriage and Family* 64, no. 3 (August 2002): 780–92.

Chapter 8: Let Doctors Be Doctors

1. Shari Rudavsky, "Health Care Sharing Ministries Offer Insurance Alternative," *USA Today*, July 8, 2012, http://usatoday30.usatoday.com/news/religion/ story/2012-07-08/health-insurance-sharing-ministries/56083586/1.

2. Ibid.

3. Alliance of Health Care Sharing Ministries, "Health Care Sharing Ministries Comparison Chart," http://www.healthcaresharing.org/wp-content/uploads/ 2012/06/Health_Care_Sharing_Ministry_Comparison.pdf.

4. Rudavsky, "Health Care Sharing Ministries."

5. Ibid.

6. Ibid.

7. Alliance of Health Care Sharing Ministries, "What Is a Health Care Sharing Ministry?," http://healthcaresharing.org/hcsm.

8. Ibid.

9. David Kirkpatrick, "White House Affirms Deal on Drug Cost," *New York Times*, August 6, 2009, http://www.nytimes.com/2009/08/06/health/ policy/06insure.html.

10. Congressional Budget Office, May 2013 estimate of the budgetary effects of the insurance coverage provisions contained in the Patient Protection and Affordable Care Act, http://cbo.gov/sites/default/files/cbofiles/attachments/44190 _EffectsAffordableCareActHealthInsuranceCoverage_2.pdf.

11. Patient Protection and Affordable Care Act, Public Law 111-148, Section 3002(b).

12. Ibid., Section 3007.

13. Deloitte Center for Health Solutions, "Deloitte 2013 Survey of U.S. Physicians," March 18, 2013, http://www.deloitte.com/assets/Dcom-UnitedStates/Local%20 Assets/Documents/us_chs_2013SurveyofUSPhysicians_031813.pdf, 3.

14. Concierge Medicine Research Collective, "Three Year Analysis of Concierge and Direct Care Medicine Shows Encouraging Signs for Boosting Primary Care," May 17, 2013, http://www.prweb.com/releases/2013/5/ prweb10734184.htm.

15. Betty Ann Bowser, "Concierge Medicine: Greater Access for a Fee," *PBS News-Hour*, July 9, 2012, http://www.pbs.org/newshour/bb/health/july-dec12/medicine_07-09.html.

16. Concierge Medicine Research Collective, "Three Year Analysis."

17. Kaiser Family Foundation and Health Research and Educational Trust, *Employer Health Benefits: 2012 Annual Survey*, September 2012, http://kaiserfamilyfoun dation.files.wordpress.com/2013/03/8345-employer-health-benefits-annual -survey-full-report-0912.pdf, 1.

18. Elizabeth O'Brien, "Why Concierge Medicine Will Get Bigger," *Market-Watch*, January 17, 2013, http://www.marketwatch.com/Story/story/print?guid=431D2B2C-6018-11E2-AD22-002128040CF6.

19. Kaiser Family Foundation, *Employer Health Benefits*, Exhibit 1.11, 30.

20. PBS Report, Air Date: July 9, 2012: "Concierge Medicine: Greater Access for a Fee," http://www.pbs.org/newshour/bb/health/july-dec12/medicine _07-09.html.

21. O'Brien, "Why Concierge Medicine Will Get Bigger."

22. Regina Herzlinger, *Who Killed Health Care? America's $2 Trillion Medical Problem—and the Consumer-Driven Cure* (New York: McGraw-Hill, 2007), 76–82.

23. Regina Herzlinger and Peter Stavros, "MedCath Corporation (A)," Harvard Business School Case No. 303-041, rev. August 2006, 10.

24. Herzlinger, *Who Killed Health Care?*, 76–77.

25. Ibid., 77.

26. Jordan Rau, "Doctor-Owned Hospitals Prosper under Health Law," Kaiser Health News, April 12, 2013, http://www.kaiserhealthnews.org/Stories/2013/April/12/doctor-owned-hospitals-quality-bonuses.aspx.

27. Ibid.

28. Ibid.

29. Ibid.

30. National Council of State Legislatures, "Certificate of Need: State Laws and Programs," March 2012, http://www.ncsl.org/issues-research/health/con -certificate-of-need-state-laws.aspx.

31. Alicia Mundy, "Doc-Owned Hospitals Prep to Fight," *Wall Street Journal*, May 14, 2013, http://online.wsj.com/article/SB10001424127887324059704578475233553298840.html.

32. Patient Protection and Affordable Care Act, Public Law 111-148, Section 6001.

33. Mundy, "Doc-Owned Hospitals."

34. Pew Research Center, "Baby Boomers Retire," December 29, 2010, http://www.pewresearch.org/daily-number/baby-boomers-retire/.

Chapter 9: Education and the Power of Choice

1. J. P. Greene and Josh B. McGee, "Suburban Schools Post Low Global Grades," *Hartford Courant*, October 9, 2011.
2. U.S. Department of Education, Institute of Education Sciences, National Center for Education Statistics, National Assessment of Educational Progress (NAEP), 2013 Mathematics and Reading Assessments, Trend in fourth-grade NAEP reading average scores and score gaps, by race/ethnicity, at http://nationsre portcard.gov/reading_math_2013/#/student-groups
3. U.S. Department of Education, Institute of Education Sciences, National Center for Education Statistics, National Assessment of Educational Progress (NAEP), Trial Urban District Assessment, 2011, grade 4 district results, at http://nationsreport card.gov/reading_2011/district_g4.aspx?tab_id=tab2&subtab_id=Tab _1#chart
4. President Barack Obama, State of the Union address 2013.
5. Michael Puma et al., "Third Grade Follow-up to the Head Start Impact Study Final Report," U.S. Department of Health and Human Services, Administration for Children and Families (Washington, DC: Office of Planning, Research and Evaluation, October 2012), Exhibit 4.2, 78, and Exhibit 4.1, 77, http://www.acf.hhs.gov/sites/default/files/opre/head_start_report.pdf, as found in Lindsey Burke and David B. Muhlhausen, Ph.D., "Head Start Impact Evaluation Finally Released," Heritage Issue Brief #3823, January 10, 2013, http://www.heritage.org/research/reports/2013/01/head-start -impact-evaluation-report-finally-released#_edn11.
6. Andrew Coulson, "The Impact of Federal Involvement in America's Classrooms," Testimony before the Committee on Education and the Workforce, United States House of Representatives, February 10, 2011, at http://www.cato .org/publications/congressional-testimony/impact-federal-involvement-americas -classrooms
7. Patrick F. Fagan and Nicholas Zill, "The Second Annual Index of Family Belonging and Rejection," Marriage and Religion Research Institute, November 17, 2011.
8. "Remarks in a Tribute to Milton Friedman," *Public Papers of the Presidents of the United States: George W. Bush*, May 9, 2002, http://www.gpo.gov/fdsys/pkg/ PPP-2002-book1/html/PPP-2002-book1-doc-pg759-2.htm.
9. Milton and Rose Friedman, *Free to Choose: A Personal Statement* (New York: Avon, 1979), 148.
10. Virginia Walden Ford, *Voices, Choices, and Second Chances: How to Win the Battle to Bring Opportunity Scholarships to Your State* (Washington, DC: D.C. Parents for School Choice, 2005), 79.

11. Virginia Walden Ford, "School Choice: An Activist's Guide," cited in *Choosing to Succeed*, edited by Lindsey M. Burke, Heritage Special Report #125, January 28, 2013, 20.

12. Ibid., 22.

13. Lindsey Burke and Rachel Sheffield, "13 Ways the 113th Congress Can Improve Education in America," Heritage Backgrounder #2796, May 15, 2013.

14. Mark Zimmermann, "D.C. Opportunity Scholarship Opened Doors for Carroll Valedictorian, *My Catholic Standard*, June 18, 2013, http://www.cathstan.org/main.asp?SectionID=2&SubSectionID=24&ArticleID=5721.

15. Barack Obama, "Renewing American Competitiveness," address at Kettering University, Flint, Michigan, June 26, 2008.

16. Ford, *Voices, Choices, and Second Chances*, 79.

17. Greg Forster, "A Win-Win Solution: The Empirical Evidence on School Choice," Friedman Foundation for Educational Choice, April 17, 2013, http://www.edchoice.org/Research/Reports/A-Win-Win-Solution--The-Empirical-Evidence-on-School-Choice.aspx.

18. Lindsey Burke, "Creating a Crisis: Unions Stifle Education Reform," Heritage WebMemo #2967, July 20, 2010, http://www.heritage.org/research/reports/2010/07/creating-a-crisis-unions-stifle-education-reform.

19. Terry M. Moe, "Special Interest: Teachers Unions and America's Public Schools," Brookings Institution, Washington, DC, 2011. 208

20. Sherif Matar and Tracy Oppenheimer, "What We Saw at the National School Choice Week's Kickoff in New Orleans," Reason.com, January 23, 2012.

21. James Madison Institute, *Policy Brief*, February 2013, 5.

22. Sutherland Institute, "Fostering Educational Innovation in Choice-Based Multi-Venue Settings and Government Single-Venue Settings," April 8, 2010, 44.

23. http://www.eagleforum.org/publications/educate/aug13/nea-resolutions-passed-2013-convention-atlanta-georgia.html

24. Sandra Martin-Chang, Odette N. Gould, and Reanne E. Meuse, "The Impact of Schooling on Academic Achievement: Evidence from Homeschooled and Traditionally Schooled Students," *Canadian Journal of Behavioural Science / Revue Canadienne des Sciences du Comportement* 43, no. 3 (July 2011): 195–202; HSLDA, *Homeschool Progress Report 2009: Academic Achievement and Demographics*, http://www.hslda.org/docs/study/ray2009/2009_Ray_StudyFINAL.pdf.

25. Mother of Divine Grace School, "Letter from Laura Berquist—Founder & Director," http://www.motherofdivinegrace.org/aboutus/letterfromthedirector.

26. Laura Berquist, *Designing Your Own Classical Curriculum*, 3rd ed. (San Francisco: Ignatius Press, 1998).

27. "Ron Paul's Congressional Farewell Speech," *Target: Freedom*, http://target freedom.typepad.com/targetfreedom/2012/11/ron-pauls-congressional-farewell-speech-11142012.html.

28. Laura Berquist, *The Harp and the Laurel Wreath* (San Francisco: Ignatius Press, 1999), 8.

29. *Pierce v. Society of Sisters*, 268 U.S. 510, 534–35 (1925) (UNANIMOUS Supreme Court).

Chapter 10: Loving Work

1. Marquis James and Bessie R. James, *Biography of a Bank: The Story of Bank of America* (New York: Harper & Brothers, 1954), 2.

2. Ibid., 3.

3. Ibid., 28.

4. Jim Drinkard, "Crack Appearing in Once-Solid Farm Marketing System," Associated Press, April 22, 1985.

5. James R. Hamby, Testimony Before the House Oversight and Investigations Committee, July 19, 2012, http://oversight.house.gov/wp-content/uploads/2012/07/Hamby-Vision-Bank-Testimony-07-19-12.pdf.

6. Kaitlyn Evans, "Free Checking No More: Thanks, Dodd-Frank!" *The Foundry*, September 25, 2012, http://blog.heritage.org/2012/09/25/free-checking-no-more-thanks-dodd-frank/.

7. "Global Company Lays Off 100 in U.S., Blames ObamaCare," FoxNews.com, February 1, 2013, http://www.foxnews.com/politics/2013/02/01/memphis-based-medical-company-lays-off-100-blames-obama-care/.

8. Heritage Foundation, "The Death-Tax Burden on American Business," http://www.heritage.org/research/projects/the-death-tax-burden-on-american-business.

9. Agis Salpukas, "Falling Tax Would Lift All Yachts," *New York Times*, February 7, 1992, http://www.nytimes.com/1992/02/07/business/falling-tax-would-lift-all-yachts.html.

10. Drs. Robert Carroll and Gerald Prante, "Long-Run Macroeconomic Impact of Increasing Tax Rates on High-Income Taxpayers in 2013," http://www.nfib.com/LinkClick.aspx?fileticket=OMV7uZczVaM%3d&tabid=1083.

11. Cited in Edwin J. Feulner and Brian Tracy, *The American Spirit: Celebrating the Values and Virtues That Made Us Great* (Nashville: Thomas Nelson, 2012), 221–22.

12. James L. Gattuso and Kiane Katz, "Red Tape Rising: Regulation in Obama's First Term," Heritage Backgrounder #2793, http://www.heritage.org/research/reports/2013/05/red-tape-rising-regulation-in-obamas-first-term.

13. Ibid.

14. Diane Katz, "Tales of the Red Tape #36: USDA Lays a Regulatory Egg," *The Foundry*, October 13, 2012, http://blog.heritage.org/2012/10/13/tales-of-the -red-tape-36-usda-lays-a-regulatory-egg/.

15. Diane Katz, "Tales of the Red Tape #25: EEOC Disables Employers," *The Foundry*, January 25, 2012, at http://blog.heritage.org/2012/01/25/tales-of -the-red-tape-25-eeoc-disables-employers/.

16. See Jonathan Gruber, "The Incidence of Mandated Maternity Benefits," *American Economic Review* 84, no. 3 (June 1994): 622–41; Patricia M. Anderson and Bruce D. Meyer, "The Incidence of a Firm-Varying Payroll Tax: The Case of Unemployment Insurance," NBER Working Paper No. W5201, August 1, 1995; Jonathan Gruber and Alan B. Krueger, "The Incidence of Mandated Employer-Provided Insurance: Lessons from Workers' Compensation Insurance," NBER Working Paper No. W3557, December 1990; Price Fishback and Shawn Kantor, "Did Workers Pay for the Passage of Workers' Compensation Laws?," *Quarterly Journal of Economics* 110, no. 3 (August 1995): 713–42.

17. U.S. Department of Labor, Bureau of Labor Statistics, "Employee Benefits Survey: Leave Benefit Access," Table 32, March 2012, http://www.bls.gov/ncs/ebs/benefits/2012/ownership/civilian/table21a.htm.

18. Luis Garicano, Claire LeLarge, and John Van Reenen, "Firm Size Distortions and the Productivity Distribution: Evidence from France," National Bureau of Economics Working Paper No. 18841, February 2013.

19. Department of Labor, Bureau of Labor Statistics, "Job Openings and Labor Turnover Survey," Table B, December 2007–June 2009.

20. Morris Kleiner and Alan Krueger, "Analyzing the Extent and Influence of Occupational Licensing on the Labor Market," *Journal of Labor Economics* 31, no. 2 (April 2013): S173–S202.

21. Dick Carpenter et al., "License to Work: A National Study of Burdens from Occupational Licensing," Institute for Justice, May 2012, http://www.ij.org/licensetowork.

22. City of Annapolis, Office of the City Clerk, "Fortune Telling License Application," http://www.annapolis.gov/docs/default-source/forms-permits-and -licenses/fortuneteller%27s-procedures-and-application.pdf?sfvrsn=2.

23. Morris M. Kleiner, *Licensing Occupations: Ensuring Quality or Restricting Competition?* (Kalamazoo, MI: Upjohn Institute Press, 2006), 31.

24. Carpenter et al., "License to Work."

25. Burt Helm, "Do Not CrossFit," *Inc.*, July–August 2013, http://www.inc.com/ welcome.html?destination=http://www.inc.com/magazine/201307/burt -helm/crossfit-empire.html.

26. Jessica Sidman, "Curbed: Could New Regulations Kill DC's Food Culture?," *Washington City Paper*, March 20, 2013.

27. Tim Carman, "It's Status Quo on Food Trucks After D.C. Council's Vote," *Washington Post*, June 5, 2013.

28. *Castelle v. St. Joseph Abbey*, petition for certiorari, filed in No. 13-91, July 17, 2013.

Chapter 11: Loving the Poor

1. Marvin N. Olasky, *The Tragedy of American Compassion* (Washington, DC: Regnery Gateway, 1992), 13.

2. Ibid., 8.

3. Ibid., 13.

4. Ibid., 19.

5. Ibid.

6. Ibid., 14.

7. Ibid., 11.

8. Harvest of Hope, "About Harvest of Hope," http://www.harvestofhopefamily .com/about.php.

9. Bud's Warehouse, "About," http://budswarehouse.org/about/.

10. Brian Prioleau, "Bud's Warehouse: Home Improvement Like You Have Never Seen Before," Homelessness Resource Center, http://homeless.samhsa.gov/ resource/bud%E2%80%99s-warehouse-home-improvement-like-you-have -never-seen-before-55978.aspx.

11. "The Gift of Brokenness," Faithventure Forum, http://www.faithventureforum .org/2011/04/gift-of-brokenness.html.

12. "Viana's Story," Faithventure Forum, http://www.faithventureforum.org/ search/label/Bud%27s%20Warehouse

13. Lyndon B. Johnson, "Proposal for a Nationwide War on the Sources of Poverty," special message to Congress, March 16, 1964, http://www.fordham.edu/ halsall/mod/1964johnson-warpoverty.html.

14. Lyndon B. Johnson, "Annual Message to the Congress on the State of the Union," January 8, 1964, http://www.presidency.ucsb.edu/ws/index.php?pid=26787.

15. Lyndon B. Johnson, "Remarks upon Signing the Economic Opportunity Act," August 20, 1964, http://www.presidency.ucsb.edu/ws/?pid=26452.

16. Johnson, "Proposal for a Nationwide War on the Sources of Poverty."

17. Olasky, *Tragedy*, 174.
18. "Obama to Spend $10.3 Trillion on Welfare: Uncovering the Full Cost of Means-Tested Welfare or Aid to the Poor," Heritage Special Report #67, September 16, 2009, http://www.heritage.org/research/reports/2009/09/obama-to-spend-103-trillion-on-welfare-uncovering-the-full-cost-of-means-tested-welfare-or-aid-to-the-poor.
19. Charles Murray, *Losing Ground: American Social Policy, 1950–1980* (New York: Basic Books, 1984), 219.
20. Ibid., 9.
21. Ibid.
22. Robert L. Woodson Sr., "Testimony before the United States Senate Committee on the Budget," February 13, 2013, http://www.budget.senate.gov/democratic/index.cfm/files/serve?File_id=799c8541-a525-4ad5-9dba-0ae41b27beea.
23. Marianne E. Page, "New Evidence on Intergenerational Correlations in Welfare Participation," National Bureau of Economic Research, April 2002, 15.
24. Steve Forbes and Elizabeth Ames, *Freedom Manifesto: Why Free Markets Are Moral and Big Government Isn't* (New York: Crown Business, 2012), 168–69.
25. Rector and Marshall, "The Unfinished Work of Welfare Reform."
26. Ibid.
27. Murray, *Losing Ground*, 185.
28. Robert Rector and Rachel Sheffield, "Understanding Poverty in the United States: Surprising Facts About America's Poor," Heritage Backgrounder #2607, September 13, 2011, http://www.heritage.org/research/reports/2011/09/understanding-poverty-in-the-united-states-surprising-facts-about-americas-poor.
29. Food and Nutrition Service, U.S. Department of Agriculture, "SNAP Outreach and Nutrition Education Materials," http://snap.ntis.gov/download.aspx.
30. Eli Saslow, "In Florida, a Food-Stamp Recruiter Deals with Wrenching Choices," *Washington Post*, April 23, 2013, http://www.washingtonpost.com/national/in-florida-a-food-stamp-recruiter-deals-with-wrenching-choices/2013/04/23/b3d6b41c-a3a4-11e2-9c03-6952ff305f35_story_3.html.
31. Ibid.
32. "Welfare Quotes: They Said It," Heritage WebMemo #126, July 11, 2002, http://www.heritage.org/research/reports/2002/07/welfare-quotes-they-said-it.
33. Robert Rector, "Why Congress Must Reform Welfare," Heritage Backgrounder #1063, December 4, 1995, http://www.heritage.org/research/reports/1995/12/bg1063nbsp-why-congress-must-reform-welfare.

34. Ibid.

35. "Welfare Quotes: They Said It."

36. Robert Rector and Patrick F. Fagan, "The Continuing Good News About Welfare Reform," Heritage Backgrounder #1620, February 6, 2003, http://www.heritage.org/research/reports/2003/02/the-continuing-good-news.

37. Rector and Marshall, "The Unfinished Work of Welfare Reform."

38. Woodson, "Testimony before the United States Senate Committee on the Budget."

39. Ibid.

40. Personal communication, March 2012.

41. Barbara J. Elliott, *Street Saints: Renewing America's Cities* (West Conshohocken, PA: Templeton Press, 2004), 111–12.

42. Ibid.

43. "At Budget Hearing, Sessions Presents Moral Case for Welfare Reform," Senate Budget Committee Republicans press release, February 13, 2013, http://www.budget.senate.gov/republican/public/index.cfm/press-releases?ID=7ce1a64b-5598-4075-a886-304b0b8525cf.

44. Rector and Marshall, "The Unfinished Work of Welfare Reform."

45. Charles Murray, *Coming Apart: The State of White America, 1960–2010* (New York: Crown Forum, 2012), 180.

46. Kim Burton, "Is Work Good for Your Health and Well-Being?," http://www.aei.org/files/2013/04/15/-kim-burton-presentation_123049656774.pdf.

47. Rasmussen Reports, "Americans Favor Work over Welfare As Response to Poverty," March 29, 2013, http://www.rasmussenreports.com/public_content/business/general_business/march_2013/americans_favor_work_over_welfare_as_response_to_poverty.

48. Rasmussen Reports, "83% Favor Work Requirement for Welfare Recipients," July 18, 2012, http://www.rasmussenreports.com/public_content/business/jobs_employment/july_2012/83_favor_work_requirement_for_welfare_recipients.

49. Rector and Marshall, "The Unfinished Work of Welfare Reform."

Chapter 12: Freedom: America's Inexhaustible Energy Source

1. "Primary Resources: Proposed Energy Policy," *American Experience*, PBS, http://www.pbs.org/wgbh/americanexperience/features/primary-resources/carter-energy/.

2. Joseph W. Kutchin, *How Mitchell Energy and Development Corp. Got Its Start and How It Grew*, updated ed. (Boca Raton, FL: Universal Publishers, 2001), 378.

3. Scott Tong, "George Mitchell, 94, Dies: Oil Man Unlocked Fracking," Market-place.org, December 7, 2012 (updated July 26, 2013), http://www.marketplace.org/topics/sustainability/oil-man-who-figured-out-fracking.

4. Ibid.; "George Mitchell—Father of Fracking," GoHaynesvilleShale.com, March 20, 2012, http://www.gohaynesvilleshale.com/forum/topics/george-mitchell-father-of-fracking.

5. Institute for Energy Research, "North American Energy Inventory," December 2011, http://www.energyforamerica.org/wp-content/uploads/2012/06/Energy-InventoryFINAL.pdf.

6. U.S. Energy Information Administration, "Petroleum & Other Liquids," March 15, 2013, http://www.eia.gov/dnav/pet/hist/LeafHandler.ashx?n=PET&s=MTTEXUS1&f=A.

7. Nicolas Loris, Jack Spencer, and Katie Tubb, "Ernest Moniz: In His Own Words," Heritage Issue Brief #3897, April 8, 2013, http://www.heritage.org/research/reports/2013/04/ernest-moniz-in-his-own-words.

8. National Economic Research Associates, Inc., "Macroeconomic Impacts of LNG Exports from the United States," December 3, 2012, http://www.fossil.energy.gov/programs/gasregulation/reports/nera_lng_report.pdf.

9. Brandon Stewart, "A Fracking Miracle: North Dakota's Bakken Boom," *The Foundry*, June 19, 2012, http://blog.heritage.org/2012/06/19/a-fracking-miracle-north-dakotas-bakken-boom-video/.

10. Bryan Gruley, "The Man Who Bought North Dakota," *Bloomberg Businessweek*, January 19, 2012, http://www.businessweek.com/magazine/the-man-who-bought-north-dakota-01192012.html.

11. "Pennsylvania's Electricity Generation Composition," http://www.eia.gov/todayinenergy/chartdata/PennElecGen.csv.

12. Ben Casselman and Russell Gold, "Cheap Natural Gas Gives New Hope to Rust Belt," *Wall Street Journal*, October 24, 2012, http://online.wsj.com/article/SB10000872396390444549204578020602281237088.html.

13. Ibid.

14. "A Fracking Miracle."

15. Casselman and Gold, "Cheap Natural Gas Gives New Hope to the Rust Belt."

16. "EPA Director Speaks Out About Shale Boom," WFMJ.com, April 25, 2013 (updated July 29, 2013), http://www.wfmj.com/story/22082629/epa-director-speaks-out-about-shale-boom.

17. Interview with Lisa Jackson, *Rachel Maddow Show*, November 22, 2011, http://video.msnbc.msn.com/the-rachel-maddow-show/45395747#45395747.

18. Interstate Oil and Gas Compact Commission, "Hydraulic Fracturing: State Progress," http://groundwork.iogcc.org/topics-index/hydraulic-fracturing/state-progress.

19. Georgia Power, "Facts and Figures," http://www.georgiapower.com/about-us/facts-and-financials/facts-and-figures.cshtml.

20. Ron Bridgeman, "Plant Branch Closing 'Official,'" *Eatonton Messenger*, January 10, 2013 (updated April 3, 2013), http://www.msgr.com/news/localnews/articleabcfaaec-5b3f-11e2-9e9f-0019bb2963f4.html.

21. Phillip Lucas, "Ga. Power Shutdown Request Would Close 3 Plants," *Independent Mail* (Anderson, SC), January 7, 2013, http://www.independentmail.com/news/2013/jan/07/ga-power-shutdown-request-would-close-3-plants/.

22. Ron Bridgeman, "Plant Branch Closing 'Devastating,'" *Eatonton Messenger*, January 10, 2013 (updated April 3, 2013), http://www.msgr.com/news/local_news/article_f17e9b02-5b3f-11e2-a948-0019bb2963f4.html.

23. Ailun Yang and Yiyun Cui, "Global Coal Risk Assessment: Data Analysis and Market Research," World Resources Institute, http://pdf.wri.org/global_coal_risk_assessment.pdf.

24. Paul Knappenberger, "Analysis of U.S. and State-by-State Carbon Dioxide Emissions and Potential 'Savings' in Future Global Temperature and Global Sea Level Rise," Science and Public Policy Institute, April 2013, http://scienceandpublicpolicy.org/images/stories/papers/originals/state_by_state.pdf.

25. American Coalition for Clean Coal Electricity, "Energy Cost Impacts on American Families, 2001–2012," February 2012, http://www.americaspower.org/sites/default/files/Energy_Cost_Impacts_2012_FINAL.pdf.

26. Patrick Jenevein, "Wind Power Subsidies? No Thanks," *Wall Street Journal*, April 1, 2013, http://online.wsj.com/article/SB10001424127887323501004578386501479255158.html.

Chapter 13: Loving the Planet (and People Too!)

1. Ronald Reagan, "Remarks to the California Association of Water Agencies," Sacramento, April 27, 1973, quoted by Becky Norton Dunlop in "Base Environmental Policies on Liberty, Not Socialism," *Human Events*, January 5, 2007, http://www.humanevents.com/2007/01/05/base-environmental-policies-on-liberty-not-socialism/.

2. Pacific Legal Foundation, "Historic Supreme Court Ruling Allows the Sacketts ot Fight EPA Takeover of Their Land," March 21, 2012, http://www.pacificlegal.org/releases/Historic-Supreme-Court-ruling-allows-the-Sacketts-to-fight-EPA-takeover-of-their-land.

3. Tina Korbe, "Drilling Moratorium Devastating to Gulf," *The Foundry*, August 9, 2010, http://blog.heritage.org/2010/08/09/drilling-moratorium-devastating -to-gulf/.

4. Quest Offshore, "The State of the Offshore U.S. Oil and Gas Industry," http:// www.api.org/policy/exploration/upload/quest_2011_december_29_final.pdf .

5. Diane Katz and Craig Manson, "The National Environmental Policy Act," Heritage Foundation, July 2012, http://thf_media.s3.amazonaws.com/2012/Environmen talConservation/Chapter5-The-National-Environmental-Policy-Act.pdf.

6. Ibid.

7. Kristen Lombardiand, "Obama Administration Gives Billions in Stimulus Money Without Environmental Safeguards," *Washington Post*, November 28, 2010, http://www.washingtonpost.com/wp-dyn/content/article/2010/11/28/ AR2010112804379_2.html?sid=ST2010112903774 .

8. Stephen Lathrop, "One Man's Regulatory Nightmare," *The Freeman*, March 1, 2003, http://www.fee.org/the_freeman/detail/one-mans-regulatory-night mare#axzz2OexUyfom.

9. 33 Code of Federal Regulations Section 328.3(a)(3).

10. Lathrop, "One Man's Regulatory Nightmare."

11. Letter from Senators Claire McCaskill and Ron Johnson to Lieutenant General Thomas P. Bostick, commanding general of the U.S. Army Corps of Engineers, March 25, 2013, http://www.ronjohnson.senate.gov/public/index.cfm/files/ serve?File_id=f80cbc9f-ac8c-41b5-96eb-201ec82cc92b.

12. U.S. Chamber of Commerce, "Extreme Enviros Harbor Dangerous Views on Society," April 2000, http://www.uschamber.com/node/5333/%252Fmay.

13. Ronald Reagan, February 27, 1975, cited by William Perry Pendley in *Sagebrush Rebel: Reagan's Battle with Environmental Extremists and Why It Matters Today* (Washington, DC: Regnery, 2013), 83.

14. Theodore Roosevelt, "Conservation as a National Duty," May 13, 1908, http:// voicesofdemocracy.umd.edu/theodore-roosevelt-conservation-as-a-national -duty-speech-text/.

15. Nicolas Loris and Katie Tubb, "EPA Administrator Nominee Gina McCar thy: In Her Own Words," Heritage Issue Brief #3904, April 10, 2013, http:// www.heritage.org/research/reports/2013/04/epa-administrator-nominee -gina-mccarthy-in-her-own-words.

16. Warren Brookes, "How Government Turns the Learning Curve from Green to Brown," Center of the American Experiment, April 18, 1991, http:// www.americanexperiment.org/publications/reports-books/how-government -turns-the-learning-curve-from-green-to-brown.

17. Laura Legere, "Debate over Proposed Dimock Waterline Divides Community," *Scranton Times-Tribune*, October 24, 2010, http://thetimes-tribune.com/news/debate-over-proposed-dimock-waterline-divides-community-1.1053233; http://dimockproud.com/history-2/.

18. Dee Depass, "3M, Others Share Their Secrets for Energy Savings at Summit," *Minneapolis Star Tribune*, September 11, 2012, http://www.startribune.com/business/169258466.html.

19. Julie Wernan, "Shedd Aquarium Looks to Slice Energy Bill," *Chicago Tribune*, January 26, 2013, http://articles.chicagotribune.com/2013-01-26/business/ct-biz-0126-shedd-energy-20130126_1_shedd-aquarium-light-bulbs-shedd-plans.

20. Heritage Foundation, "Eight Principles of the American Conservation Ethic," July 2012, http://thf_media.s3.amazonaws.com/2012/Environmental Conservation/Eight-Principles-of-the-American-Conservation-Ethic.pdf.

Chapter 14: And the Greatest of These...

1. Mark Steyn, *America Alone: The End of the World as We Know It* (Washington, DC: Regnery, 2008), 44.

Chapter 15: Falling in Love Again

1. Barry Goldwater, *The Conscience of a Conservative* (Shepherdsville, KY: Victor Publishing Company, 1960), 10–11.

2. U.S. Border Patrol, "Southwest Border Sectors: Southwest Border Deaths by Fiscal Year," http://www.cbp.gov/linkhandler/cgov/border_security/border_patrol/usbp_statistics/usbp_fy12_stats/border_patrol_fy.ctt/border_patrol_fy.pdf.

3. Ronald Reagan, "Farewell Address to the Nation, January 11, 1989," http://www.reaganfoundation.org/tgcdetail.aspx?p=TG0923RRS&h1=0&h2=0&sw=&lm=reagan&args_a=cms&args_b=1&argsb=N&tx=1749.

4. Points of Light Award Number 5,000, July 15, 2013.

Acknowledgments

The idea for this book began in 2012 when I was still in the U.S. Senate. As the Republican leader of the Joint Economic Committee (JEC), I was responsible for researching, analyzing, and publishing economic data and trends to guide policy development. Michael Connolly, an excellent analyst and writer, was my staff director at JEC. Mike and I did extensive work comparing the economic growth of our fifty states and assessing the root causes of their economic successes and failures. It became apparent that the least successful states were following the top-down, big government, centrally controlled model of Europe, and the most successful states were competing to create the best economic environment by using proven, uniquely American, free-market principles.

We kept asking ourselves why some states continued to follow a failed economic model despite compelling, indisputable evidence that they were creating unsustainable debt and headed for almost certain bankruptcy. Our research led us to a long list of perverse incentives from the federal government and the political control of government unions. More digging brought us to the conclusion that the sheer "bigness" of the federal government was destroying the foundations of America's success.

The states were not the only victims of the institutional bigness spawned by the federal government. Our research provided evidence beyond a reasonable doubt that big banks, big corporations, big unions, big cronyism, and big political corruption were all directly related to a big, blundering federal government that had grown too big to succeed.

Mike and I began to write a book, at night and on weekends, about "the Bigs," and several of the chapters in this book reflect that early work. I am deeply grateful for Michael Connolly's early help. But we were just getting started. When I came to The Heritage Foundation in 2013, I was soon inspired by our team to develop a much more positive concept for the book. Heritage is all about solutions. Their research identifies the principles and public policies that work...that make life better for everyone. Americans didn't need another book about what was wrong with America, we needed an inspiring, positive book about what makes America the most wonderful, prosperous, and compassionate nation in history.

I asked for the help of Heritage author and scholar Dr. Lee Edwards. Lee assembled a team of researchers and writers who are experts on every issue that affects the lives of Americans. When we met to discuss the book, we didn't talk about politics. One by one, these Heritage scholars shared stories about individual Americans, families, churches, businesses, associations, communities, and states that were, without federal assistance, solving problems, helping people, and building a better America. As we shared these success stories, we all fell in love with America again. And that became our title.

I'm often asked what was it like to join The Heritage Foundation after serving in the Senate and the House. My answer is simple: It was like coming home to my family. Heritage was my greatest ally when I was in the Congress, and former Heritage interns stocked my Senate staff as bright young conservative champions.

The Heritage Foundation really is an extended family. There's

ACKNOWLEDGMENTS

the founding father, Ed Feulner, whose kindnesses to me are too numerous to mention; the wise old uncles—Phil Truluck, John Von Kannon, and Stuart Butler—who carry the family lore in their well-stocked minds; women of valor like Becky Norton Dunlop, Genevieve Wood, and Bridgett Wagner, who wage the good fight every day; and the extraordinarily talented team of scholars, communicators, fund-raisers, and marketers, who have made me feel more welcome than I ever thought possible.

I thank them all from the bottom of my heart.

I'd like to give special thanks to four collaborators without whose help this book would not have seen the light of day: Lee Edwards, Joseph Shattan, Billy Gribbin, and Linda Bridges. Don't ask me how they did it, but these folks helped make writing this book a fun project as well as a labor of love.

I also want to acknowledge the assistance of my colleagues Matthew Spalding, Jennifer Marshall, Alison Fraser, Nina Owcharenko, Collette Caprara, Chris Jacobs, Katie Tubb, Lindsey Burke, Sarah Torre, Rachel Sheffield, Andrew T. Walker, James Gattuso, Curtis Dubay, Diane Katz, Nicolas Loris, Leslie Grimard, and Jack Spencer. These men and women are all specialists in their fields who have retained the ability to communicate with ordinary folks like me.

A special word of thanks to David Addington, Jan Smith, Anthony Campau, Elizabeth Slattery, and Tiffany Bates for their keen editorial eyes, and even keener policy intellects.

I'm deeply grateful to my editor at Center Street, Kate Hartson, for her confidence in me, her encouragement, and all her hard work.

Last but most definitely not least, I want to thank my nuclear family: my wife Debbie and our children and grandchildren. Their abiding love sustains me in everything I do.

Appendix

There are far too many little platoons around the country deserving of recognition to honor them all here; these are some I've mentioned in this book, and organizations that help preserve them.

Center for Neighborhood Enterprise
http://www.cneonline.org
1625 K Street NW, Suite 1200
Washington, DC 20006
Phone: (202) 518-6500
Fax: (202) 588-0314

Friedman Foundation for Educational Choice
http://www.edchoice.org
One American Square, Suite 2420
Indianapolis, IN 46282
Phone: (317) 681-0745
Fax: (317) 681-0945

Home School Legal Defense Association
http://www.hslda.org
P.O. Box 3000
Purcellville, VA 20134
Phone: (540) 338-5600
Fax: (540) 338-2733

Prison Fellowship
http://www.prisonfellowship.org
44180 Riverside Parkway
Lansdowne, VA 20176
Phone: (800) 206-9764

American Legislative Exchange Council
http://www.alec.org
2900 Crystal Drive, 6th Floor
Arlington, VA 22202
Phone: (703) 373-0933
Fax: (703) 373-0927

Mackinac Center
http://www.mackinac.org
140 West Main Street
P.O. Box 568
Midland, MI 48640
Phone: (989) 631-0900
Fax: (989) 631-0964

Outreach, Inc.
http://www.outreachprogram
.org
301 Center Street
P.O. Box 361
Union, IA 50258
Phone: (641) 486-2550
Fax: (641) 486-2570

Victory Ministries
http://outcryofaustin.org
P.O. Box 6250
Austin, TX 78752
Phone: (512) 480-9628

Step 13
http://www.step13.org
2029 Larimer Street
Denver, CO 80205
Phone: (303) 295-7837

H.I.S. BridgeBuilders
http://hisbridgebuilders.org
2075 West Commerce Street
Dallas, TX 75208
Phone: (469) 621-5900

First Things First
http://firstthings.org
620 Lindsay Street, Suite 100
Chattanooga, TN 37403
Phone: (423) 267-5383

House of Help/City of Hope
http://www.hollowayministries
.org/index.php/house-of-help

Christian Care Center Ministries
http://www.christiancarecenter
.org/home
115 North 13th Street
Leesburg, FL 34748
Phone: (352) 314-8733

Harvest of Hope
http://www.harvestofhopefamily
.com
727 Franklin Boulevard, Suite 1
Somerset, NJ 08873
Phone: (732) 247-1270
Fax: (732) 247-1710

Bud's Warehouse
http://budswarehouse.org
4455 East 46th Avenue
Denver, CO 80216
Phone: (303) 296-3990

Good Samaritan Ministries
http://www.goodsamministries
.com/
513 East 8th Street
Holland, MI 49423
Phone: (616) 392-7159

Wait No More
http://icareaboutorphans.org

The Heritage Foundation
http://www.heritage.org
214 Massachusetts Avenue NE
Washington, DC 20002-4999
Phone: (202) 546-4400

DISCARD